Raising Venture
Capital in the UK

Raising Venture Capital in the UK

John Ormerod MA, FCA
Partner, Arthur Andersen & Co
Chartered Accountants

Ian Burns BA, FCA
Director, Lloyds Development Capital Ltd

Butterworths
London and Edinburgh
1988

United Kingdom	Butterworth & Co (Publishers) Ltd, 88 Kingsway, LONDON WC2B 6AB and 61A North Castle Street, EDINBURGH EH2 3LJ
Australia	Butterworths Pty Ltd, SYDNEY, MELBOURNE, BRISBANE, ADELAIDE, PERTH, CANBERRA and HOBART
Canada	Butterworths. A division of Reed Inc., TORONTO and VANCOUVER
New Zealand	Butterworths of New Zealand Ltd, WELLINGTON and AUCKLAND
Singapore	Butterworth & Co (Asia) Pte Ltd, SINGAPORE
USA	Butterworths Legal Publishers, ST PAUL, Minnesota, SEATTLE, Washington, BOSTON, Massachusetts, AUSTIN, Texas and D & S Publishers, CLEARWATER, Florida

© Arthur Andersen & Co 1988

All rights reserved. No part of this publication may be reproduced or transmitted in any form or by any means, including photocopying and recording, without the written permission of the copyright holder, application for which should be addressed to the publisher. Such written permission must also be obtained before any part of this publication is stored in a retrieval system of any nature.

This book is sold subject to the Standard Conditions of Sale of Net Books and may not be re-sold in the UK below the net price fixed by Butterworths for the book in our current catalogue.

British Library Cataloguing in Publication Data

Ormerod, John
   Raising venture capital in the U.K.
   1. Great Britain. Companies. Financing — Manuals
   I. Title II. Burns, Ian
   658.1'522'0941

ISBN 0 406 10310 0

Reproduced from copy supplied, Printed by Biddles Ltd, Guildford Surrey

Preface

This book was written to fill a significant gap in current venture capital literature. The venture capital industry is now well served by both books and periodicals analysing the various types of funding on offer and current trends in the marketplace. To a greater or lesser extent however, these are all focused on the investor or student. At the other end of the scale, practical advice written specifically for the *entrepreneur* on how to raise venture capital is more limited and fragmentary, and is largely confined to individual press articles or specific chapters of more general financial textbooks. There is no single work in the UK today written to synthesise these two strands, ie to set out for the entrepreneur looking for equity finance what is on offer and how to raise it, *from his point of view*.

Raising Venture Capital in the UK is an attempt to fill this gap. Although the book is designed to be of relevance to other interested parties — we hope for example that the solicitor and accountant advising the small businessman, the student, academic and journalist, and even the venture capitalist himself will find no difficulty in reading it as an analysis of the workings of the industry — it is primarily written to be of practical help to the entrepreneur at all stages of the venture capital process. As a result, the book is more analytical than descriptive. For example, although the entrepreneur needs to be aware of the sorts of venture capital on offer — and a large part of the book is taken up discussing this — we have tried to confine the discussion to points of specific relevance to him. We have also not hesitated to include lists of 'points to watch' and 'do's and dont's' at points where in our experience these represent issues of particular importance to the entrepreneur or the company executive. To those who feel that advice written from experience merely reflects the prejudices of the authors, we can only hope that the fact that we wrote the book sitting on both sides of the investor:investee fence has subsequently cancelled them out!

Preface

The completion of this work has relied on the contributions of many, and it is among the most pleasant obligations of authorship to mention them. In this case however it would be impossible to discharge this task fully. For, as a book written largely from our own experience, our first and most basic debt of gratitude is to the sources of this experience, ie to all our entrepreneurial and small company clients, contacts and investee companies, and to our past and present colleagues at Arthur Andersen & Co, British Technology Group, and Lloyds Development Capital.

Turning to the emergence of the book in its final form, we are specifically indebted to Ian Krieger and Arthur Hunking at Arthur Andersen, and Ron Hollidge and Tim Ingelfield at Lloyds Development Capital for their review of and input to its various drafts. We are also especially grateful to Derham O'Neill at Clifford Chance for his perceptive comments on the legal aspects of the venture capital industry and process set out in the book. Any remaining errors, omissions or prejudices are strictly our own.

The facts and opinions in the book also owe much to our colleagues throughout the venture capital industry. We would in particular like to thank John Coyne and Mike Wright of the Centre for Buy-Out Research at Nottingham University for their permission to quote extensively from their works on buy-outs, and Susan Lloyd from Venture Economics for allowing us to make such generous use of her treasure trove of information on the UK venture capital industry in general. We would also like to acknowledge the following: The Boston Consulting Group for Figure 3; the National Economic Development Office for Figure 13, reproduced with the kind permission of the Controller of Her Majesty's Stationery Office; the UK Venture Capital Journal for Figures 11 and 17; and the British Venture Capital Association for Appendix II and the extracts from their Code of Conduct.

Sarah Larkham deserves a special word of thanks for her unfailing tolerance and perseverance in the typing of the original manuscript, and for her detective abilities in deciphering what were euphemistically known as our handwritten drafts and amendments. Our final and greatest debt of gratitude is to the patience and support of Pamela and Nicky, our wives, to whom this book is truly dedicated.

London	John Ormerod
March 1988	Ian Burns

Contents

Preface v
List of Figures xi

PART 1 INTRODUCTION

Chapter 1 Introduction 3

PART 2 THE NEED FOR RISK CAPITAL

Chapter 2 Sources of Finance 9
Cash versus control — the entrepreneur's dilemma 9
Types of finance 10
Choosing the financing package 15

Chapter 3 Choosing Equity Finance 17
Types of risk capital 17
Venture and development capital 18
The entrepreneur's choice 21

PART 3 RISK CAPITAL ALTERNATIVES

Chapter 4 The Risk Capital Funds 27
Types of funds 28
Current investment patterns — issues for the entrepreneur 34
The risk capitalists 39
Sources of information 43

Chapter 5 Management Buy-outs 44
What is a management buy-out? 49
The key questions 51

Critical success factors   56
The buy-out process   58
Financing the buy-out: six steps   59
Five golden rules   61
Appendix — structuring the buy-out: Newbrand   62

Chapter 6   The Business Expansion Scheme   65
BES as a corporate finance alternative   65
The Scheme in practice   67
Advantages of BES finance   72
Practical problems   73
Current and future trends   75
Conclusion   79

Chapter 7   Corporate Venturing   80
What is corporate venturing?   80
Corporate venturing: motivators   82
How it is done?   84
Advantages for the smaller company   88
Problems and pitfalls   90
Do's and dont's   96

Chapter 8   Other Methods of Raising Risk Capital   99
Replacement capital   99
Issuing shares to other members of the public   101
Joint ventures   108

PART 4   RAISING THE FINANCE

Chapter 9   Getting Started   113
Is risk capital for me?   113
The preliminaries   115
Choosing professional advisers   115
Setting out the stall   121

Chapter 10   The Business Plan   124
The investor's view: a two-stage process   125
Some common questions answered   125
The key points   132
Appendix — outline business plan   139

Chapter 11   Obtaining Offers   150
Surviving the evaluation   150
The initial offer   153

Contents ix

Chapter 12 Optimising the Offer 159
Management objectives 159
Shaping the deal 160

Chapter 13 Detailed Negotiations 167
Specialists' investigations and reports 167
Completion documentation 171
Negotiations — do's and dont's 179

PART 5 AFTER INVESTMENT

Chapter 14 Aftercare 183
Types of aftercare 183
Problems and flashpoints 190
Do's and dont's 192

Chapter 15 Exit Routes 194
Types of exit route 194
Choice of alternatives 199

PART 6 THE FUTURE

Chapter 16 The Future 209
The present — issues and opportunities 209
The future 214

Appendix I   A Practical Example — Leader Electronics Limited 217

Appendix II Extracts from 'British Venture Capital Association Report on Investment Activity (1986)' 228

Appendix III Negative Covenants and Warranties — Some Examples 237

Appendix IV Pricing Risk Capital Investments — An Example 241

Appendix V   The Business Expansion Scheme 244

Index 251

List of Figures

1 Types of Finance   11
2 Venture and Development Capital Contrasted   20
3 Growth/Share Matrix   22
4 UK Management Buy-outs: Recent Rewards   44
5 Total Number and Value of Management Buy-outs 1967–85   45
6 Value of 1985 Management Buy-outs   46
7 Industry Distribution of 1985 Buy-outs   47
8 Sources of 1985 Management Buy-outs   48
9 Management Buy-outs — The Basic Problem   52
10 Investments by BES Funds   68
11 Early Stage Investments   70
12 Three Types of Corporate Venturing — Examples   85
13 NEDO Corporate Venturing   98
14 History of OTC and USM Entrants to June 1986   106
15 Illustrative Offer Letter   156
16 Main Factors Affecting the Choice of Market for Flotation   196
17 Venture-backed New Issues and Acquisitions   198

PART 1
INTRODUCTION

Chapter 1

Introduction

In 1977 a committee headed by Sir Harold Wilson was appointed to review the financing of small firms. Its report in 1979 (the so-called 'Wilson Report') painted a gloomy picture. 'There is no doubt,' it concluded, 'that, compared to large firms, small firms are at a considerable disadvantage in the financial markets'. 'In particular,' it noted, 'venture capital is particularly hard to obtain'. Its remedies for the encouragement of equity investment in such companies, however, were somewhat less than revolutionary. With the exception of a passing nod in the direction of what eventually was to emerge in a much-changed form as the Business Expansion Scheme, its major recommendations were that the National Research and Development Corporation (the then major government-backed technology investor) should consider making more investments, and that they and Technical Development Capital (one of the few other major players in the field) should increase their publicity profile!

This was consistent with the pessimism of the times, and the political ambivalence towards small business then current. Its content and tone were, however, hardly prophetic for by the end of 1985 billions of pounds had been made available by financial institutions for investments in unquoted companies, the vast majority of which was provided by the private sector. This explosion of what is popularly known as venture capital has emerged as one of the most important industrial phenomena in the UK in the 1980s, which itself may well with hindsight be seen as the decade of the entrepreneurial revolution.

Several factors have combined to generate this explosion. In the USA the late 1970s saw an upsurge in venture capital activity, coupled with the emergence of new, often high technology, businesses. Many of these grew rapidly and the news of their successes crossed the Atlantic and provided a model which could act as an incentive for similar activity in the UK. This opportunity was quickly capitalised on as several American venture capitalists established operations in the UK in the early 1980s. At the same time, other factors had fuelled the formation of Britain's second tier stockmarket, the Unlisted Securities Market. Together with the increasing pace of merger and acquisition activity in general, this provided investors in young, unquoted companies with a real chance of cashing in on their investments within a reasonable time-frame by way of flotation or trade sale. Finally, and fundamentally, lying behind all this was the political will to use the development of new businesses to revive a stagnant economy and create employment. This resulted in specific measures such as the establishment of the Business Start-Up Scheme (later the Business Expansion Scheme), tax favourable treatment for employee share options, and a series of measures aimed at relieving the administrative burdens on smaller businesses.

The early 1980s have as a result seen a significant growth in the availability of equity finance for young and unquoted companies. After a number of years when venture capital was the preserve of the Industrial and Commercial Finance Corporation (now Investors in Industry (3i)) and a handful of other institutions prepared to make investments in unquoted companies on a very selective basis, a venture capital industry has now been established in the UK which is comparable as a percentage of gross national product with that of the USA. In its report on investment activity for 1986, the British Venture Capital Association reported that its 77 members had during the year provided nearly £430m of finance to over 700 companies — and these statistics exclude the continuing and very large investment in this sector by 3i and a number of other non-member institutions.

Growth in the sector continues apace. If it is true (as if often said) that the single most critical element in any new business venture is the quality of management, then the growth in the number of proposals for new business ideas finding their way on to the risk capitalists' desks must be encouraging. Increasingly these proposals are put forward by experienced managers who, only ten years earlier, would not have contemplated a career outside a major company. The many successful examples of investments in unquoted companies (especially management buy-outs) which have yielded spectacular returns, both for the venture capitalists and for the management teams which led them, have provided role models to act as a catalyst for other venture capital activity.

Venture capital is not, however, a new phenomenon. It has existed in an organised form in the UK since 1945 and has its roots in the financial patrons of the industrial revolution and the merchant adventurers of Renaissance times; the title of 'the world's first venture capitalist' is often given to Christopher Columbus, and can almost certainly be pushed further back in time. Why then, if the concept has such a long and distinguished pedigree, was venture capital apparently so deeply in the doldrums by the 1970s?

In fact, despite the above examples, the historical popularity of venture capital has been distinctly uneven; this in turn is a function of the difficulty of practising it successfully. The delay of the entrepreneurial revolution until the 1980s was not the only reason why the venture capital climate was as cool as it was in the days of the Wilson Committee. As we shall see in subsequent chapters, it has never been and still is not always easy for the investor to build fruitful continuing relationships with his portfolio companies without over-interference. In addition, and possibly more importantly, many British small company owners and managers have had unrealistic expectations of what they can expect from investors, and many frustrated seekers of venture capital should not have tried in the first place. Even today it is commonly believed that less than 10% of all applications for risk capital finance end in success; despite the vastly increased supply of funds, putting them in place does not seem to get any easier.

This book has been written with these problems in mind. It deals with the role of equity finance in funding growing businesses from start-up, through the stages of expansion, to maturity and regeneration through the provision of new money on the buying-out of existing shareholders. It is primarily written for the entrepreneur who is considering raising capital for his or her own company, although the points we make will also be relevant to the professional adviser or student of venture capital. As such, we have tried to concentrate on those practical issues he will come up against in his search for the ideal backer. Conversely, we will not deal with some subjects which deserve and are receiving increasing current attention from outside commentators on the overall venture capital scene — management buy-ins and the structural and fiscal problems of the venture capital funds are two examples — but will not normally be relevant to the entrepreneur on the Clapham omnibus.

In the following Part 2, we discuss the question of why the entrepreneur might need capital, and the alternatives open to him. Concentrating particularly on equity finance, we set out the differences between the various types of risk capital (including our own definition of venture capital) and we try and assess which will best suit different types of companies. Part 3 deals in more detail with the various sources of equity finance for smaller companies, including management buy-outs, the Business Expansion Scheme, and the emerging phenomenon of corporate venturing.

Part 4 returns to the process of raising risk capital, up to the point when the investment is made. In discussing how investors typically evaluate investment proposals and structure and negotiate their investments, we have tried to identify the process by which the investors' overall aims are translated into action (including the key question of how they evaluate investment proposals); to highlight some of the areas which commonly give rise to problems; and suggest ways in which these can be surmounted or, better still, avoided entirely.

Part 5 deals with what the risk capitalists know as 'aftercare' or life after investment. This is of critical importance for, as we will see, with very few exceptions the relationship between the risk capital investor and his portfolio companies is a continuing process, and can if not properly nurtured lead to recrimination, ill-feeling and unproductive conflict. This can be especially true when considering exit routes — the way in which the investor gets his money back — for the ending of the risk capital relationship can be just as difficult as the beginning. Finally, in Part 6, we suggest some ways in which the industry may move in the future and its likely impact on the relationship between the institutional investor and his potential investees.

If there is a dominant theme throughout the book, it is the importance of an understanding by the venture capitalist and the entrepreneur of each other's objectives. This, combined with continuing good communications between the two, can help both achieve more from their partnership. The aim of the book is to help achieve this.

PART 2
THE NEED FOR RISK CAPITAL

Chapter 2

Sources of Finance

'The small business person goes into business for himself; entrepreneurs go into business for others' (David Silver: President, the Association of Venture Capital Clubs).

CASH VERSUS CONTROL — THE ENTREPRENEUR'S DILEMMA

The issue raised by David Silver, the well known American venture capitalist, in the above quotation provides the starting point for every entrepreneur thinking of raising what is called 'venture capital'. It immediately begs the key question of his own objectives, which will lie at the heart of every company's financing plans. An imperfect understanding of these objectives will often explain the reasons why so many businesses fail to raise new equity capital; conversely, honest analysis can identify why many more should not even try.

People go into business for a wide variety of reasons, but underlying this in the vast majority of cases is the desire to work for themselves at jobs they like doing. Many, however, and maybe the majority of businessmen — David Silver's 'small business person' — turn this into an overriding objective rather than an underlying motive. The craftsman who lives for the quality of his product, and the small employer who is driven by a personal obligation to his customers and a desire to provide a good service, are recognisable examples of this type. Such businesses are not primarily driven by the desire of their owners to accumulate wealth, and by and large do not tend to grow to a large size. Indeed, many owners of such businesses would actively prefer to stay small, in order to maintain close day-to-day control over all the activities of the business.

As such, they will in many cases not require significant amounts of finance, and would typically seek to avoid having to raise any unless absolutely necessary, in view of the obligations to the outside financiers this would entail.

The entrepreneur of Silver's definition, however, — which we will use in this and succeeding chapters — differs critically from his counterpart, the small businessman, in his acceptance of the fact that he will have to grow his business in order to amass the wealth he desires. This will require him in the fullness of time to develop from a businessman into a manager, involving not only the ability to work through, rather than with, people but also the necessity of obtaining, allocating and controlling the resources at his disposal, an important part of which will be the company's finances.

The entrepreneur will accordingly be faced at an early stage with a major issue which will run through this book: cash versus control. For the financier will not only look for a financial return from his investment; he will also seek in some way, however indirectly or subtly, to influence the conduct of the company to protect his money. The greater the opportunity for the entrepreneur to grow his business, the greater will be the need for finance and the greater the dilemma, for as the need for finance increases, so will the potential for a corresponding loss of control.

The degree and type of influence desired by the financier will, however, vary according to the type of finance on offer. It is thus important for the entrepreneur seeking finance to be aware of the ways in which his freedom of action is likely to be circumscribed under the different forms of finance available to him.

TYPES OF FINANCE

This is not a textbook on corporate finance. We need, however, at this stage briefly to look at how the various types of finance available are likely to fit in with the entrepreneur's concern to balance cash and control.

A diagrammatic division of the main types of business finance available is reproduced in Figure 1 (the special case of joint venture project finance is dealt with in Chapter 8). The table broadly divides corporate finance into two — debt and equity capital. Equity is essentially permanent risk capital: the investor has no assurance that his capital will be returned or that he will receive payment for the use of his money. On the other hand, the whole of the profits of a business, after debt service and tax payments, is the property of the equity shareholders.

FIGURE 1

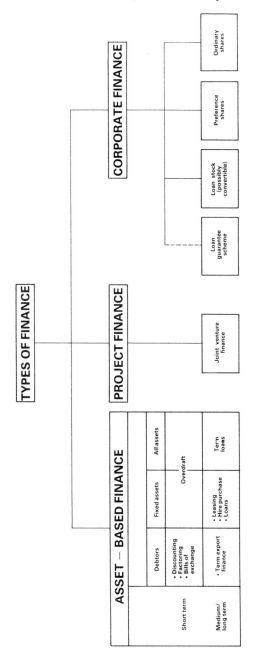

Debt finance, in contrast, is seldom if ever permanent, and both repayment terms and servicing costs are normally agreed at the outset. More importantly, lenders assume less risk than equity investors because their claims, often secured on the assets of the business, have preference over the shareholders in the event of business failure. As lenders are not usually in a position to see the value of their loans rise, they tend to be more concerned with ensuring the repayment of their capital and interest, and less in influencing the direction of the business to maximise its worth.

If this might seem to imply that the entrepreneur should always seek to borrow money rather than widen his equity base, then Figure 1 will give him some comfort in the number of alternative ways in which debt finance can be supported. It also suggests that debt can be seen as a spectrum of types of finance more or less directly related to specific assets, from highly specific financing (eg, hire purchase, invoice discounting, etc) where the finance for a single transaction (eg, a specific sale, giving rise to a debtor) is secured on the asset itself, to finance which is in effect part of the long term capital of the company (eg, unsecured long-term loan stock) which is sometimes known as quasi-equity. Generally, the more specific the type of finance required, the less direct influence on operations the lender can be expected to have.

Limits of debt financing

Sadly, however, companies will not always have unlimited access to borrowed funds. Borrowing capacity will always be limited to reflect the lender's assessment of the risks involved in financing the business (will he get his money back?) and the rewards. In assessing this risk the lender will typically take account of:

(a) The security available. The lender's risk can be significantly reduced if he can obtain a specific charge (ranking before all other creditors) over an asset which has a reasonably certain market value. The most obvious example is hire purchase on vehicles which is available to some extent to almost all businesses, whatever their financial standing, because of the security of the vehicle which can be easily re-possessed and sold.

(b) The financial strength of the business. The lender will also look to the ability of the company to service the debt out of income. He will typically look at the ratio of profit before interest to interest charges (interest cover) as a measure of this strength. Beyond that he will look at the profits and cash flow of the business to repay debt in accordance with the agreed terms. Finally, he will look at the ratio of debt to equity finance as a measure of the ability of the business to sustain adverse results and still have assets available to repay debt (a one-to-one debt equity ratio is often quoted as the golden rule here although in certain situations, such as buy-outs, the ratio can often be as high as ten to one).

Frequently the managers of smaller businesses are heard saying that banks are too conservative in their lending. In particular they feel that the assets of the business should provide the bank with sufficient security, while the bank takes a different view. It must be remembered, however, that the book value of assets reflected in accounts drawn up on a going concern basis are often significantly higher than the values which can be realised if a business fails and the bank calls in its loans. In addition, in such circumstances other costs, like redundancy costs and lease termination payments, may arise. A not untypical example is given below:

Assets of business	Book value (going concern)	Forced sale value
Fixed assets		
Property	100	75
Machinery	100	25
Net current assets (liabilities)		
Stocks	350	70
Debtors	200	150
	550	220
Creditors	(450)	(550)
	100	(330)
Net assets — surplus (deficiency)	300	(230)

The cost of debt finance will reflect the risks involved; generally younger and less financially sound businesses have to pay a higher rate of interest for their money. An extreme example of this is the government Loan Guarantee Scheme. Under this Scheme, where a bank considering a long-term unsecured loan considers that the business is sound but does not have the necessary security, the bank can seek approval of a guarantee of a proportion of the loan from the Department of Trade and Industry. For the payment by the business of a guarantee fee (which accordingly increases the cost of the money) the Department provides the lending bank with a guarantee of up to 70% of the funds advanced.

In exceptional cases, lenders may look to alternative means of increasing their return on funds lent to a business. This might be achieved, for example, by providing that part of all of the loan can be converted on agreed terms into share capital. Such lending, especially when it is unsecured or subordinated to some or all of the company's creditors, is often referred to as quasi-equity. Indeed, Figure 1 shows both Loan Guarantee Scheme finance and convertible loan stock on the equity side of the corporate financing spectrum, as to many entrepreneurs they are in practice very little different from, say, raising money by way of preference shares.

We will deal specifically with the special case of the Loan Guarantee Scheme in Chapter 4. Quasi-equity debt instruments such as convertible loan stock, and their role in the structuring of debt: equity packages, are discussed further in Chapter 12.

Equity finance

Just as lenders will provide funds on a variety of terms which reflect their perception of the risk and reward, the same considerations apply to providers of equity finance. This may be achieved by investing through a single type of security (eg, 'straight' ordinary shares) or a package of different types of shares to provide the right blend of current return, growth potential and priority to repayment of capital. The number and types of such packages is as varied as the number of businesses requiring finance. However, some of the principal equity type instruments include:

(a) Preference shares carrying a fixed dividend. These shares provide the investor with a fixed return in priority to any other dividend payments. They also typically rank preferentially for repayment of capital in the event of liquidation. These shares may also be redeemable (but generally this can only be achieved out of retained profits of the business or from a new issue of shares) or convertible on agreed terms into ordinary shares of the business at the request of either the company or the investor.

(b) Preferred participating shares. These typically provide the investor with a dividend which varies with the profits of the business and which is paid in priority to any other dividends. Again, these shares may be redeemable and/or convertible.

Preferred shares of one type of another are commonly seen in risk capital investments. Some of their uses are discussed further in Chapter 12.

(c) Ordinary shares. These shares have the lowest priority in terms of ranking for dividend or repayment of capital. They do, however, typically offer the opportunity for the greatest gain in that all of the residual profits (after the payment of preference dividends, etc) accrue to the ordinary shareholders.

CHOOSING THE FINANCING PACKAGE

How will all this affect the typical owner of the small growing business with a continuing appetite for new finance?

Although each case will be different, the entrepreneur will typically be confronted with the following issues:

(a) The limits on debt capacity will in most cases severely restrict his ability to expand the business on the back of debt finance alone. In most cases the lenders will impose the limit on the debt capacity of the business. Exceptionally, however, particularly where sufficient security can be provided, a lender may be prepared to advance more than it is prudent for the business to borrow. In such cases the entrepreneur needs to make his own risk assessment and obtain funding which can cope with reasonable fluctuations in the fortunes of the business.

(b) Raising further equity capital can be expected of itself to increase a company's debt capacity. It is therefore possible, and indeed common, to raise new capital for many purposes via a combined loan-equity package, which will often be heavily weighted towards the type of securities found in the centre of the financing spectrum in Figure 1, eg, subordinated loan stock, or preference shares, which do not typically require dilution of the owner's equity.

(c) Any package containing a significant amount of equity is likely to appear 'expensive' to the entrepreneur. A high return is necessary in order to compensate the investor for the risk associated with investing in an unquoted company. For higher risk (typically early stage) ventures, the investor may look for an *annual* compound internal rate of return in excess of 50%–60%, while equity or quasi-equity investors in more stable and mature companies (thus hopefully with a lower risk profile) will not look closely at any opportunities which do not promise a return in excess of 25%–30% per annum on their total investment. This will usually involve the recipient company in either a significant annual cash drain, by way of dividends or loan interest, or the surrender of significant equity which the investor will hope will grow in value over the years.

(d) This in turn can lead to other more subtle pressures from the investor on the entrepreneur. Investors seeking exceptionally high returns may, for example, see a Stock Exchange quotation as the best way to achieve this, and may consciously or unconsciously influence management throughout the investment period to move in this direction, whether or not it matches with their own interests. These indirect pressures, predisposing the entrepreneur to think in terms of the expectations of his investors as well as his own objectives, should not be underestimated, whatever type of finance is sought and the entrepreneur needs to be confident that the pressures will not become unbearable.

So how does the entrepreneur go about resolving these issues? In particular, if he is reconciled to the fact that he will require some form of equity capital to finance future growth, how should he evaluate the various types of finance available, and the institutions which provide them? We will leave further discussion on the choice between debt and equity financing until Part 4 of this book. For we first need to find out more about the providers of equity finance.

Chapter 3

Choosing Equity Finance

The first problem in any discussion about choosing between the various types of equity finance available is one of terminology. We will find as we go on through the book that many of the terms used are defined in different ways by different people — corporate venturing and mezzanine financing are two examples — to the extent that many remain confused about their application. Neither are some of the basic concepts of venture capital defined consistently by all its practitioners. At the risk of adding to the number of definitions in current use, but to avoid confusion, we will throughout this book use our own definitions which we have found most relevant in practice.

TYPES OF RISK CAPITAL

One of the most obvious definitional problems arises in the case of the term around which this book is based — venture capital. Many definitions of the concept of venture capital are in current circulation, but not all of them fit very easily into the operations of the institutions which provide it. The British Venture Capital Association for example, the 'trade association' of the British venture capital industry, has not published a formal definition of 'venture capital' but opens its membership to '[institutions] who are active in managing funds for long term equity investment in British unlisted companies.'

We would prefer to call these members '*risk capitalists*', as many tend to specialise in investments in different types of companies, requiring them to accept different types of risks.

These companies and their attendant risks form a continuum, the ends of which require two distinct types of risk capital to finance them, widely known as *venture capital* and *development capital*. This is a key distinction, which underlies much of the message of the book, for venture capital and development capital in most cases will be mutually exclusive; a company looking for equity finance, if suited to one, is unlikely to be suited to the other, and as most risk capital institutions tend to be biased towards either venture or development capital, it is important for the entrepreneur to know which type he needs, in order to save time and effort in searching for the right backer.

So what is venture and development capital? What sort of companies need it? What institutions provide it? Risk capital institutions are discussed in Chapter 4; the remainder of this chapter concentrates on the first two questions — the application of these two types of risk capital finance to different companies.

VENTURE AND DEVELOPMENT CAPITAL

The first of these two questions — what is venture and development capital? — is easier to answer than the second. 'Pure' venture and development capitalists have completely different objectives and operating practices, and tend to make completely different demands on the companies they invest in (their so-called 'portfolio companies').

Development capital

Development capital has historically grown out of the traditional financing activities of the City's lending institutions — today all the clearing banks and many of the merchant banks have their own dedicated development capital arms. This has been reflected in the aims, and consequently the structures, of their investments. The development capitalist typically will look for a better than average return on investment while seeking to limit his financial exposure as much as possible consistent with the equity risk he is taking. Most of his investments will be made in established companies with a proven track record, and — most critically — a reasonable prospect of immediate or early cash generation to provide him with a running yield.

Development capital is thus usually invested in a mix of preponderantly cash-generating securities — long-term loans, preference shares, or ordinary equity with preferred dividend rights are some of the more common variants.

The running yield generated from these securities will typically account for a major portion of the development capitalist's overall return on any individual investment, supplemented hopefully by the capital gains resulting from the eventual sale of any ordinary equity stake taken as part of the package. (Obviously, the greater the running yield the less the investor looks to the equity gain to achieve his overall required return.) Within these constraints, many development capital organisations are highly flexible when designing capital structures to achieve their aims, although they will typically seek to secure their investment as much as is practicable. A common way of achieving this is to insist on preferential dividend rights when investing by way of equity, or taking legal charges over assets in the case of loan stock investments.

Finally, in view of the type of ventures they are seeking to invest in, it is unusual to find development capital funds taking a truly active 'hands-on" management role in their investee companies. In those cases where their role is more than 'hands-off' (eg, where a representative of the fund takes a seat on the board) their input tends to be reactive rather than pro-active. Provided the business is achieving results broadly in line with those anticipated when the investment was made, the entrepreneur is unlikely to feel any significant demands being placed upon him by the investor.

Venture capital

The venture capitalist, on the other hand, represents an entirely different breed. The impetus for his success derives from the principle of limited liability, which limits the loss incurred by the investor on any one company to the cost of his investment, but sets no limit other than that imposed by the market on the upside potential from his successes.

The aim of the venture capitalist is to achieve the maximum possible return on his investments, over whatever period this may take (usually five to seven years). This is a risk-accepting rather than a risk-averse strategy (although not necessarily risk-seeking!), made possible by the portfolio effect implicit in spreading his investments over a number of companies (usually more than ten) and the spectacular returns achievable on successful portfolio investments.

It is, however, important that each company in the venture capitalist's portfolio should show very substantial growth potential sustainable over a number of years. Classically, this presumes that they will be operating in areas of large market potential, protected from competition by proprietary products or services which cannot be duplicated.

To achieve this, all venture capitalists rely on the crystallisation of the capital growth of their investments, whether by way of a public offering or a third party sale, rather than any running yield. This is because almost all fast-growing companies are cash-consuming, and cannot afford a capital structure with an associated cash drain. Venture capital investments therefore typically include a major portion of ordinary equity finance, and substantially deferred payout terms for preference or loan capital.

Finally, and again of critical importance, venture capitalists recognise that, to minimise risk and maximise the potential of their investments, management experience and expertise will be at least as important to the fast-growing company as will the availability of finance. A key role of the venture capital executive is to provide this to the companies in his charge, using either his own experience or his network of contacts to access the necessary expertise. Examples of this 'pro-active' involvement may include assistance in the formulation of corporate strategy and plans, definition and selection of an appropriate management team, negotiations with suppliers, agents or partners, and many other functions. Some commentators believe that this distinction between 'hands-on' and 'hands-off' management is the major distinguishing feature between venture and development capital.

The contrasts between typical venture and development capital are summarised below.

Figure 2

Venture and Development Capital Contrasted

	Venture Capital	*Development Capital*
Objectives	Substantial capital gain	Combination of running yield and capital gain
Investee	Cash-consuming	Cash-generating
Typical investment structure	Predominantly equity	Loan/equity package
Running yield?	Unusual	Normal
Relationship with investee	Active — 'hands-on'	Passive

THE ENTREPRENEUR'S CHOICE

So how does the entrepreneur know whether he needs venture or development capital?

The most useful way we have found to illustrate this is by use of a variation of the 'growth/share matrix' originally developed by the Boston Consulting Group, and still widely used in strategic planning analysis, adapted for our own purposes. This is shown in Figure 3 — and every company will fit somewhere within it. The matrix has four quadrants, defined by:

(a) the annual sales growth of the company, divided into high and low ('high' for these purposes is typically defined as in excess of 25%–30%); and

(b) the size of the company relative to the rest of its market as a whole, ie, the vertical middle line represents the median market share.

The companies in each of the four quadrants are known as:

Question-mark — high sales potential, low market share.

Star — high sales growth, high market share.

Cash cow — low sales growth, high market share.

Dog — low sales growth, low market share.

For the purposes of this exercise, as we will see, it is not necessary to calculate precisely the company's position on the matrix — in most cases this will be intuitively obvious. It will also be apparent that for many companies the matrix will represent the various stages in their life-cycle, starting from the top right and moving anti-clockwise. Following this life-cycle through, the need for venture of development capital should become clearer, as follows.

The *'question mark'* company, with a low market share and high growth potential (annual percentage sales growth must be high when starting from nil!) classically describes a start-up or early stage venture. It will need cash to establish a track record and probably fund initial losses. It may well also need help from outside to ensure the company's survival, for example, in assembling the necessary

"GROWTH/SHARE MATRIX"

FIGURE 3

rounded management team. The finance required will be pure risk finance, and will usually be provided principally by specialist venture capital companies if personal or bank finance is unavailable.

As a company becomes more established and hopefully begins to grow, it assumes the characteristics of a '*star*'. Such companies tend to be fast growing but cash consuming, with funding necessary for fixed and working capital investment, and for the marketing and R & D expenses which eat into margins. Such companies may also need management expertise to cope with this growth; both cash and management skills are offered by the venture capital funds to such companies.

When an operation reaches its optimum market share, and growth slows, the investment requirement also typically decreases. Working capital investment will in particular automatically slow down in well managed companies as sales growth tails off. The profitable company should then begin to generate cash, ie, become a '*cash cow*'. The cash cow, however, may still need equity finance for a number of reasons: to restructure its balance sheet if necessary after a period of losses; to fund new projects; to finance any necessary diversification, and so on. If the company is going into new business areas which are large enough in relation to its size and with attractive enough growth prospects which together can be expected to turn the company around into a cash consumer for the foreseeable future, the company will move back towards the 'star' category, and should look for venture capital finance. Most companies in this position, however, would see themselves as returning to modest growth cash generators again after a relatively short period of time.

Cash cows should be able to support a degree of running yield required by a risk capital investor, thus minimising the equity dilution involved in the issue of ordinary shares. Financing such companies thus not surprisingly tends to be the speciality of the development capital institutions, and they are likely to be the natural first port of call for their owners in the absence of any special factors, eg, the need for specific industry expertise on the part of the investor which the development capitalist may not be able to provide.

In due course, changes in the market place will cause the market share of the '*cash cow*' to decline. The matrix defines a company in this position as a '*dog*'. The resuscitation of sick dogs and their reincarnation as 'cash cows' can often, however, be very successfully practised, either by a turnaround of the company internally, organic expansion into new business areas, or by successful acquisition. This may require additional share capital, or alternatively might be accomplished by a change in ownership of the companies concerned, by buying out some of the existing shareholders (management buy-outs are an example of this type of 'replacement capital'). Either way, however, this will involve an initial investment which if successful should quickly generate cash — and a number of very successful quoted companies (eg, BTR, Hanson Trust) have adopted precisely this strategy of using cash to buy mature businesses, which are then turned round to generate cash to start the process again. As with the 'cash cow' above, financing of such companies tends to be the natural preserve of the development capitalist, for similar reasons.

This is a rough and ready guide to how to choose between venture and developmnent capital, which can, however, be successfully applied to almost any business. The key thread which runs through it is the need to match the type of finance required to the *cash profile* of the company (ie, whether it is likely to be cash consuming, cash neutral, or cash generating) over the short and medium-term future. This will be heavily conditioned by the company's anticipated *growth rate* over the foreseeable future, which in turn will heavily influence whether any outside *management assistance* will be required from the investor. It is these three factors together which should determine whether the entrepreneur should concentrate on development or venture capital in his search for finance.

Before we discuss how to raise this finance, however, we must look at some length at what is currently on offer. This is the subject of the next part of the book, which deals with:

Chapter 4 — The Risk Capital Funds
Chapter 5 — Management Buy-Outs
Chapter 6 — The Business Expansion Scheme
Chapter 7 — Corporate Venturing
Chapter 8 — Other Methods of Raising Risk Capital.

PART 3
RISK CAPITAL ALTERNATIVES

Chapter 4

The Risk Capital Funds

The authors of the Wilson Report mentioned in Chapter 1 could be forgiven for their lack of foresight in anticipating the emergence of the risk capital funds. For the size and scale of this explosion of capital is impressive by any measure. It is estimated that over 130 British institutions are currently dedicated to providing risk capital to unquoted companies. The European Venture Capital Association Year Book suggests that together these have raised over £2.1 billion for the purpose. According to the British Venture Capital Association, its members invested over £420m in 1986 in over 700 companies. Indeed, it can be legitimately argued that this type of finance currently on offer will meet the needs of virtually any unquoted company, of whatever type or size, as long as it is good enough. Whether this is true of not, it is certain that there have never been so many alternative sources of finance for the risk capital seeker as there are today, or such competition to invest in businesses with good prospects.

It is not the aim of this chapter to provide a list of risk capital funds, or an evaluation of individual investors. This field is well served on a regular basis by a number of specialised journals, and periodically by the business press. Where individual funds are named, they are given as examples rather than recommendations. We have also not set out in detail here the facts and figures cataloguing the detailed trends in risk capital activity in the UK since the start of the boom in 1980. The latest available figures (for the year ended 31 December 1986) analysing the investment activity of the members of the British Venture Capital Association prepared by the independent consultants Venture Economics Limited, are, however, summarised in Appendix II.

We will, however, look at the distinctive characteristics of the different types of funds on offer, and draw out some issues of relevance to the entrepreneur raised by the current patterns of risk capital activity detailed in the above Appendix.

TYPES OF FUNDS

Continuing activity

We said in Chapter 1 that 'venture capital' had been a feature of the British scene for some time. The City has always been proud of its flexibility and willingness to take equity risks in smaller companies whose prospects were felt to justify this. As a result, before the start of the 1980 'venture capital boom' a large number of unquoted companies were being directly financed, with relatively little publicity, by major City institutions, including pension funds, insurance companies, investment trusts and merchant banks.

This still goes on today — an example is given in the case study in Appendix I — and a congenial investment relationship with a major institution happy to sit back passively for many years waiting for its investment to mature can have its advantages for the entrepreneur. However, as risk capital investment in unquoted companies has never represented the core business of these institutions, and is often made as a 'one-off', it is not always easy to identify likely sources of serious interest in this area, even if knowledgeable professional advisers are used. Furthermore, as we shall see, more and more of such institutions are concentrating their involvement in the unquoted sector on indirect investment, by taking stakes in venture and development capital funds, rather than doing it themselves.

So what can the entrepreneur expect to find behind the doors of the venture and development capital funds?

Development capital funds

The basic investment philosophy of the development capital funds is set out in Chapter 3. They can broadly be divided into three types. First, are the so-called *captive funds*, direct subsidiaries or divisions of larger financial institutions. The most obvious examples of these are the subsidiaries of the major clearing banks (eg, Lloyds Development Capital, Barclays Development Capital, etc). They are typically financed largely or wholly by their parent, and many enjoy effectively unlimited access to funds. At the other end of the spectrum are the *independent funds*, managed usually by small teams of risk capitalists who raise funds which they invest on behalf of their members. These funds come from a variety of sources. Principal sources have been UK pension funds, although substantial funds have also been obtained from other financial institutions and, to a very limited extent, from companies. These funds are usually 'closed-end' funds, with a finite size (typically in the range of £5m–£30m and often substantially larger) and defined life (often seven to ten years) at the end of which the assets of the fund will be distributed to its members. Many management groups today, however, have raised and now manage a number of funds. Managers of independent development capital funds include such names as Causeway Capital and Grosvenor Venture Managers.

Finally, somewhere between these two extremes lies a group of funds which share some similarities with both types. Tony Lorenz in his book *Venture Capital Today* calls them *semi-captives*. Their distinguishing feature is that they raise the bulk of their finance in the same way as the independents — ie, from outsiders, largely in the form of closed-end funds — but at the same time are closely tied to a 'host' institution, through an agreement with the fund's management company or similar arrangements. These host institutions embrace a wide range of city institutions (especially after the 'Big Bang') including stockbrokers such as Phillips & Drew (Phillips & Drew Development Capital), merchant banks such as Hill Samuel (Fountain Development Capital) and Charterhouse (Charterhouse Development Capital).

Implications of captive versus independent funds

The above analysis may appear somewhat academic to the entrepreneur who is first and foremost looking for money, at least if he has identified the development capitalist as his first port of call. The distinction drawn above can, however, hide a number of important issues of particular relevance to the businessman and should raise in his mind, inter alia, the following key questions:

(a) *Risk Capital Commitment.* The independent funds will almost certainly be dedicated to the risk capital business. This may not be true, however, of every captive or semi-captive fund, to whose parent they may represent an insignificant part of their total business. It has been known for captive funds to be wound up, and the entrepreneur needs to be convinced not only of the current enthusiasm of the fund of his choice, but also its long term commitment, and that of its parent, to risk capital investment.

(b) *Second Round Financing Capability.* Conversely, all of the captive and some of the semi-captive funds can be expected to have access to large sums of money if required for subsequent financing rounds. This may not always be true in the case of the independent funds, whose financing capability will depend upon their ability periodically to raise new funds in a competitive marketplace.

(c) *Conflicts of Interest.* The entrepreneur will also want to ensure that a link up with a specific fund will not involve him in unacceptable pressure to make use of the services of its associates, eg, the use of the fund's merchant banking arm in the event of a subsequent flotation. This will apply most obviously to the captive and semi-captive funds, but the entrepreneur should also check up carefully on the backers of any independent funds with whom he is thinking of doing business. In particular he should be wary of any preferred rights they may have negotiated, including for example a first refusal to buy any investments from the fund should it wish at any time to sell.

(d) *Affiliated Services.* Conversely, the closer a fund's connections to the rest of its host organisation, the more efficiently it can be expected to utilise their services for the benefit of the business. Perhaps the most obvious advantages here will lie with the bank-backed funds in financings involving a significant level of conventional secured debt finance, and those funds with strong international links in the case of companies whose success is heavily export dependent.

Chapters 14 and 15 discuss further the roles of the various types of funds in this area at the aftercare stage.

Investment focus

Within the confines described in Chapter 3, the development capitalist will typically be relatively unfocussed in terms of the industries he invests in. Indeed, as relatively risk averse institutions, it is in their interests to diversify their portfolios across a number of industries. Especially in the case of the captive and semi-captive funds which can benefit from the powers of patronage of their host organisations, they can often afford to be more opportunistic in their approach to deal flow. In view of their typically wide range of investee companies, they tend to be staffed by executives with qualifications which cut across industry boundaries (eg, business graduates, accountants).

Venture capital funds

Some of the characteristics noted above apply equally to both the venture and development capital funds. There are, however, some important differences. First, the balance between independents and captives is significantly different from the development capital scene. There are few captive funds involved solely in venture capital, and although a number of semi-captive funds are big players (eg, Baring Brothers, Hambrecht & Quist, Charterhouse Venture Capital) the influence of the independent funds is much greater. Of special interest are the links which many British venture capital funds have with overseas venture capital organisations, especially in the USA. Advent, APA and Alta-Berkley are just three examples of major British funds with strong formal links with established American venture capital funds. This can give important advantages at the aftercare stage to portfolio companies considering international experience, an issue discussed in more detail in Chapter 14.

Secondly, the venture capital funds are often more focussed in their investments than is typical of the development capital sector. This operates on two levels. First, at a more general level, a number of funds have concentrated heavily on, or confined themselves to, investments in technology companies. More specifically, however, in recent years we have witnessed the emergence of a number of funds whose investments have been targetted at specific industry sectors.

This trend began in the technology field, where information technology (eg, Octagon, Syntech) and health care/bio-technology funds (eg, Transatlantic Capital, Bio-Technology Investments) are popular; this is now, however, also beginning to spread to non-technology sectors, with specialised leisure and franchising funds already up and running. It is interesting to observe how many of these specialist venture capital funds include as investors a number of the major risk capital funds without a specific industry focus.

This concentration of investments in specific areas also makes for a different attitude to fund staffing and identification of potential deal flow. Specific industry knowledge is much more of an advantage here, and most of the venture capital funds now include within their ranks a significant number of executives recruited for their experience in specific industries rather than the generic skills of the accountant or the business school graduate.

It is also more difficult to make the most of opportunities in a particular industry sector by sitting back and waiting for the mature and well structured business plan to appear on the desk. As a result, the venture capitalists tend to be more active in promoting their own deal flow and raising their profile in their target industries. They will also typically look at projects in an earlier stage of formulation, and will often take a major role in shaping business plans. This aspect of the venture capitalist's 'hands-on' approach is discussed further in Chapter 14.

Composite funds

We mentioned earlier how the City has traditionally prided itself on its flexibility. This has found expression in the unquoted sector by the existence of a number of funds which together represent an important part of the risk capital sector and which sit somewhere in between the venture and development capitalists.

Composite funds have emerged for a number of reasons. They may be the result of the amalgamation of what were previously separate venture and development capital organisations, such as occurred after the merger between Development Capital Group (confusingly, a venture capital fund group) and Lazards, or the combination of the high and the low technology investment arms of the Prudential Assurance Company into Pruventure. Alternatively, institutions such as Citicorp (part of the giant American CitiBank), CIN Industrial Investments (the unquoted investment arm of the National Union of Mineworkers' Pension Fund) and Equity Capital for Industry have consciously chosen to straddle both the venture and development capital spectrum. These institutions include examples of both captive, semi-captive and independent funds.

Finally, a small number of funds are big or well established enough to have developed under their wing separate venture and development capital operations. Perhaps the prime example of this is 3i, which is often (although, we believe, misleadingly) referred to as 'the largest venture capital fund in the world'. Formerly the Industrial and Commercial Finance Corporation (ICFC), 3i has as its shareholders a number of major banks and raises additional funds through borrowing in the money markets. As a result, in ownership it has a structure closer to the independently managed rather than the captive funds; in size and culture, however, in most respects it is closer to the captives.

Information on 3i is often excluded from statistics on British venture and development capital investment. This arises principally because of the difficulty of analysing relevant information concerning various types of investment within the very broad scope of activities of 3i, and because of its different year-end from the majority of British risk capital funds. The organisation does, however, invest in all stages and sizes of transactions and across all industry sectors. A large proportion of the money invested is provided by secured debt, and arguably for that reason alone falls outside the scope of venture capital. Figures revealed to Venture Economics appear, however, to suggest that in the year to 31 March 1986, 3i's investments of a risk capital nature exceeded £140m.

On the basis of these figures, the size of 3i, operating from 20 regional offices throughout the country, dwarfs any other risk capital fund in the UK. This is primarily a legacy of the length of time it has been investing and the fact that for over 25 years it had few serious rivals in the field. The more sedate competitive environment which characterised its earlier years has been cited by some as the reason for its predominantly low-risk development capital oriented portfolio. It is equally true, however, that it is only because of its size and the consequent portfolio effect that 3i is able to invest so significantly in smaller and start-up companies — nearly 50% of its investments by number in 1986 were in amounts of less than £100,000, compared with 30% by the risk capital industry as a whole.

In addition, 3i has for many years run its own separate high technology group, 3i Ventures, formerly Technical Development Capital. This is a small specialist unit based in London with branch offices in the USA which specialises in making true venture capital investment with a strong technology focus. It operates in a very similar way to the 'pure' technology based independently managed funds.

Government and public sector funds

The public sector, and especially government involvement in the risk capital process, has been significant for a number of years. Indeed, as noted in Chapter 1, it appears to have monopolised the venture capital thinking of the Wilson Report in 1979, largely because of the relative lack of private sector alternatives. With the burgeoning of the venture and development capital funds after 1980, the public sector profile in the risk capital industry has been significantly lowered, although it is still active on a wide front in its encouragement of venture backed enterprises, from fiscal incentives and grants to direct risk capital investment.

This direct investment is currently channelled on two fronts. Active nationwide is the British Technology Group (BTG), a merger between the National Research and Development Corporation (NRDC) and the National Enterprise Board (NEB). BTG invests significant sums annually in technology based companies. A large percentage of this investment, most of which can be categorised as high risk, high return venture capital, is represented by joint venture project finance, which is described in more detail in Chapter 8. BTG's pre-eminence as a technology investor has been diminished somewhat since the recent loss of its right of first refusal to exploit technology developed in government-backed research institutions. It still, however, has one of the largest teams of technologically qualified executives in the country, and should be seriously considered as a financing source by all technology companies.

The main focus of the public sector risk capital presence today is currently, however, concentrated at regional level. Wales, Scotland and Northern Ireland have long had their own development agencies, formed to encourage small business growth in their localities. This has spread into England in the 1980s with the establishment of local Enterprise Boards in such regions as Greater London, Manchester, West Yorkshire and the West Midlands. All these regional bodies have a wider brief than the pure provision of risk capital finance (acting also as a source of industrial factories and warehouses) and a general marketing role to attract business to the area. They have, however, over the years invested significant amounts of venture capital (including a large number of start-ups) and 'rescue capital' for local businesses experiencing trading difficulties. In this context they can be seen as similar to many of the other regional funds within the UK, whose influence is discussed later in this chapter.

CURRENT INVESTMENT PATTERNS — ISSUES FOR THE ENTREPRENEUR

A summary of the investment patterns of the members of the British Venture Capital Association (excluding the majority of 3i investments) in 1986 can be found in Appendix II. Some of the major issues emerging from these statistics for entrepreneurs seeking to raise capital are discussed below.

Type of industry

Much publicity has been given in the press to risk capital investment in high technology companies, which are often thought to account for the majority of funds invested. As Table 5 of Appendix II on page 233 shows, however, this is far from the case. Even if we include all companies in the computer, electronics, medical/health and communications fields in our definition of technology companies, including distributors, they still together barely account for one-third of the investments made by the funds in 1986. The two most popular technology hunting grounds for the risk capitalists, computer and electronics, together have not proved as attractive as consumer related businesses. Furthermore, this is not a new trend; consumer related industries have been at the head of the league table for the past three years.

The signs are that this wide spread of activity will remain a feature of the risk capital scene. There is a common view among industry professionals that the increasing number and appetite of the funds now operating has intensified the competition for good deals to the point where many are being forced to look further afield for investment opportunities, even at the risk of diluting their industry focus. This can be seen in the 'people-based' industries (eg, advertising/PR and financial services) in which some of the venture capital funds are now investing significant sums. It is doubtful whether this trend, which would appear to transgress the venture capitalists' classic insistence on a proprietary product, would have risen to prominence in the absence of such competition.

Stage of finance

Risk capital investors are conversely, however, becoming more concentrated in terms of the stage of the life-cycle of their investee companies. More and more investments, both by number and by amount invested, are now so-called 'later-stage' investments, made in companies which are already profitable, and largely requiring development capital. The increasing amounts of money invested in such companies are to some extent distorted by the recent emergence of a significant number of very large management buy-outs, often involving purchase prices in excess of £100m. The overall trend towards such later stage investments has also, however, been underpinned and reinforced by the increasing number and size of the composite and development capital funds raised in recent years, with their predisposition towards investments in companies of this type. A further reason, some commentators believe, lies in the poor performance of some of the first start-up and early stage investments made by some of the funds in the early 1980s, especially in the now-troubled computer and related sectors.

This is not to say, however, that the sources of early stage finance are drying up. As can be seen from Table 3 of Appendix II on page 231, start-up and early-stage ventures accounted for nearly 30% of 1986 financings, a figure not much changed from 1985. More worrying for the entrepreneur contemplating a start-up, however, the average size of those start-ups which were financed in 1986 rose to £512,000, over 50% up on the comparable 1985 figure of £343,000. If start-up funding is still available, it would appear that more of it is finding its way to the large projects and, by implication, less to the smaller scale ventures which in popular belief represent the essence of entrepreneurship.

Size of finance

The question of whether small companies are more or less likely to find the risk capital they are looking for has generated some controversy. It is also difficult to answer by statistical analysis above. The British Venture Capital Association (BVCA) summary in Appendix II does not address the issue directly, and the relevant figures which do exist are not easy to interpret meaningfully. For although it has been suggested that well over 40% of companies successfully raising risk capital finance receive less than £200,000, this represents little over 5% of the total funds invested each year. More importantly, there are no figures available on small company *failure rates* — the number of rejected applications for risk capital funding for each success — compared with its large company equivalent.

A more meaningful, if less precise, answer can be obtained by looking at the attitudes of the funds themselves to small investments. Here the position is much clearer, for apart from a number of regionally-based funds, and with the notable exception of 3i, few risk capitalists concentrate on making investments of less than £150,000. Many set a minimum investment size of £250,000 and a number have a preference for investments of £500,000 plus.

The main reason for this lies in the internal structure of the funds themselves, and in particular the way the fund managers are remunerated. Aside from any participation in the eventual capital gains of the funds under management, their day-to-day running expenses (in particular executive salaries) are typically covered, at least in the case of the independent funds, by a combination of fees earned from portfolio companies and an annual management fee (typically in the regional of 2%) from investing institutions. It is therefore very much in the interests of the managers to minimise

Chapter 4 The Risk Capital Funds 37

their running expenses, the best way to achieve which is to cut down the time spent in making and monitoring investments. As many market professionals would say that there is maybe twice as much work involved in a £50,000 as in a £500,000 funding, the best way of achieving this is to concentrate on larger deals.

As a result, obtaining small amounts of finance, particularly for early stage companies, is a difficult and in many ways unsolved problem. Somewhat surprisingly, many respected commentators have argued that this so-called 'equity gap' is more acute within the £50,000–£200,000 range than at its lower end. Not only does it appear as though the number of companies receiving risk capital in these amounts have fallen consistently over the last three years, they can also point in support of this contention to the vast majority of small start-ups which have been funded by bank debt backed by personal guarantees of their owners, or by the Loan Guarantee Scheme (which, with a maximum borrowing limit of £75,000, is confined to the very small investment). How true this is, however, remains a matter of opinion. The Loan Guarantee Scheme in particular has had a chequered existence; although many millions of pounds were lent under its aegis in its initial stages, its popularity among bank managers sharply decreased after a number of well publicised failures. It remains open to doubt whether any scheme which attempts to meet a need for equity finance by the provision of debt can provide a long term answer to this real problem.

Regional investments

Ths risk capital community has also been accused by many in the press of perpetrating and even exacerbating the so-called 'north-south divide' by concentrating its investments exclusively in the affluent south-east, to the detriment of the rest of the country.

Table 6 of Appendix II on page 234, analysing the regional breakdown of BVCA members' investments in 1986, initially appears to give some support to this contention, for London and the south-east cumulatively account for 64% of all amounts invested in that year. Further research by Venture Economics also suggests that this figure has risen steadily over the past three years, from a figure of around 55% in 1984.

The position is, however, a little more complicated that these figures imply. For the total *number of companies* financed in London and the south-east in 1986 (a more directly relevant measure to the businessman) amounted to only 46% of the total, in an area which contains some 35% of the population of the UK. Furthermore, comparable figures again prepared by Venture Economics suggest that this percentage has remained constant over the same three-year period. It would thus appear that this apparently increasing predominance of the south-east is not so much the product of more investments as of bigger investments; this in turn is not so surprising in view of the emergence of the large risk-capital backed management buy-outs, often businesses operating on a national scale but headquartered in London or the south-east.

Whatever the details, however, the basic message to the entrepreneur emerging from the figures is clear. Although there is a natural concentration by the funds in investments in the south-east, significant investment activity is continuing throughout the UK; and more and more companies in other parts of the UK are succeeding in obtaining risk capital finance. This is despite the fact that the vast majority of risk capital funds are still London-based, and reflects their willingness and ability to invest nationally.

In addition there are a growing number of regional risk capital funds which focus their investment in a particular local area. As a result of their lower overhead structures these funds typically compete for the smaller investment which requires closer post-investment monitoring and which, when the business is located some distance from London, can involve a significant cost for the larger London-based funds. The number and scope of activity from regional funds continues to increase, and they will probably provide a source of opportunities for second round investment by the larger funds.

Syndications

Table 1 of Appendix II on page 228 shows that BVCA members in 1986 made 1105 investments in 708 companies. The main reason for the difference lies in those companies in whom investments were made by more than one fund at a time.

Following the pattern established in the USA, there is a growing trend in the UK for venture capital funds to share, or syndicate, participation in investments. Many funds feel most comfortable investing in blocks of around £500,000, and it is still the exception rather than the rule to find institutions investing in excess of £1m in any one company, unless this is spread over more than one round of finance. As a result, the vast majority of larger risk capital equity financings involve some syndication.

Syndication has a number of advantages. By sharing the effort involved in assessing new investment opportunities and subsequent monitoring across a number of fund managers participating in the syndicate, the individual funds are able to participate in a larger number of investments and, as a result, share their risk. In addition, participation in syndicates increases the flow of deals to which any individual fund manager has access. By sharing deals with other funds, a fund can expect reciprocal treatment from syndicate partners who are offered participation in their good deals. Dealing with a syndicate of investors can be time-consuming and difficult for management, both during negotiations and after an investment has been made. This can and often is, however, minimised by a lead investor taking on the burden of the investor 'due diligence' work and the conduct of detailed negotiations on behalf of the other investors, thus insulating management as far as possible from uncoordinated enquiries and unstructured negotiation.

Syndication can also benefit management in other ways, not least of which is the prestige arising from the backing of a group of reputable risk capitalists. In addition, a number of funds with a large capital base are now willing to invest in amounts over £1m, or to syndicate larger investments with the fewest possible partners. Again, the choice is there for the entrepreneur with something to sell.

THE RISK CAPITALISTS

We mentioned earlier the different skills of the executives typically recruited by the venture and development capital funds, but who are these executives, and what implications do their experience and training have for the entrepreneurs they will be dealing with?

Risk capital fund executives

We will deal in more detail later with some of the specific qualities the entrepreneur may be looking for in his chosen risk capitalist. It is worth, however, at this stage setting out some general characteristics of the funds and their executives which may be of relevance to the small business seeking finance.

Size

Most funds, both venture and development capital, are small; the average size is around six executives and there are few funds with more than 12. This may be an advantage to their portfolio companies, if by linking up with a small team of executives they can reasonably be assured of continuity of staff, and in particular of the executive they will be working with. This can, however, be taken too far if the fund allows its executives to become too widely stretched by taking on too many companies. We will deal with this point further in Chapter 14, but it can often be a problem, especially with 'hands-on' funds whose executives may be spending considerable amounts of time with their existing portfolio companies.

Training and qualifications

With the major City institutions so involved in the current risk capital scene, it is perhaps not surprising that so many risk capital executives (in total well over half) have been trained in the 'traditional' City disciplines of accounting, corporate finance, management consultancy, or the business school, rather than in industry. This is not necessarily a bad thing from the entrepreneur's point of view, as this may be precisely the expertise he is looking for from his financial backers. In addition, many of the executives he will be dealing with will also have worked in industry at some stage in their careers. Perhaps of more importance is the balance of skills available in each particular fund, and their compatibility with their target portfolio companies. Here the position is changing, with many funds actively recruiting seasoned industrialists onto their executive teams, or augumenting their skills base by the use of specialist outside associates.

Common experience

In common with many of the industries it invests in, the risk capital business is a small place. Although there may be as many as 400 executives practising in the industry today, the significant market segmentation and increase in syndication which we have already mentioned means that many of the funds know each other very well, as collaborators as well as competitors. The marketplace is characterised as a result not only by a high degree of shared knowledge but also, more importantly, of shared values and expectations. This has been accentuated by the not infrequent personnel moves from one fund to another, but also by the way in which certain funds (notably 3i, but also BTG and others) have acted as an 'industry training ground', in the sense that many of their executives now work for other funds or have formed their own.

This is an important feature of the industry, which is often lost sight of by seekers of risk capital finance. Although the marketplace is competitive, many financing proposals from otherwise sound companies will in practice prove unfundable across the industry because they transgress one or other unshakeable industry-wide axioms, for example an inadequate financial commitment to the venture by management. It can be difficult for the outsider to know at what point he is likely to hit this barrier, or conversely, which parts of his proposal he can reasonably hope to persuade one or more funds to be flexible on. Again, specialist advice will be essential here.

The significant commodity of common experience and attitude within the industry has recently been strengthened by a more formal move towards industry-wide standards with the creation of a nationally representative voice of the risk capitalists in the form of the British Venture Capital Association.

Role of the British Venture Capital Association

The British Venture Capital Association is the trade association for the risk capital industry. It was founded in 1982, as the current venture capital boom began to approach critical mass. By December 1986 it numbered as full members 77 funds or fund managers, together with 32 associate members who are generally involved in advising fund managers or their portfolio companies on risk capital investment.

The primary role of the BVCA is to identify and research the issues facing the industry as a whole and to lobby the government for changes in company law, tax legislation, etc, which are likely to help the risk capital industry and its portfolio companies grow. These are communicated throughout the membership by a series of workshops, seminars and newsletters, which also seek to share cumulative experience on operational matters.

The BVCA also monitors the investment activity of its members. Its annual review analyses the funds raised (for example by source, nature of fund) and funds invested (by industry sector, region, stage of financing, etc). A summary of the latest review covering investment activity for 1986 is included in Appendix II.

Arguably of more relevance to the entrepreneur, however, the BVCA also provides a code of conduct for its members. This is set out overleaf.

Code of conduct

Membership of the BVCA implies support for the development of the British venture capital industry, the advancement of technology and productivity and the creation of an encouraging climate for companies seeking venture capital.

1. Members shall promote and maintain ethical standards of conduct and at all times deal fairly and honestly with each other and with companies seeking venture capital.
2. Members will conduct their business in a professional way and will not engage in practices which would be damaging to the image of the venture capital industry.
3. Members recognise that their primary business is building the strength of their investee companies which will result in the funds under management making long-term capital gains.
4. Membership of the BVCA implies an active involvement by members in the companies in which they invest and this involvement shall be applied constructively to the benefit of the company concerned.
5. Members who sponsor investment syndications with other parties, whether members of the BVCA or not, must operate on the basis of full disclosure to such other parties.
6. Members shall be accountable to their investors and keep their investors fully and regularly informed including the provision of regular financial reports.
7. No member shall take improper advantage of his position in the BVCA nor of any information addressed to the BVCA.
8. Members shall respect confidential information supplied to them by companies looking for venture capital or by companies in which they have invested.

The BVCA requires members to ensure that their directors, employees, representatives and nominees comply with these standards. Members are also required to avoid financing enterprises or participating in activities which are inconsistent with these goals. As all the major risk capital funds are members of the BVCA, this should give real encouragement to the entrepreneur, not only as a sign that the industry is maturing, but also that it is taking itself and its professional standards seriously.

SOURCES OF INFORMATION

Finally, where can the entrepreneur seeking risk capital find out more about what the funds have to offer?

There are a number of sources of information on the names, size and investment focus of British venture capital funds. In addition to information available in a number of trade directories, there are periodic surveys in a number of magazines such as *Investors Chronicle* and newspapers such as the *Financial Times*. Venture Economics, an independent research organisation, also publishes a bi-monthly journal on venture capital activity and a directory of venture fund managers. Finally, the British Venture Capital Association publishes annually a directory of its members including details of investment preferences and contact names.

None of these sources can, however, provide a sufficiently detailed or current analysis of the areas of interest of the risk capital funds for a businessman to be certain that his company will be attractive to a particular fund. This is in part due to the subjective nature of the assessment of any risk capital project. In addition, however, the risk capitalist's interest in a project will be affected by the spread of other investments in his portfolio. However good a new project may appear, if making the investment would involve an excessive exposure in a particular sector it is unlikely to receive the support of that particular fund.

Approaching the funds can be a daunting task, which is best attempted with the aid of specialist advice. We deal with this subject in more detail in Chapter 9, after looking at some more specific sources and applications of risk capital finance.

Chapter 5

Management Buy-outs

'Who really makes the big money? The inside stockholders of a company do, when the market capitalises the earnings of that company' (Adam Smith, *The Money Game*).

The truth of the above quotation is increasingly being seized upon by British managers working for large companies, more and more of whom are seeking to buy their company or division from its existing owners by the process known as a *management buy-out* (MBO). As most MBO's are financed by the risk capital community, the success of the MBO phenomenon has in the 1980s provided an important engine of growth for the British venture and development capital industry.

There has so far been no shortage of spectacular successes. Figure 4 below gives examples of some of the more successful MBO's of recent years in terms of demonstrating the truth of Adam Smith's doctrine by achieving a Stock Exchange quotation for their companies shortly after buy-out at a valuation far in excess of the purchase price.

Figure 4

UK Management Buy-outs: Recent Rewards (£m)

	Parent	Purchase price (£m)	Market capitalisation on listing (£m)	Completion to listing (years)
DPCE	DPCE Pty (Australia)	1.75	20.0	2
Amari	BP	5.0	31.4	0.5
Sarosota Technology	Redland plc	5.4	23.3	2

The wide publicity achieved by these and similar examples has rightly focused considerable attention on management buy-outs as a means both of releasing entrepreneurial talent into the economy, and enabling managers to 'get rich quick', to the point that the investment community is as anxious to invest in soundly-based buy-outs as are management themselves. This is perhaps most obviously demonstrated by the establishment in recent years of specialised management buy-out funds and the emergence of many banks (both domestic and foreign) as major players in the buy-out game.

This increasing interest is reflected in the figures. It is generally accepted that over 1,000 MBO's have been completed in the 1980s so far, with current activity running in excess of 200 per annum. Billions of pounds have been invested to date, and billions more are available for investment in companies of all sorts and sizes, from those little bigger than the corner shop to amongst the largest companies in the land.

The most authoritative current source of information on management buyouts in the UK today can be found in the *Review of UK Management Buy-outs*, produced jointly by Venture Economics and John Coyne and Mike Wright of the Centre for Management Buy-out Research at Nottingham University, from which source the following tables have been extracted.

Figure 5

Total Number and Value of Management Buy-outs 1967–85

Year	No.	Cum No.	Value (£m)	Cumulative Value (£m)	Average value in year (£m)
1967–76	43	43	n/a	n/a	n/a
1977	13	56	n/a	n/a	n/a
1978	23	79	n/a	n/a	n/a
1979	52	131	26	26	0.50
1980	107	238	50	76	0.47
1981	124	362	114	190	0.92
1982	170	532	265	455	1.56
1983	205	737	315	770	1.54
1984	210	947	255	1,025	1.21
1985	229	1,176	1,150	2,175	5.02

Figure 5 shows the cumulative value of MBO's identified by the *Review* since 1967, representing an estimated, 1,176 individual transactions. 229 of these were completed in 1985, with an estimated value of over £1,150m. This implies an average size of just over £5m per transaction, although as shown by Figure 6 below, this is significantly skewed by the existence of a small number of very large buyouts

Figure 6

Value of 1985 Management Buy-outs

Value (£000's)	No. of MBO's	% of MBO's
Less than 100	10	6.5
100 — 499	51	33.1
500 — 999	15	9.7
1,000 — 4,999	46	29.9
5,000 — 9,999	12	7.8
10,000 — 49,999	14	9.1
50,000 and over	6	3.9
Total	154	100.0

These figures, based on an analysis of 154 1985 management buy-outs where the value range is known, show that nearly half of all buy-outs by number involve amounts of less than £1m, with a further 38% in the £1m — £10m range. Although in money terms an analysis of the amounts involved suggests that the biggest 20% of buy-outs account for 80% of funds committed, the bulk of activity in the sector clearly remains at the smaller end of the spectrum.

As Figure 7 below shows, MBO investors also tend to be more omnivorous in the type of industries they invest in than other venture and development capital investors. Although industrial and manufacturing companies represent the most popular targets, all types of industries (including financial services) are represented. A much more definite concentration emerges, however, when the type of risk capital invested is examined. Although there is no reason to stop venture capitalists investing in early stage high growth buy-outs — and indeed many have been financed with conspicuous success — the vast majority, both by number and by value, appear

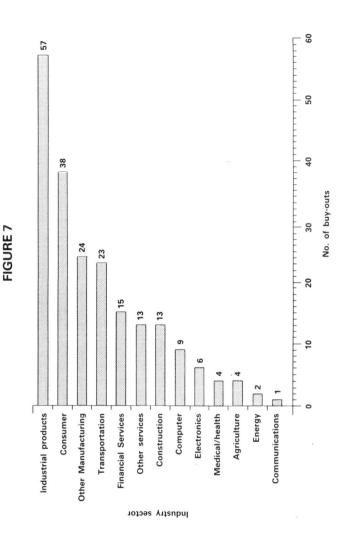

INDUSTRY DISTRIBUTION OF 1985 BUY-OUTS

FIGURE 7

to have been financed with development capital. We discuss the reasons for this later.

A similar degree of concentration in sources of management buy-outs can be observed from Figure 8 which shows that 78% of 1985 management buy-outs were as a result of divestitures from existing groups.

Figure 8

Sources of 1985 Management Buy-outs

Source	No. of MBO's	% of MBO's	% 1976-1983
Divestment — British parent	147	69.6	52.7
Private/Family	35	16.6	20.5
Divestment — Foreign Parent	20	9.5	7.1
Privatisation	5	2.4	1.8
Receivership	3	1.4	17.9
Public Company	1	0.5	—
Total	211	100.0	100.0

Divestitures have increased as a percentage of the total since 1983, especially those from foreign parents. The major change in recent years however, can be seen in the sharp decline in buy-outs from the receiver. In a study by Coyne and Wright of 110 buy-outs between 1976 and 1983 (reproduced in their book *Management Buy-outs*), receivership buy-outs represented 18% of the total during this period, a figure heavily influenced by the effects of the recession. The third major category of management buy-out shown in the above table — involving the transfer of ownership of family companies to non-shareholder managers — has and is likely to continue as a significant vehicle of industrial continuity. Many of these transactions can alternatively be seen as another form of replacement capital, which is dealt with further in Chapter 8.

Overall, however, there appears to be no end to the appetite of all parties for management buy-outs. Not only is more money becoming available to finance the demand for buy-outs, but more and more companies are coming to regard the sale of the subsidiary to management as a main stream corporate finance alternative to divestiture via a trade sale. STC and Hanson Trust are just two of the many examples of this emerging trend in recent years. In fact it has been estimated that in 1985 more subsidiaries of British companies were sold to their existing management than to other companies. It is this increasing willingness of large companies to consider management buy-outs as a natural alternative which lies at the heart of the current MBO explosion, and it is this question (ie, why should the parent sell?) which any entrepreneur seeking to buy into the company he works for will need to examine at the outset.

WHAT IS A MANAGEMENT BUY-OUT?

First, however, we should attempt to define the terms we have been using — for, as with so much of the risk capital business, there seem sometimes to be as many definitions as there are practitioners — and look at the major sources of buy-out activity.

Perhaps the best definition of an MBO would define it as the purchase of a company as a result of which its managers come to assume day-to-day control of all aspects of the business and acquire a substantial stake in its ownership.

This wide definition of on MBO has led some to try and subdivide the phenomenon further, by the use of such terms as:

(a) *Leveraged buy-outs*, where the post-financing capital structure of the company is heavily geared (or leveraged). As few management teams can afford to buy into their companies unaided without a financing structure which will give them a greater percentage of new equity capital than their percentage contribution to the purchase price, most buy-outs will contain at least some leveraged element.

The leverage referred to here is typically achieved either by way of traditional debt leverage (by the use of the sort of borrowing described in Chapter 3) or equity leverage, in cases where the company's capital structure is heavily weighted in favour of preferred or other forms of non-voting shares. The 'gearing' here arises from the fact that management will typically only invest by way of ordinary shares, thus ensuring that for every per cent of the *total* share capital they invest, they will receive more than 1% of the *voting* shares.

(b) *Employee buy-outs*, a variant of the above where ownership of the company is extended to as many of the work force as possible.

(c) *Management buy-ins*, whereby a team of outside managers take both operating and ownership control of the 'target' company. This is becoming increasingly popular in the UK and many risk capitalists have helped in the financing. The phenomenon, however, will be seen by many entrepreneurs as having more similarities with the process of corporate acquisition than with the provision of risk capital, and buy-ins are not dealt with further in this book.

(d) *Sponsored spin-offs*, whereby existing management of a large corporation allows management of one division or project to form a separate company to continue in business under their own control. This is really a form of corporate venturing, which is dealt with in Chapter 7.

In addition, as noted above, we have seen in recent years the emergence of a number of very large management buy-outs, often involving purchase prices of up to and over £100m. In many cases these have involved mature companies with capable and well-rounded management structures, where the vast majority of the purchase price has been financed by debt secured directly or indirectly on previously under-utilised assets of the target company. One such example was Haden plc, the publicly-quoted engineering group which was bought out by its management as a defence to a hostile take-over bid from Trafalgar House. The background to some of these 'mega-deals' can also appear more than somewhat esoteric to the average entrepreneur. Although many of these transactions have been backed by risk capital funds, the main value added by the institutional investor in such cases will often lie in his financial engineering ability rather than his skills in working with management after investment to help the company grow. We are moving into a grey area here, away from the core expertise of the risk capitalist and into the domain of the corporate finance expert, and some would doubt whether such transactions should properly be considered as venture or development capital. Throughout the rest of this chapter therefore, we will exclude them from further consideration.

THE KEY QUESTIONS

Regardless of how we define our terms, however, how does management go about converting the dream of buying-out its employers into reality?

The problem

It is at this stage that anyone thinking of a management buy-out, either as a buyer, seller, or backer, will come across the fundamental problem inherent in the process, which is illustrated by way of example in Figure 9.

This effectively boils down to one of price. If we assume that the host company will generally want to sell at a fair value and that the management and investors are looking for an exceptional return, then this implies that the target company must have unrealised potential, either as a result of under-utilised assets or the ability to increase future profits. In either case this begs the questions of:

(a) why should the parent want to sell? and
(b) if it were willing to sell, why would it be likely to sell to management?

Finally, management will also need to answer the question of how the outside investor can be persuaded to back the project.

It is the answers to these questions which will, if applicable, provide the management team and their backers with the confidence to initiate the buy-out process and drive it successfully to a conclusion.

Why should the parent want to sell?

Disregarding 'receivership' and 'management succession' buy-outs, there are many factors which may incline groups of companies to sell one or more of their subsidiaries.

(a) *Incompatibility with corporate strategy.* First, the subsidiary may be peripheral to the group's core business, as a result of:

    (i) the move from a conglomerate to a more focused strategy. Many groups in recent years have re-cast their corporate

Figure 9

Management Buy-outs — The Basic Problem

Consider the following two companies, which we will assume are cash generating and have established good competitive positions in industries which are stable but with limited growth prospects. Let us also assume that in both cases management are examining the possibility of an MBO, although their own cash resources are negligible.

	Company A (£000's)	Company B (£000's)
Net assets	1,000	1,000
Net profit (post-tax)	100	250
Return on capital	10%	25%

Company A is extremely unlikely to be an attractive MBO proposition at a purchase price anywhere near net asset value. The potential development capital investor (neither of the above companies would be likely to interest the venture capitalist in the absence of special circumstances) would require a running yield on the bulk of his investment at market rates. An investment of £1m would at current rates of profitability absorb substantially all the company's annual income in the debt and equity service costs required to meet the investors' own cost of funds, leaving little behind to support the extra returns the investor will require to compensate him for his investment risk.

The investor is therefore unlikely to consider financing a buy-out at anything other than a heavy discount to net assets (maybe of the order of 50% in the absence of significant turnaround prospects), a figure which the current owners might find hard to accept.

Company B appears to be earning a high enough return on capital to justify financing any proposed buy-out at net asset value. The question is, however, why the parent company would want to sell any of its subsidiaries which is already earning a return on capital of this magnitude or, if it did, would it accept a purchase price which could be supported by the institutions. For example, a full market price of, say eight times earnings, would imply a purchase price of £2m, the debt and equity servicing costs of which again would be expected to absorb substantially all the company's annual cashflow.

> **Solution**
>
> The above scenario might well call the viability of both the projected buy-outs into question. The classical answer to this dilemma can be found when the two companies in fact represent *the same company seen through different eyes*. The parent company may see the target company as Company A, a poor performer under current conditions.
>
> Management, however, may see the target as Company B, in terms of future potential. This *turnaround potential* may give both sides the opportunity to strike a price which the vendor feels properly reflects current performance and the investor feels is supportable from the promise of future results.

        strategy around the concept of 'sticking to the knitting', reversing the corporate orthodoxy common in the 1960s;
  (ii) a re-definition or change in the core business of the group, in response to the availability of more attractive business areas or other changing circumstances. A good example of this is Dataserv, which was quoted on the Stock Exchange in 1984 as a lease-broker, but within two years was earning over half of its profits from computer maintenance;
  (iii) the acquisition of unwanted subsidiaries 'by accident', ie, as a result of take-overs or mergers with other diversified groups. The Hanson Trust example quoted above represents an instance of this.

(b) *Resource starvation*. In some cases the parent may not be able to provide the resources needed by subsidiaries in peripheral businesses, both in terms of cash, for necessary investment, and people, ie, experienced executives to manage subsidiaries and top management at group level to monitor their performance.

(c) *Force majeure*. Finally the group may be forced to sell certain subsidiaries to raise cash. Going-concern sales typically realise higher prices than piecemeal disposals or break-ups, especially when closure costs are taken into account. Closure costs, including redundancy payments, lease cancellation costs, etc, can often be of fundamental importance because of their size, and can be a useful negotiating point for management in their attempt to buy their own business at a price which does not over-strain the company's capacity to finance it.

Why should the parent company sell to management?

The MBO boom of the early 1980s was fuelled by many recession-induced forced sales at heavy asset discounts to managements who at that time represented the only possible buyers. This is now changing as corporate earnings increase, enabling sellers realistically to ask for more, and third party buyers to pay more. This is especially true of acquisitive quoted companies with the ability to use their own paper to fund the purchase, but, although the environment is now becoming more competitive, a determined management group may still retain many advantages denied to a third-party alternative buyer including:

(a) *Better information.* This can be a key advantage. Existing management should have a better appraisal of the real operating potential of the business than anyone, and a sharper sense of the value of their own contribution to it. This knowledge can have its own deterrent value which management can use in the negotiation process. For example, the implication that existing management would resist any alternative to an MBO, including maintenance of the status quo, can be a powerful lever both in persuading the parent to sell to management, and in driving down the purchase price.

This superior information should theoretically enable management to judge what is the right price more accurately than anyone else, without taking up the weeks or months of time involved in an outside evaluation of the business. Time-scales may also be speeded up by the fact that the parent will not normally need to give extensive warranties about the business (see Chapter 13) to a management team who are intimately familiar with it.

(b) *Confidentiality.* An MBO will not normally involve trade competitors. Should the sale fall through, it is unlikely that competitive information will have been given away in the attempt.

(c) *Continuing relationships.* The vendor may be unwilling to sell a subsidiary with whom he has a continuing trading relationship, when after the MBO he would otherwise have to trade with a competitor or third party; this is, for example, a major consideration in many sales by manufacturers of their distribution operations. If a continuing trading relationship is likely to be important to him, he may prefer to deal with people he knows well, especially if the customers of the subsidiary have indicated they will only do business with existing management.

(d) *Intangible factors* can also be important. Many groups concerned with their outside image would rather sell off unwanted subsidiaries to existing management than surrender control to other (possibly overseas) companies or close the business down. Finally, but by no means unimportantly, many MBO's have succeeded because of the wish of the parent to reward the past loyalty and performance of the managers concerned.

Why should the investor fund the buy-out?

As mentioned above, MBO's have recently been very attractive to risk capitalists; virtually every venture or development capital fund is interested. Why should this be so?

(a) *Historic success.* The MBO failure rate according to 3i, Britain's leading investor in MBO's in terms both of number of companies and amounts invested, is running at approximately one in seven, as against the figure of one in three conventionally associated with start-ups. The main reason for this is the low-risk nature of the bulk of projects financed, in keeping with the tendency of the development capitalists to dominate the process. There is however some evidence to suggest that, in addition to this, management teams have by and large managed their companies more efficiently after the buy-out.

(b) *Improved performance.* It is widely agreed that among companies in receipt of MBO funding, the most critical subsequent improvement has been in *cash flow management*. This has to some extent been forced on new owners by the need to pay off the debt commonly incurred in financing the buy-out, whereas previously there may have been little meaningful incentive to maximise cash generation within the previous group, especially if finance were provided from the centre. As a result, improved debtor and stock control systems and more sophisticated cash planning have characterised many companies in the post-buy-out period.

This has similarly been reflected in many cases in tighter *cost control*, both in terms of production and overheads. Again, this may result from the removal of pre-buy-out central overheads charged to the company, or alternatively the subsequent freedom to simplify a management structure previously made unnecessarily complex by old group policies.

Management should not, however, overestimate these savings, important though they may be, or underestimate the replacement cost of essential services previously provided by head office, such as computer or accounting charges.

Finally, many managers have used their freedom to *enhance competitiveness by significant investment* in marketing, R & D or capital equipment. In the Coyne and Wright study of 110 MBO's between 1976 and 1983, referred to previously, 71% of the companies in question subsequently significantly upgraded their product range, and 30% entered new markets. This was felt to be a major factor in the reporting of improved profitability by 75% of respondents, half of whom increased profits substantially.

CRITICAL SUCCESS FACTORS

As noted above, no MBO can succeed without a *willing seller* in circumstances which are likely to give a competitive edge to any bid from existing management. This is not all. A successful MBO will also require:

(a) *A sound business.* Capable of generating the return required by the investor. To the development capitalist, this will mean the ability to generate sufficient cash to service his running yield and repay his invested capital on schedule; for the venture capitalist, this will require the potential for sustained rapid growth.

(b) *Able management.* The key to success in every MBO is an *entrepreneurial* management team. The new owners (and especially the chief executive) will need to be able to take risks, anticipate and respond to change, and motivate the work force, as well as continue the conventional management functions which dominated their working lives in their old group. This will often require a sea-change in outlook, and some never rise to the task.

To be successful, the management team will also need drive and commitment, and a balance of skills including specialists in all major relevant management functions. It is rare for an investor to back a buy-out without a rounded management team already substantially in place. Finally, the team needs to be able to walk the tightrope between the action-oriented dictatorship and the consultative commune where nothing gets done. It is important to ensure that the personal chemistry between the team is right at the outset, and it is here above all that the non-executive director nominated by the investor can play a positive role.

(c) *Appropriate investors.* The right investor will depend on the nature of the finance sought. The venture capital investor requiring a high equity stake will be of little use to a cash-generating company with asset backing to support significant amounts of debt finance; likewise the development capitalist will be unlikely to fund the buy-out of an early stage high technology venture.

Whatever the type of buy-out, however, the investor will need to be extremely flexible, and move quickly when necessary, especially when the vendor decides to change the terms of the deal at the last minute or threatens to sell to a third party who says he can complete within a week!

(d) *Experienced advisers.* The subject of professional advisers is dealt with more fully in Chapter 9. Management will rely significantly on advisers throughout the MBO process, especially the *lead adviser*.

In rare cases, eg, where one of the management team has specific MBO experience, the lead can be taken internally. It is usual, however, for an outsider to be appointed, and critical that one person takes overall responsibility for all phases of the deal.

The lead adviser can be an accountant or solicitor with relevant experience or a consultant, merchant banker or broker. A number of firms specialising in MBO advice and negotiations have recently emerged, and can provide an excellent 'turnkey' lead advisory service.

The lead adviser's role is complex and includes:

(i) organising the management team (and their intra-group relationships);
(ii) appointing and instructing other advisers;
(iii) negotiating with the vendor and financiers, including the critical issue of determining the purchase price.

As a result, we would generally not advocate that the lead investor assumes the role of lead adviser, because of the conflicts of interest this will inevitably entail, notably when negotiating the terms of the finance he is subscribing.

THE BUY-OUT PROCESS

Complexity

The process of how venture and development capital investments are made is described more fully in Part 4. MBO's follow an essentially similar course, although they are typically more complex than normal risk capital transactions, as:

* they involve three parties (vendor, management, financiers) rather than two;
* there are at least two sets of agreements (the purchase agreement with the vendor and the investment agreement with the backers) to be negotiated rather than one.

This commonly has the following effects:

(a) *Legal and tax implications* are important. Issues can include:

   (i) *Tax:* whether to purchase the assets of the target company or its shares; the possibility of obtaining tax relief for individuals on the interest cost of borrowings; and the need to avoid if possible those sections of the Taxes Acts which would normally have the effect of taxing any subsequent capital gains of management on their shares as income rather than a capital gain.

   (ii) *Legal:* the structuring of the purchase so as to ensure that the provisions of the Companies Acts prohibiting the financial assistance by the company in the purchase of its own shares are not breached; the mechanics of ensuring the trouble-free assignment of assets and liabilities to the purchasing company in asset-based purchases.

   These issues can be complex and are not always encountered in conventional venture and development capital financings. As such it is even more important than usual for management to be well advised.

(b) *Personalities and timing.* The progress of two sets of negotiations at the same time, involving three different parties, can lead to some of the protagonists 'wearing different hats for different occasions'. For example, management will be trying to minimise the price when negotiating with the parent, but trying to maximise its value when in discussions with financiers. This can lead to problems of personality and timing, including:

(i) The problem of management attempting to negotiate with its current employers, which can be a great strain to both sides. One of the most important services a lead adviser can provide on such occasions is to take the lead in acting for management throughout the negotiations, to help maintain a businesslike atmosphere at all times.

(ii) It is possible to hit 'catch 22' timing problems throughout the process. A common stumbling block often rears its head prior to achieving agreement in principle to the buy-out. Specifically, the vendor may not be willing to give an agreement in principle to sell without a firm commitment that the necessary finance will be available, while the financiers may similarly be reluctant to give any commitment in the absence of a written undertaking to sell from the vendor. Lead advisers will need to take some care to ensure that this does not become insuperable by the creation of suitably worded conditional undertakings or letters of intent.

(c) *A long haul.* The net effect of such complexities is commonly to prolong the process — MBO's can in some cases take as little as three weeks to finance, but sometimes will take over two years. Anyone thinking of buying the business he works for should not underestimate the time it could take, and should prepare himself mentally for a three to six months timeframe even in the case of the smallest deals, and longer if any significant problems are anticipated.

(d) *Structural flexibility.* The MBO process also demands considerable flexibility from all participants to adapt their initial aims and operating policies to the facts of a constantly changing situation. Nowhere will this be more necessary than in structuring the terms of the financing.

FINANCING THE BUY-OUT: SIX STEPS

The risk capitalist of whatever type will, however, go through essentially the same thought process in structuring the terms of any MBO, as set out in the six steps below:

(a) *Determine the amount of financing required.* This will comprise the purchase consideration to the vendor, plus any continuing cash requirement of the target company itself.

(b) *Ascertain the amount of management's contribution.* This need not represent a significant percentage of the total purchase consideration. Indeed, except in the case of the smallest deals or other special cases, it would be unreasonable for the investor to insist on it. He will nevertheless look for evidence of commitment from management, ie, for management to go 'on risk' for an amount which is material to its own circumstances. A figure of around £25,000 (for *each* member of the management team) is often cited as representing a norm for this purpose, although this can be subject to significant variation when considered alongside the managers' personal circumstances, the equity stake they are seeking and the overall amount of finance required.

(c) *Determine the company's debt gearing capacity.* This will usually be calculated on the principles outlined in Chapter 2. In general, however, this can be high in the case of development capital-backed MBO's, but will usually be low in the case of venture-backed projects.

(d) *Agree management's equity percentage.* This is a key decision which is discussed in more detailed in Chapter 12. In general, however:

   (i) Single investors do not like taking control, although in cases of syndicated financings investors are usually happy for no one party (counting the managers as one for these purposes) to have a majority.
   (ii) As a tentative rule of thumb, a contribution by management in excess of 20% of the purchase price will in most cases give them control. It used to be said that less than 10% will not, although this nostrum has become somewhat eroded in recent years as able management teams are increasingly realising the attractiveness of their companies to investors.

(e) *Determine the method of equity gearing.* For example, preference shares, deferred shares, unusual voting rights, etc.

(f) *Agree on the share rights,* These are required to secure acceptable rates of return for the investors, eg, preferred dividend rights, provisions for conversion into equity (possibly related to performance), redemption premiums, etc.

A worked example of how such an approach was used in practice to structure a development capital-backed buy-out can be found in the Appendix to this chapter.

FIVE GOLDEN RULES

All MBO's are different, and each has its own lessons for its participants. Some, however, recur time after time. Here are five of the most important lessons for management from our own experience:

(a) *Organise yourselves.* Clear agreement between the management team as to the respective roles of each member, and their delegated powers, etc, is essential at the outset. It should not be forgotten that while they are trying to buy the company, the management is still employed to run the business.

(b) *Have you got a sale?* Unless there is good reason to believe at the outset that the vendor will not be averse to selling to management, the whole process could be useless and possibly prejudice the prospects of the management team within the group. This is often a many-layered issue, and a difficult decision to make, but one which must be faced up to at the start.

(c) *Choose the right advisers and backers.* Ensure that your advisers — and especially the lead adviser — are the best you can get. It is difficult to imagine a case where you will not need their expertise. Use your advisers to help you avoid the other obvious pitfall here — getting tied up with the wrong fund.

(d) *Do not pay too much.* If you do, and as a result the company is saddled with too much debt, or equity carrying a running yield, you will have succeeded only in exchanging one owner for another (ie, the backers). This is an understandable temptation, but one which too many managers are prone to fall into, to their eventual detriment.

(e) *Do not panic.* One leading MBO practitioner tells us that 'all successful deals go through at least three crises before completion'. Many believe that the psychological strain on the management team is the biggest problem involved in the MBO process because of the unique pressures at work. Patience and optimism are important qualities which management will need to develop to see the deal through to a finish.

APPENDIX — STRUCTURING THE BUY-OUT: NEWBRAND

The following is a somewhat simplified practical example of how a development capital management buy-out (using an assumed name) was structured.

Background

Newbrand is an established company in the fashion business, which had over the last three years recently experienced some hard times in an increasingly competitive market. Heavy investment by the parent company over a number of years to reposition the company more profitably in the marketplace had been slow to take effect, although current management estimated that the company would break even at the end of the current year before exceptional items (largely redundancy costs), and improve thereafter.

Newbrand's net assets were estimated by management at approximately £1.25m, on which they believed that, in the absence of group management charges, a profit before tax in the region of £500,000 could be achieved in future years (it was anticipated that no tax would be payable for some years in the future, in view of large historic accumulated tax losses).

Management approached the parent company as to the possibility of purchasing the company for themselves, and believed that the sale could be negotiated at a price around £1.5m.

Structuring the deal

The advisers of management structured the proposed terms of the MBO using the six-step approach outlined previously.

Step 1 — determine the amount of financing required. The advisers first assumed that both the purchase price could be negotiated at the price estimated by management, and that the company would not need further finance to support its projected future activity. Although some might consider this a rather high price to pay for a loss making company, the advisers were happy to take this figure as a starting point.

Chapter 5 Management Buy-outs 63

Step 2 — *ascertain the amount of management's contribution.* This was assessed at not more than £150,000, which limited management's freedom in manoeuvre in considering the next step.

Step 3 — *determine the company's debt gearing capacity.* By a process not detailed here, this was determined at £800,000.

Step 4 — *agree management's equity percentage.* After some discussion, it was felt that management could not expect to achieve control in the new company in exchange for the 10% of the total capital they were subscribing, but that they could ask for a significant stake. It was finally agreed to propose that management should take a 33% ordinary equity stake for their subscription.

Step 5 — *determine the method of equity gearing.* This left £250,000 to be funded by some other form of equity; it was decided to make up this balance with preference shares, carrying a market rate of interest.

At this stage, the capital structure required to fund the buy-out looked like:

	£000's
Ordinary equity — Management (33%)	150
— Outside investors (67%)	300
	450
Balance required	
— debt	800
— preference shares	250
	1,500

Step 6 — *agree on investors' share rights.* Two problems here had to be solved — how to provide the development capitalist with an appropriate running yield, and how to protect him against non-redemption of preference shares and loan stock, or non-payment of dividends or interest. This was accomplished by giving the investor ordinary shares with preferred rights to dividends based on a percentage of subsequent profits, and providing for conversion of the preference shares into ordinaries in the event of non-payment of capital or interest on the due dates.

The final proposed capital structure looked like (all figures in £000's):

	Ordinary shares 'A'	Ordinary shares 'B'	Preference Shares	Loan Stock	Total
Management	150	—	—	—	150
Investors	—	300	250	800	1,350
	150	300	250	800	1,500

Finally, the proposed scheme was checked to ensure that the resulting cash drain on the company was supportable, especially in the event of a reasonable degree of slippage in the forecast figures. Had this not been the case, the advisers would have had to alter certain of the variables in the equation (eg, the purchase price, amount of management contribution, etc) in order to put together a convincing package.

Chapter 6

The Business Expansion Scheme

The Business Expansion Scheme (BES) is not in itself a form of risk capital. It is a piece of legislation giving significant tax relief to certain individual investors, which can give them the latitude to finance a wide range of companies in a number of different ways. It has given rise, however, to an important source of equity finance for unquoted companies, which should be seriously considered by all entrepreneurs looking for money.

The decision whether or not to raise finance taking advantage of the BES as opposed to more conventional institutional funding is, however, complicated by a number of issues arising largely from the provisions of the Scheme itself. Some of these will be short term and immediately apparent, but others can be more long term and subtle. In this chapter, we will attempt to draw out the more important of these issues as they affect the finance-raising process by discussing:

(a) How the BES fits into the corporate finance alternatives described in Chapter 2.
(b) How the Scheme has been operated in practice, and its impact on entrepreneurs.
(c) The prospects for the Scheme in the future.

BES AS A CORPORATE FINANCE ALTERNATIVE

The Scheme

An outline of the major provisions of the Business Expansion Scheme is provided in Appendix V.

In summary, however, the BES was established in 1983 as a successor to the 1981 Business Start-Up Scheme. It offers *individuals* income tax relief for investment in *qualifying* unquoted British trading companies with which they are not connected. In this context:

(a) *Individuals* must be residents in the UK and hold their shares for at least five years.
(b) *Investments* must be in new, full-risk ordinary share capital; the purchase of existing shares from current shareholders, or the subscription for preference shares or convertible loan stock will not qualify for relief.
(c) *Qualifying* companies for the purposes of the Scheme should have the bulk of their business located in the UK, and not be quoted on the Stock Exchange or Unlisted Securities Market (but somewhat illogically may have their shares traded in the Third Market or an Over-The-Counter (OTC) market). Certain types of businesses are excluded from the Scheme, including those dealing in land, shares and commodities, leasing and letting assets and providing financial services. Farming, property development and certain heavily asset-backed ventures, originally included, have been excluded by subsequent legislation.
(d) The Scheme also provides for individuals to make their investments directly, or through an investment fund, although the investor owns the shares in both cases.

Finance raising

Within the bounds set out above, BES finance is thus theoretically available to all companies of all types and sizes. Furthermore, the emergence of the BES funds has given the growing company two ways to raise BES finance, either by:

(a) *Direct investment by the public:* this in turn can be subdivided into informal and more formal arrangements. Informal arrangements typically involve a small number of individual investors (often friends of management) agreeing on the terms of their investment directly with the owners, usually with a minimum of formal investigation and documentation. Alternatively, and more formally, management may enlist the aid of an intermediary (for example a stockbroker, merchant bank or licensed dealer in securities) to raise money from the public on their behalf, requiring the preparation of a prospectus complying with the Companies Act.

Public fund-raising as a source of risk capital is dealt with specifically in Chapter 8.

(b) *Via the funds:* these are professionally managed, and use disciplines similar to those used by the venture and development capitalists to evaluate and process their investments; many are in fact part of established venture or development capital groups.

However, despite this theoretical flexibility and wide applicability, BES investments to date have in practice been significantly concentrated around certain types of ventures and have given rise to a number of problems in their structuring and negotiation. Some of the reasons for this are outlined below.

THE SCHEME IN PRACTICE

First, some facts and figures.

Size and importance

The BES has during its life attracted big money. In 1983/84, its first year of operation, Inland Revenue statistics suggest that over £105m was invested under the Scheme. The majority of this was invested directly by the public, largely through public issues sponsored by stockbrokers or licensed dealers in securities involving a formal prospectus. This trend has continued throughout the following three years with the total amounts of money invested under the Scheme during the period rising steadily to over £150m per annum. Over the same period, however, an increasing percentage of the total money raised has come from larger issues of shares direct to the public by way of a prospectus. The implication of this for the BES is considered at the conclusion of this chapter.

Amounts invested — funds

According to figures compiled by Venture Economics, however, the BES funds have also continued to play an important part in the operation of the Scheme. The following paragraphs set out some of their major characteristics.

The BES funds have continued to invest significant amounts throughout the life of the Scheme, as shown in the accompanying Figure 10.

Figure 10

Investments by BES Funds

	1983/84	1984/85	1985/86
Number of Funds	26	38	31
Total Capital Raised (£m)	46.7	48.7	37.3
Average Fund Size (£m)	1.73	1.28	1.20

(Source: Venture Economics)

The above figures demonstrate a high continuing level of interest by the risk capital community in the BES. The average fund size, however, is much smaller than the average venture or development capital fund, at £1.2m in 1985/86. In this year only four funds (12% of the total) raised more than £2.5m, and 58% raised less than £1m. This is perilously close to the minimum economic fund size for such a vehicle, and many managers have as a result been sufficiently discouraged to withdraw from the field in 1986/87. As a result of this and other factors, amounts raised by the BES funds in this year are estimated to have fallen somewhat, to around £33m.

Industry sector

BES fund investments have continued to be made across a wide range of industrial companies. A number of trends, however, stand out. Investment in manufacturers and distributors of industrial products has for example become increasingly important, while the popularity of technology-related businesses has fallen sharply over the period of operation of the Scheme, accounting for only 9% of investments in 1985/86.

In common with the rest of the venture and development capital industry however, consumer-related industries are most popular, accounting in 1985/86 for 55% of such investments. This is somewhat higher than 'mainstream' risk capital fund investment, largely due to the high level of investment in companies owning and operating ventures with significant asset backing, eg, hotels, restaurants, nursing homes and public houses. In 1985/86, such companies accounted for 16% of all investments made by BES funds. This has not gone unnoticed by the press, and has focused considerable attention on the type of companies financed by the Scheme.

Types of financing

Although the Business Expansion Scheme only applies to one type of investment, ie, subscriptions for ordinary shares, relief can be obtained for such investments in companies which conventionally require both venture capital and development capital. It is widely believed, however, that the overwhelming majority of BES investments, both by the funds and by direct investment, have been concentrated in low-risk ventures, especially those with high asset backing.

This, so the theory runs, is a direct consequence of the terms of the Scheme itself, and their impact on the risk-reward profits of the investor, for, as illustrated in Appendix V, a BES investor paying tax at 60% who does no better than recover his original investment after five years will, by the arithmetic inherent in the timing of his tax relief, have earned a 20% annual compound rate of return net of tax. Surely then, the investor will plump for the safest possible investment to secure this exceptional rate of return, rather than risk his original capital in the hope of greater gain? What, the argument continues, is the safest investment? Well established low growth companies will be safer than high growth, high-risk propositions, but best of all will be companies whose assets can be expected to keep their value, notably property and certain types of stock. If the company does well, then the investor wins, but if it does not, the investor still wins, taking the tax relief into account, by liquidating the company and selling the assets to recoup the initial investment.

This may be somewhat overblown, but in fact many of the BES funds have gone through a not dissimilar thought process in setting their investment policies. The majority of the BES fund managers have raised their money with 'City backing' or are offshoots of established City institutions, with reputations they are understandably and rightly keen to protect. As such, especially in the early years of the Scheme, they have not wished to attract criticism by making injudicious, risky investments. As a result, very few BES funds have been set up to concentrate on high-risk or early-stage ventures, and a large number have openly stressed their risk-averse nature.

Do the figures of sums actually invested by the BES funds bear this out? Analysis by *UK Venture Capital Journal* enables us to compare the proportion of early-stage investments made by the BES funds in 1985/86 with those made by the risk capital industry in general. These are summarised in Figure 11 on page 70.

70   Part 3   Risk Capital Alternatives

FIGURE 11

EARLY STAGE INVESTMENTS

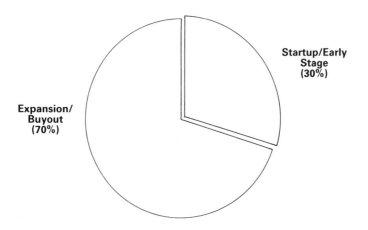

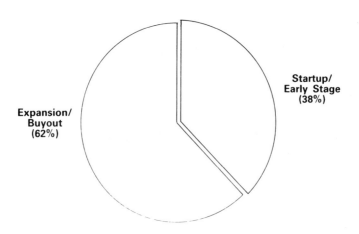

Somewhat surprisingly, it would appear from the figure that proportionately *more* early stage and start up investments (38% of the total) have been made by the BES funds than by the rest of the industry (30% of the total) as a whole. These figures should, however, be treated with some caution, as more than half of the companies classified as 'start-ups' for the purposes of the BES figures (in fact some 14% of the total) are accounted for by asset backed start-ups (eg, hotels, nursing homes, etc), the risk profile of which in many ways has more in common with expansion financings than the conventional early stage venture. Adjusting for such companies would decrease the percentage of 'young company' BES investments to 24% of the total, significantly less than the industry as a whole.

Thus there would appear to be some truth in the contention that the BES funds are somewhat more conservative in the companies they invest in than the rest of the industry. It would also however probably be true to say that the degree of this conservatism has been somewhat exaggerated by the financial press, given the significant minority of higher risk young companies who have received funding from this source. Finally, many commentators expect the percentage of young company investments to rise again following the disqualification of many asset backed start-ups under the terms of the Scheme in 1986.

Size of investments

The average size of BES fund investment has varied little over the life of the Scheme, averaging out at £168,000. This is significantly lower than the average venture or development capital investment. The main reason for this lies in the small size of most of the funds, and their unwillingness to concentrate too much of their portfolio in a single company, in line with guidelines from the Department of Trade and Industry setting a limit of no more than 20% to be invested in one company by any fund.

Detailed statistics show that 53% of all BES fund investments in 1985/86 involved sums between £50,000 and £200,000. For companies seeking such relatively small amounts of finance, BES funds thus represent an attractive potential source, given the unwillingness of many conventional funds to invest in 'small ticket' projects, as noted in Chapter 4.

Timing

Driven by timing of available tax relief, there is a significant concentration of BES investments made in the last quarter of each tax year (the basic principle of the Scheme is that investors in BES funds receive tax relief only on those amounts invested in target companies by the fund managers in the tax year, ending on 5 April, not in respect of amounts invested in the fund). In 1983/84, the only year for which detailed authoritative figures are available, some two-thirds of investments were made in the last quarter, and 56% of investments were made in the last month of the year.

This is to some extent a function of the opening dates of the various BES funds, although many fund managers are attempting to stagger this seasonality of financing by raising funds in the summer months. In addition, recent legislation has slightly eased this seasonal pressure by enabling certain small investors to carry back a proportion of the tax relief on investments made in the first six months of the tax year into the previous year. It is too soon, however, to tell whether this measure will have a significant impact. Timing thus remains a significant factor for companies raising BES funds, and should be accordingly borne in mind by their owners and professional advisors.

ADVANTAGES OF BES FINANCE

So why has BES finance proved so popular with recipient companies?

A survey carried out by accountants Peat Marwick Mitchell for the Treasury in 1986 suggested the following answers.

(a) *No running yield.* As BES investments can only be made by way of ordinary shares, and in view of the rigorous anti-avoidance provisions concerning taking value out of the company during the five year relief period, it has been unusual for dividends to be paid to BES shareholders during this time. This represents a major benefit to companies who could otherwise have expected to pay out a significant proportion of their profits to shareholders in the form of dividends.

(b) *Lack of pressure from outside investors.* This was held to be especially true in the case of BES investments made directly by the public, but also felt to apply in the case of a number of investments made by the BES funds.

(c) *Broadened shareholder base.* Longer established companies in particular, who might normally be reluctant to involve institutional investors in their affairs, regarded a broadened shareholder base and reduced loss of control as a significant advantage of BES finance. Many companies still fear significant and powerful outside shareholders who could potentially exert an unwelcome influence on strategic or operational questions. A number of these did not see the BES funds in this light as they felt that after five years they would be dealing with a large number of small investors with limited collective influence.

(d) *Ready exit route.* The willingness of many of the funds to secure an exit route by encouraging the company to repurchase the BES shares after five years, ie, suffering a temporary dilution of equity only, was also felt to be a major advantage of this form of finance.

Price

Some people hold the view that BES finance is cheaper than conventional venture or development capital funding, ie, less equity typically has to be surrendered for the funding required. This appears to be especially true amongst recipients of BES finance, although to what extent this represents the wish to be convinced that they have acquired a bargain remains to be seen.

There is in fact little hard evidence to prove or disprove this contention. Most BES fund managers would vigorously deny it and the arguments advanced previously to explain the caution of the BES funds in investing in high-risk ventures, if true, would suggest that they would be similarly unwilling to pay 'over the odds' for the investments they do make. An explanation for the apparent contradiction may possibly revolve round the issue of *additionality* — research suggests that many companies receiving BES financing would have had the greatest difficulty in raising equity finance at any price from conventional risk capital sources, thus suggesting that what many recipients of BES financing considered the best price they were offered was in reality the *only* price which was ever seriously on the table.

PRACTICAL PROBLEMS

The operation of the Scheme in practice has also, however, revealed a number of problems of which the seeker of finance should be aware.

Perhaps the most immediately apparent of these relates to the *reduced flexibility of operations* which has often resulted from BES investments. To avoid withdrawal of tax relief to the investors, the company, as noted previously, cannot engage in a non-qualifying activity or acquire a Stock Exchange quotation for a period of three years after the commencement of a qualifying trade. The definition of what constitutes a qualifying trade can be difficult in practice, especially in the case of certain companies receiving their income in the form of rentals or royalty payments (which may be defined as leasing, a non-qualifying activity) and in the case of certain heavily asset-backed companies. In addition, the tax legislation contains a number of widely drawn anti-avoidance provisions which may actively discourage investee companies from transactions which in other circumstances may be normal commercial practice.

Of course this does not stop the company from doing any or all of these things. It is standard practice, however, at least in the case of all BES fund investments, for the investee company shareholders and directors to agree as part of the investment contract to seek at all times during the qualifying period to ensure that the company does not lose its qualifying status. As this to a large extent will depend upon tax law and practice, which is not always straightforward to the layman, this is an undertaking which is not to be given lightly by any company, and may for some represent a significant constraint upon their freedom of action.

Recipients of BES finance may also experience *difficulties in raising second round finance*. Unless second round financing is obtained from a separate BES fund (or another fund managed by the same fund managers), the logistical problems involved in offering each existing investor his rights to take up further shares, and the cost involved, may be prohibitive. Between 1983 and 1986 approximately 8% of companies who raised finance from BES funds secured second round financing (a lower figure than is typical in the UK venture capital industry). It can also be difficult to obtain second round finance from non-BES funds if they are unwilling to accept the constraints on the company's freedom of action noted above.

Competition from other funds

In addition, many executives of conventional venture and development capital funds would argue that they have a lot more to offer than the BES funds. Because of their larger size, they may be able to finance larger deals without resorting to time-consuming widespread syndication. They may also have an advantage where more complex financing packages are required (eg, including a mixture of loan and equity) from which the BES funds are precluded. Finally, although there are a small number of BES funds catering for earlier-stage ventures, there are very few focused BES funds or management groups with the time and ability to provide a 'hands-on' monitoring service, especially for technology projects.

These are important issues, and the advantages and disadvantages of each should be weighed up carefully before deciding whether to seek BES or non-BES finance. In this connection it can, however, be possible to obtain the best of both worlds by seeking finance from a management group with both a BES fund and a conventional venture or development capital fund under its wing. A number of fund managers fall into this category, and it is not uncommon to see for example one of their development capital investments containing the usual mix of loan, preference and ordinary equity shares provided by the development capital fund to be supplemented by a simultaneous tranche of ordinary equity provided by the BES arm.

CURRENT AND FUTURE TRENDS

It is still too early to assess with any certainty whether the BES will continue to provide significant amounts of risk capital financing for small growing British companies. The signs are, however, that BES finance has some significant long term attractions for both investors and companies seeking finance.

On the one hand, there are indications that the attractions of BES investment via the funds are losing their early bloom. As we have seen, the size of the average BES fund is very small, and according to some commentators may be approaching the point below which the creation of further funds is not justified because of the costs involved. Many fund managers are currently reappraising whether the executive time involved in administering such small funds is adequately compensated for by their remuneration (which is commonly tied to a percentage of money invested), and some of the leading BES funds managers have decided to withdraw from launching further funds. This has been reflected in a further fall in the number of BES funds raised in 1986/87.

Conversely, however, we are also currently witnessing an accentuation of the trend concentrating BES investments on larger financings. These are typically achieved by way of direct offer for subscription to the general public (usually via a stockbroker or licensed dealer in securities) involving a formal prospectus, rather than in the small ticket, small company investments favoured by the funds or arranged through private offerings. This is because the typical BES investor is relatively financially sophisticated and, so the argument runs, he is increasingly likely as time progresses to have the confidence to make his own choice of BES investments rather than delegate this to a fund; if this is true, then we can expect this trend to become more marked in the future.

Finally, whatever the split of BES investments between the funds and direct public offers, published research strongly suggests that the popularity of BES investment in one form or another from high tax paying individuals continues at a high level. Overall, the future of the Scheme would seem to depend as much as anything on its ability to avoid certain major pitfalls which could constrict its scope or destroy its credibility as a viable investment alternative in the eyes of its subscribers. The most obvious of these are detailed below.

Changes in legislation

The government certainly has confidence in the future of the BES, having extended its life indefinitely in the Finance Act 1986. This may not, however, always be the case, especially given any future change of government, although it should be pointed out that the bulk of the politically inspired criticism of the Scheme has tended to concentrate on its detailed method of operation (eg, the type of companies in which BES finance has been invested, and its alleged failure to encourage start-up companies and create jobs) rather than its basic principles.

Excessive fund manager remuneration

Again to some extent a function of the small size of most BES funds, the typical methods of BES fund manager remuneration have attracted some criticism.

Typically, BES fund managers will levy a management fee from subscribers (usually in the range 3%–5% of funds subscribed) at the date of investment, and/or retain the entitlement to interest earned on uninvested cash. While the fund managers bear the costs of raising money for the fund, as with most venture capital funds, they will seek to pass on all professional costs involved in making investments to the companies concerned, and many will charge director's fees if executives of the fund are appointed to the board of portfolio companies. In addition, it is common for the fund managers to take options on the share capital of investee companies, to be exercised after five years at a price equal to the original subscription price by the fund. These commonly amount to up to 15% of the BES fund's investment — thus, if the fund purchased 20% of the equity, the fund managers would have an option on 3% of the company's capital base.

The major comparative disadvantage of these arrangements to the entrepreneur is the granting of options. A number of existing shareholders have, however, got round the dilutive effect of these provisions by securing the grant of an equal number of options to themselves, thus confining the dilution to the individual investors in the fund. Taken to excess, however, the cumulative impact of all the above provisions could materially depress investor enthusiasm for this form of investment. The danger arising from this for companies considering BES fund finance is that, in reaction to this, fund managers will seek to shift the burden of their remuneration from individual fund investors to their investee companies.

Commercially unsuccessful investments

As is the case with the venture capital industry as a whole, it is too soon to judge the commercial performance of the Scheme in view of the long time scales involved. There are, however, a number of well publicised examples of companies who have received large amounts of funding from the Business Expansion Scheme (or its predecessor, the Business Start-up Scheme) being forced into liquidation, and a number of funds have attracted considerable adverse press comment at the supposed poor performance resulting from the disclosure of a number of failed or troubled investments.

This is somewhat unfair, as it is a basic truth of the venture capital industry, in the USA as in the UK, that 'the lemons ripen before the plums', and that the best time to judge the performance of a fund is at its closing date. Such figures as exist also appear to cast doubt on the assertion that BES investments are not performing. Of the investments made in 1983/84 by the BES funds, 78% were still trading in July 1986, 14% were in receivership or liquidation, and 8% had been purchased by other companies. Acquisition prices ranged from nominal amounts (in cases where acquisition represented the only alternative to receivership) to amounts equal to four times fund cost. Information available on all BES investments made over the same period paints a similar picture. These figures are not as bleak as suggested by some press comment, and they in fact compare quite favourably with the failure rate of one in seven quoted by 3i for its management buy-outs (see Chapter 5), an area whose increasing popularity is commonly ascribed to its low-risk nature.

By the same token, however, it is true that there have been few spectacular examples of significant capital gains generated from BES investments to foster enthusiasm for the sector, as has happened in the case of the Unlisted Securities Market. The success of the BES funds in the long term will depend critically upon the ability of the early funds to generate real returns for their investors. In this context the BES funds may not have as much to do to satisfy their backers as the conventional venture and development capital funds. The majority of BES investors are higher rate tax paying individuals, many of whom have invested in the BES as a tax shelter and all of whom will have earned attractive tax free rates of return if they break even on their investment (as explained in Appendix V). Capital gains expectations may thus be modest. Most investors, however, will at the least expect to get their money back. This should not be too difficult in many cases, if typical fund target rates of return (in the region of 15–25% per annum) are anything like realised. In some cases, however, there may be a question as to whether the ultimate gains will be big enough to compensate for early losses, even of a modest amount.

Subsequent marketability

The key determinant of the ultimate profitability or otherwise of each individual BES fund will be *liquidity*, and specifically the ease with which investors will be able to dispose of their shares in portfolio companies at the end of the five year qualifying period. This may not always be straightforward, as not many BES backed companies will be willing or able to improve shareholder liquidity by way of a Stock Exchange listing or quotation on the Unlisted Securities Market. A number of companies may, however, be able to obtain a quotation on the Third Market or on one of the various Over-the-Counter (OTC) markets in the UK (the OTC is dealt with in more detail in Chapter 8), but it is unrealistic to expect in all cases that either existing management would agree or that the company could find a sponsor. In response to this, many funds have reached an understanding with their portfolio companies for the company to repurchase the BES shares after five years at a mutually agreeable price, although this may only prove practicable if the finances of the company are strong enough.

Alternatively, other funds have made arrangements that any BES shares still in the original shareholders' hands after the qualifying period will carry preferred dividend rights in order to make them more marketable to third parties. Time will tell whether or not the requisite liquidity is likely to be achieved.

CONCLUSION

Overall then, while the larger BES prospectus issues continue to attract interest, it would be fair to say that there are perhaps rather more question marks over the likely future health of the Business Expansion Scheme funds than have for example been voiced about the risk capital funds. BES finance can nevertheless offer some unique advantages to the entrepreneur seeking finance, especially those companies looking for between £100,000 and £200,000 or those for whom the necessity for second round finance is unlikely to prove a major issue. At the least, the Scheme is worth serious consideration as an integral part of all the potential alternative sources of risk capital finance open to the small business we have been discussing.

Chapter 7

Corporate Venturing

One of the more interesting differences between the venture capital markets in the USA and the UK lies in the fact that only 4% of the money raised by the British industry comes from industrial corporations, as opposed to 13% in the USA. This is of more than academic interest to the entrepreneur, as in the USA this represents only one expression of a wider trend for larger corporations to become increasingly interested in forming alliances with smaller companies, to the advantage of both sides.

Furthermore, despite the above figures, there is evidence that this trend is also on the increase in the UK. More and more small companies are finding that funding from large corporations, or *corporate venturers*, can be a viable alternative or complement to institutional sources of finance.

The entrepreneur facing the choice between corporate venture or institutional finance will typically be faced with issues of a different magnitude from those involved in choosing, say, between venture and development capital. To enter into a corporate venturing relationship goes beyond issues of financing; the company seeking corporate venture funding needs to understand the aims of the potential corporate partner, and its ability to provide more than money.

To put these issues in some perspective, however, we first need to know what corporate venturing is all about, why it has grown, and the problems and opportunities it has created in practice.

WHAT IS CORPORATE VENTURING?

As with the term 'venture capital', the concept of 'corporate venturing' as used in practice is somewhat vague, and tends to mean different things to different people. Its most basic definition would characterise it as 'the establishment of mutually beneficial working relationships between major corporations and innovative young companies.' (National Economic Development Office, 1986.)

Perhaps rather clearer is its underlying purpose, to combine the traditional advantages of the large corporation — including its capital base, management skills and marketing muscle — with the strengths of the entrepreneurial small company — innovation, flair and speed of response — to help both achieve a sustainable competitive advantage.

Corporate venturing is thus one of the tools which can be used by the large corporation to help it achieve its strategic aims. It can be practised in different ways, many of which will already be familiar to its executives. Joint ventures, externally-funded research, and licensing arrangements for example all fall within the above definition, to which some would add acquisition programmes or the creation of separate in-house new venture divisions to develop new business areas. It is possible for the small company to profit in many ways from participating in such programmes, and many have in the past and will continue to do so.

Nevertheless, in recent years, another form of corporate venturing has become increasingly popular — the phenomenon of large corporations making minority investments in smaller companies, either directly or indirectly via subscription to a venture capital fund. This is properly considered as corporate venturing when, as has occurred in the majority of cases, such investment is made with a view to earning more than the financial reward available to the portfolio investor and it is to this form of corporate venturing that this chapter is directed. Large amounts of money in the USA are being invested in this way; as well as the amounts invested via the funds as noted above, direct venture investment is also common. For example, 36 of the 50 largest American electronics companies have made direct venture investments since 1980.

There is also growing interest in corporate venturing in the UK evidenced by the results of a survey carried out in September 1986 by the National Economic Development Office (NEDO) on the subject. A diagramatic summary of the replies from 228 respondents is included in Figure 13 on page 98. The replies revealed that one-third of respondents had tried corporate venturing, nearly half of whom appeared to be satisfied with their experience to date, and a slightly smaller number finding it too early to say.

Why should the large corporation want to invest often substantial sums of money in minority stakes in smaller private companies over which they may have little effective control, and which may prove extremely difficult to dispose of at a realistic price?

CORPORATE VENTURING: MOTIVATORS

A number of factors have acted together in recent years to increase interest in venture capital investments by industrial companies, either directly or by subscription to specialised venture capital funds.

Effective diversification

The increasing competitiveness of today's business environment has forced many corporations to recognise explicitly that the management of change represents their greatest strategic challenge. To a large number this will in practice boil down to the issue of how to diversify effectively.

This can be a challenge of equal magnitude. For the two conventional alternative ways to achieve this — organically (ie, the expansion into new business areas using internal resources only) or by acquisition — are both fraught with danger, as a long list of companies have learnt to their cost. Research in the USA for example suggests that it takes on average 10 to 12 years before the return on investment of organically grown new ventures equals that of mature businesses. On the other hand, many acquisitions have come to grief as a result of the new owner destroying the competitive edge of the target company by consciously or inadvertently changing its unique culture through too many changes in management or operating policies.

Corporate venturing offers the potential to steer a middle course between these two dangers, by investing in an established business in such a way as to retain its existing character and growth potential. In addition, a number of corporations have found it easier to carry out high-risk new projects in associate companies outside the host company organisation structure, where their profile may be lower in the eyes of others within the organisation and failure easier to swallow.

Keeping pace with technology

The costs and commercial risks associated with major investment in technology have increased dramatically over the past few years as a consequence of the increasing pace of technological change, decreasing product life cycles, and continuing cost inflation.

This has created a growing need within many companies to increase and diversify their investment in technology within increasingly stringent cost and time constraints. Corporate venturing can provide an effective answer to this problem through its potential to share costs, spread risk, and diversify technology with maximum leverage by acting in partnership with smaller, technology-based companies. In addition to these direct benefits, a corporate venture programme can also provide the investor (sometimes known as the 'host' company) with the more general advantages of increased awareness of current technology and market developments, an example of what the advocates of corporate venturing call a *window on technology*.

The above two factors appear to have proved particularly attractive in the UK. As can be seen in Figure 13 on page 98 diversification into new markets or technologies was the most often-quoted benefit emerging from the NEDO corporate venturing survey.

Maintaing concentration of effort

Many organisations, even large corporations, do not have the financial or emotional resources to devote to more than a small number of individual projects the effort required to achieve the 'critical mass' necessary to secure sufficient commitment throughout the organisation and avoid ineffective diffusion of their internal technology expertise. A properly structured corporate venturing programme can help to maximise the number of technology initiatives which can be sustained at this critical mass by any one company.

Outward technology exploitation

Conversely, some companies find it difficult to commercialise all the technology they have developed internally, either through lack of specific expertise (eg, an appropriate marketing organisation) or insufficient market potential. Hiving off this technology by way of partnerships with smaller companies willing to operate in narrower markets may be an attractive solution to this problem.

Protection of supplier/customer base

The above principles do not only apply to the procurement, protection and exploitation of technology. For many companies, the quality of their supplier and customer bases will be just as important in the maintenance of a competitive edge. Corporate venturing can help maintain or enhance these assets, either opportunistically, for example by giving financial (including equity) support in times of financial trouble, or as part of a planned programme of vertical or horizontal integration.

Organisational factors

Arguably the successful exploitation of technology in recent years has often stemmed as much from the entrepreneurial culture within the small companies which have developed it as the special features of their technology. For example it can be as important to move quickly in product support or distribution arrangements in order to keep up with the requirements of the market as to make major changes in product performance and technology. This culture can be difficult to graft successfully on to the organisation structures of many large companies, as a number of major corporations learned to their cost in a series of unsuccessful technology-based acquisitions in the 1970s. Again, corporate venturing via large/small company collaboration can help to bridge this gap by combining the resources of large corporations and the flexibility and speed of response typically found in smaller companies.

HOW IS IT DONE?

The potential corporate venturer, once he has been convinced of the merits of allying himself with smaller companies, can typically use a combination of one of three approaches to carry out his programme. These are detailed below, and some examples of companies operating in the UK in this way can be found in Figure 12.

Figure 12

Three Types of Corporate Venturing — Examples

(Investee companies/funds in italics)

Direct investment	Via venture capital funds	Spin-offs
British Aerospace *(European Silicon Structures)*	Air Products *(Atla-Berkeley)*	BP *(BP Ventures)*
Ferranti *(Lattice Logic)*	GEC *(JMI Seed Capital)*	British Telecom *(Martlesham Enterprises)*
Olivetti *(Sphinx)*	Monsanto *(Advent)*	ICI *(Marlborough Technical Development)*
	Johnson & Johnson *(Transatlantic Capital)*	MOD *(Defence Technology Enterprises)*
Plessey *(Imperial Software Technology)*	Pikington *(Rainford Venture Capital)*	
Some of the companies above invest in third party venture capital funds. Others (eg, Thorn and Ferranti in the USA) have adopted an 'intermediate approach' of setting up their own venture capital funds in promising areas of technology.	The corporate venturer will seek to capitalise on his investment in the fund(s) by way of access to deal logs (lists of applications of finance), summaries of investments completed, and introductions to portfolio companies.	Formed primarily as investment vehicles for outward exploitation of the 'parent' technology. Similar programmes have been undertaken by a number of British universities (eg, Queen Mary and Imperial College, London) and government-linked research units.

Direct investment

In one sense this is corporate venturing at its simplest, where the corporate venturer subscribes directly for a minority stake in a smaller company. This can be either in an existing business area, or in an industry complementary to that of the host. It is unusual to find corporate venture investments made in areas completely unrelated to the investor's core business.

EXISTING BUSINESS AREAS

Perhaps the most common example of corporate venture investments in existing businesses areas are cases of vertical or horizontal integration. The major illustration of this can be found in the investments of the early 1980s in American semiconductor manufacturers by electronics companies anxious to safeguard what was then a scarce source of supply. The minority stake taken in Intel by IBM is perhaps the best known example of this. Transactions of this type are also common in the UK, in companies of all sizes. Some examples include the minority investment by the Amari Group (the metal and plastics distributor) in Parma Aluminium, an existing raw material supplier, and Leigh Interests in Tyrolysis, a major customer for its rubber products. Management buy-outs have also been backed in a number of cases by corporations with trading relationships with existing management, an example of which is the investment by Karloscar, the Indian energy group, in the management buy-out of its customer, the pump systems manufacturer SPP, to safeguard an important market.

NEW BUSINESS AREAS

This form of investment has been led, both in the USA and the UK, by technology companies, using either in-house corporate venturing departments, or a separate venture capital fund financed exclusively by the host company. Investments are typically concentrated in business areas which are related or complementary to the core business of the corporate venturer. This is because, where such investments are made as part of a longer term strategic development plan, the investor will not only be concerned with making money. He will typically also be interested in getting to know about the technology in the markets he is investing in, and developing relationships with successful growing companies in that field. As a result, such investments are also commonly accompanied by collateral commercial agreements. Typically, the corporate venturer's money will buy him, in addition to his equity stake, one or more of:

(a) A *licensing or distribution agreement* on some or all of the associate's existing products, and possibly the right of first refusal on new product developments.
(b) A *technology share agreement*, giving him access to the technology of the associate in certain defined circumstances, eg, where the investee cannot commercialise it.
(c) The right to *buy out the remaining share capital* of the associate at a pre-agreed price, usually in cases where the investment is realising exceptional returns.

Such investments are a major feature of the American venture capital scene, where many large corporations, including Digital Equipment, EG & G and Analog Devices, are involved in systematic programmes of continuing direct investment in smaller companies. This trend is now being mirrored in Europe, by such companies as Olivetti, Pirelli, and Elf Acquitaine.

No British company has yet developed a domestic corporate venturing programme on as large or systematic basis as the companies mentioned above. Nevertheless, activity is increasing. In addition to the companies mentioned in Figure 12, a number of the smaller British electronics companies have been actively involved in this area, including Cambridge Electronic Instruments and Micro Business Systems. A number of the overseas companies mentioned above have also made corporate venturing investments in the UK.

Via a venture capital fund

Corporate venturing can alternatively be attempted in a more indirect manner, by investing in one or more of the venture capital funds described in Chapter 4. The corporate venturer here will typically have a more limited aim, which initially may be confined to gathering market intelligence by looking through the window on technology provided by the fund's executives and contacts.

This window can work on a number of levels. On a general level, considerable evidence exists to suggest that an analysis of what industries the venture capital funds are making investments in provides a good guide to which markets are likely to emerge as major money spinners within a three to five year period. More specifically, the corporate venturer can look to the contacts he can make through the fund (including access to their deal logs (detailing all investments proposals received), summaries of all investments made, and introductions to portfolio companies) for insights and information on the markets he is interested in. In many cases, he will hope to take this further by participating in certain investments alongside the fund, or, after introductions to portfolio companies, acquiring useful product or marketing rights.

The number of companies which are practising corporate venturing in this way in the UK, although small, is expanding. To date some 18 companies have committed over £30m to British venture capital funds, including some of the largest British companies, as noted in Figure 12.

Sponsored spin-offs

Sponsored spin-offs, the name given to the process of hiving off unwanted technology by large corporations to partnerships with smaller companies, is seen by some as corporate venturing in reverse. Often this is achieved by former employees of the host company establishing their own business. Whether this can strictly be defined as corporate venturing or not, it can certainly represent a significant opportunity to the smaller company, especially if the host corporation is prepared to assist in financing the project. It is also an area where a great deal of interst has been generated in the UK as well as in the USA (and, significantly, in Japan). Both ICI and British Telecom have set up separate companies to supervise spin-off programmes, and a number of academic and government-based research establishments have formal links with private sector organisations, sometimes involving equity investments, to exploit commercially technology they have developed as part of their own core activities.

ADVANTAGES FOR THE SMALLER COMPANY

Many owners of small companies view the prospect of a formal link with the monolithic major company with more than a little scepticism. Corporate venturing would not, however, have got off the ground in such a big way in the USA if it had not held out real advantages for the smaller company.

The principal advantage of a corporate venture relationship for almost all smaller companies is the finance which the host company provides either directly or indirectly. Most larger companies making corporate venture investments do so in areas of new or emerging technology, which often involves investment in young or start-up companies. These are the very areas where conventional risk capital finance is most difficult to obtain. The host company not only invests its own cash in the ventures, but by its presence reduces the perceived risk of the project which can encourage investment by other risk capital funds. As well as funds, a corporate partner can offer potential benefits such as:

(a) *Market 'Muscle'*. With the growing internationalisation of markets, many products with short life cycles require almost simultaneous launching in the USA (and maybe Japan) as well as in the UK if they are to realise fully their financial potential. Many small companies will not have the necessary marketing resources or expertise to cope with these demands, and more of them will be looking towards some form of co-operation with larger companies to provide this.

(b) *Revenue Support*. It will often be possible for a small early stage company with corporate venture backing to gain some much-needed revenue and enhance its operating statistics by entering into consultancy or research contracts with the host company.

(c) *Prestige*. Appropriate corporate venture backing can be expected to enhance credibility and esteem in the eyes of suppliers and financiers, and help in attracting and retaining customers.

(d) *Management Expertise*. Availability of the managerial and technical expertise of the investor can be invaluable to the small growing company. Production engineering and control, and financial and management systems are two of the more common calls on the corporate venturer's resources in this area.

(e) *Congenial Exit Route*. A significant proportion, if not the majority, of venture-backed companies will eventually be acquired by larger companies rather than finding their way to the Stock Exchange. Acquisition by a partner already known to management can often prove more attractive to the owners of small corporate venture-backed businesses as a means of realising their investment than the outside scrutiny and other rigours involved in the process of going public.

(f) *Pricing*. Some people consider that industrial corporations making direct corporate venture investments are by and large prepared to pay a higher price for their investments because they are not so concerned with purely financial returns. Too few investments of this type have been made in the UK to date to say definitely whether or not this is true; it is probable, however, that, in some cases at least, the technological expertise of a major corporation seeking to invest in a complementary business area may enable it to move more quickly than some of the non-specialist venture capital funds in putting together a financing package to meet the expectations of management.

PROBLEMS AND PITFALLS

Nevertheless, if corporate venturing in the UK is expanding, many commentators are concerned that the rate of expansion still appears to be somewhat slow, especially in comparison with the USA. It is also worrying that, despite the fact that corporate venturing is such a relatively new phenomenon, one in five of respondents to the NEDO survey referred to above were already dissatisfied with the experience.

This may seem surprising, given the advantages outlined above, and no single clear explanation has emerged to explain it. Nevertheless, the following retarding factors currently seem to be at work.

Finding a partner

One of the reasons put forward for the slow take off of corporate venturing is the absence of any mechanism for matching the two potential parties. A relatively small number of professional organisations, such as BASE International, assist in this process but there is no single source or agency which collects together information on all potential interested parties. Suggestions have been made that the National Economic Development Office or British Venture Capital Association might organise such a service, but until this or something similar is implemented the prospects for a corporate venturing explosion in the UK are likely to be significantly retarded.

Resistance within large corporations

British corporate venturing activity has certainly not been held back by a widespread lack of discussion of the phenomenon. The attractions of corporate venturing have now been widely publicised and, to judge from such facts as the attendance at pioneering conferences on the subject, interest has been high. Although a number of major corporations have actively considered and implemented corporate venturing plans, the majority of companies who have considered this have not translated them into direct action. This can be put down to a combination of lines of internal resistance, including:

(a) *Anti-minority basis.* Companies have been traditionally concerned that minority investments may be difficult to control, and could expose the host corporation to possible adverse publicity if things go wrong. In particular there is a fear that outsiders will expect the corporate venturer to bail out the smaller company if it gets into financial difficulty.

(b) *'Not invented here'.* It is conventional wisdom that large British companies are hidebound, narrow minded, and innately unresponsive to new ideas from within their own organisation, let alone outside. Although this description is a caricature, there is, however, more than one example of adherents of corporate venturing within large companies failing to convince their colleagues that any technology, product or marketing benefits acquired from outside the company could possibly by materially superior to existing in-house expertise. This may represent a practical manifestation of the often-quoted difference in corporate culture between large and small companies. It is natural for executives, whatever their experience, to feel more comfortable with those of a similar background, and it would not be difficult to find examples of large/small company relationships stifled at birth by a failure to strike up any mutual understanding at the outset.

(c) *Lack of role models.* An obvious, and by no means unimportant, obstacle is the fact that, unlike say management buy-outs, there are few well publicised examples of clearly successful corporate venturing programmes, even in the USA. Information on corporate venturing activity is surprisingly limited, and the benefits of a 'window on technology' can appear remote to a board of directors of a large company which has previously had little or no contact with the venture capital or small company sector.

On the contrary, there are a number of well documented examples in the USA of corporations who have attempted corporate venturing finding it difficult to take advantage of its potential benefits in practice. Even the largest companies, with sophisticated intelligence-gathering networks, can find it difficult to identify a large enough stream of suitable potential corporate venturing partners. Many companies who have tested the corporate venture waters by investing via a fund have also had problems in utilising the venture capitalists' industry contact base and deal flow for their own account.

This can be illustrated by a survey of corporate venture capital organisations made by Tektronix in 1978, which found that only 7% of corporate venture capital organisations regarded themselves as being very successful, and over half not even rating themselves as marginal successes. Why should this be true?

Problems of past corporate venturing programmes

A number of forces have conspired against the high performance of a number of corporate venturing initiatives in the past.

STAFFING PROBLEMS

Many corporate venturing programmes have been hampered by the inability of the host company to attract executives of the appropriate calibre to run them. To some people, this may not be surprising in view of the many qualities required to create the ideal venture capitalist. In terms of experience and expertise, he should have a working knowledge or better of accounting, taxation, corporate finance, and law, in addition to any specific industry experience required. In addition, he should have the personal qualities of entrepreneurial motivation, patience, realistic optimism, negotiating skills, a persuasive manner and the ability to evaluate managers as well as the businesses they run. Not many organisations have a surfeit of such paragons available for instant transfer into the corporate venturing arm, and it may prove difficult to persuade those with the requisite skills to leave their current mainstream posts. Alternatively, if the corporation seeks to recruit outsiders, these may prove difficult to attract and retain without specially tailored compensation packages, typically containing a significant equity element, which may prove difficult to arrange within existing pay structures without causing undue resentment from existing executives.

CORPORATE INTERFERENCE

Interference from host company executives in corporate venturing programmes is seldom productive, and usually quite the opposite. In fact, according to Norman Fast, perhaps the leading authority on corporate venturing, American experience strongly suggests that success in corporate venturing is inversely proportional to the degree of contact with the host organisation, in view of its almost invariably disruptive effects on both host company corporate venture managers and the portfolio companies themselves.

Iain Steel, of BP Ventures, speaking in 1984 at a corporate venturing conference in London, illustrated well the sort of thing which can happen, by way of a horticultural analogy:

'Corporate venturing is about creating a well-cultivated market garden, a commercial nursery within the grounds of the great corporate estate. It is set up on commercial lines as a business in its own right, separate from the estate and is tended by keen, knowledgeable, hard working gardeners who do not understand the concept of demarcation and who are very commercially aware. They frequently have a financial stake in their business, and this shows in their achievement and their pride in their work. Unfortunately they are showered with goodies by their benefactors in the corporate estate: open budget accounts, the best specialist services known to man, ample supplies of fertiliser, and access to the complete range of expertise within the estate.'

'However, despite having a wall round the garden, everyone in the corporate estate has a key to the gate. This is where the fun starts. Everyone, bar no-one, is an amateur gardener. Advice is freely available; this ranges from "more water" to "less water", "prune" or "let it grow freely" and so on. Dealing with these ever-so-helpful suggestions is time-consuming and distracting and is one of the reasons why corporate venturing tends to fail. The fellows from the estate frequently enter the garden to up-root their pride and joys, which they inevitably feel are not being grown fast enough.'

'They somehow cannot accept that you, the commercial grower, must take the needs of the customer into account. He, the customer, may in fact not want the largest, he may want the most fragrant or he may want the best coloured specimens. In short the estate prima donna cannot resist the temptation of telling you how to do it; in extreme cases if you do not accept his advice he showers his favourite in fertiliser, covering you in the process! Finally, the heavies come in. These are the corporate skinheads, they embark on joyrides around the garden, invariably in bulldozers, causing chaos. You can imagine the time that our hard-working gardeners spend tidying up after these escapades, mending fences, rebuilding bridges, repotting plants and restoring the garden to some semblance of order. The heavies to whom I refer are the analysts, the internal auditors, the corporate planners in your organisation. The vehicles are the corporate estate's insatiable desire for five year plans, budgets, strategic analysis and all the rest of it.'

Hollister B. Sykes, a former head of Exxon Enterprises (the corporate venturing arm of Exxon Corporation), tells a similar story in the June 1986 *Harvard Business Review*. Owners of companies in which Exxon has acquired a stake as part of this programme were forced, amongst other things, to put up with examples of the following:

(a) 'Corporate review producers removed decision-making authority from the ventures' boards and moved it up to Exxon staff and committees. Venture managers had to spend extra time and effort bringing Exxon's management up to speed. Although justified by the inexperience of some venture managers, these additional reviews slowed the response to a rapidly changing business environment and distracted attention from venture operations.'

(b) 'Corporate concerns about publicity, image, ethics, legal liabilities, and personnel policies required frequent reports to, and reviews by, corporate staff. Exxon's high profile opened it to spurious lawsuits and complaints that would not have come up in connection with a small, independent company. Because of Exxon's high ethical and legal standards, considerable staff effort went to execute venture contracts and agreements. Worries that a venture's advertising might be misleading or affect another venture or an Exxon affiliate led corporate staff to approve all venture advertising.'

(c) 'The proliferation of new ventures led as well to a variety of financial reporting formats and MIS systems. In several cases, a venture's sales outgrew its accounting systems and caused serious control problems. To promote overall efficiency and improved control, the ventures were eventually asked to change over to compatible systems and to install additional procedures and personnel. Corporate financial staffs expanded to assist and monitor these activities.'

(d) 'Ensuring and documenting fairness and consistency in rating systems, termination policies, and salary administration proved a time-consuming challenge.

(e) 'Above certain levels, Exxon management approved all starting salaries, salary increases, and performance bonus plans. At the ventures and at head quarters, staffs grew larger.'

Sykes goes on to catalogue the effects of the above:

'Considered separately, each of these procedures made good sense. Taken together, however, they imposed on each venture the superstructure of a larger corporation and the burden of frequent reporting to the parent corporation. The whole amounted to less than the sum of its parts. In effect, this corporate bear hug amounted to death by 1,000 cuts.'

Finally, even if the above temptations can be successfully resisted, problems may still arise at a higher level if the policy of the host towards its corporate venture partner changes mid-way through its investment. This is not an unknown occurrence, for, as with conventional risk capital, corporate venturing timetables are typically longer than the average interval between major internal policy shifts within large corporations. If such a shift (maybe after an interval of say three to five years) occurs at the same time as an unbudgeted request for further finance from an associate who is behind budget, this can lead at best to a heightened level of friction, and at worst to a fundamental breach in the investment relationship.

CONFLICTS OF INTEREST

If corporate venturing is distinguished from other forms of investment by the existence of multiple aims of the investor (ie, above and beyond those of financial return from a corporate investment portfolio), then conflicts of interest can be expected to arise in a number of ways. These can include:

(a) *Commercial trading conflicts.* These could arise when, for example, the associate company is considering entering a major contract with a competitor of the host company.
(b) *Position of venture managers.* Most company corporate venturing managers may find it difficult to avoid being torn between the best interests of the host corporation and the portfolio company, especially if they sit on the board of the associate, and thus have a fiduciary duty to both sides. In a number of cases for example, rapid growth and profitability in the short term may be more popular with the shareholders of the portfolio company, whereas the parent may be more inclined

to plough back profits into longer term development programmes promising new products of greater potential for its own use.

(c) *Exit routes.* Such conflicts of interest are often crystallised round the question of the timing and method of the realisation by portfolio company management of their investment in the company. It may not be in the interests of the corporate venturer to encourage portfolio company management to cut back their day-to-day executive involvement subsequent to a flotation, for example, still less to agree to any proposed sale of the company to a competitor. Finally, heated disagreements can arise over the price to be paid should the host company wish to acquire the balance of its associate's share capital. This can place the corporate venture manager in the particularly invidious position of having to arbitrate between the natural desires of the portfolio company management to sell at the highest price, and the wish of the host corporation to effect the acquisition as cheaply as possible.

Overcoming the problems

A number of the problems identified above can to a large extent be overcome by the host company investing alongside a professionally managed risk capital fund. This can have advantages both for the host and investment companies. The host can concentrate on supporting the technology and marketing, while the risk capital fund executives can advise on issues relating to growth. In addition, the pressure of the 'independent' risk capital investor can help resolve potential conflicts of interest and limit the potential for overbearing interference by the host company.

DO'S AND DONT'S

Despite the possibility of using the risk capitalist to mitigate the impact of the above issues, the problems are real and are likely to rear their ugly head in some way in most forms of direct corporate venture investments. Nevertheless, corporate venturers can make good partners if they can provide the entrepreneur with the necessary financial and non-financial assistance, and a working relationship can be developed between the two. Any entrepreneur considering becoming involved with a corporate venturer should, however, take special care to weigh up the pro's and con's of any funds on offer. We have listed below a number of suggestions which may help:

(a) If an offer is on the table from a venture capital fund, check who the fund's own investors are; if they include industrial corporations, be sure to ascertain what sort of relationship and special powers they have negotiated with the fund executives as regards portfolio companies, and consider specifically whether such relationships would be welcome or unwelcome.

(b) In the case of direct investments, examine critically what the host company can offer. Can they give convincing *practical* examples of how they can help, and will they really be of use in solving the problems you are likely to face in the future?

(c) Ensure you establish at the outset what the investor's real aims are, both short term and long term; be especially wary of those who may appear to want a minority stake in your business but are in reality looking for a phased acquisition (unless this is your objective too).

(d) Make sure that the operating policies and practices of the corporate venturer are not likely to clash with your own, and that you will not be subjected to too much interference from the host company. This in turn will depend critically on:

(e) The people you will have to deal with — have they the practical experience and personal qualities you need? Do not hesitate to see if they match up against the executives of the risk capital funds you are looking at, if you are considering a number of alternatives. Finally, ask yourself how long the corporate venture executive with whom you will be dealing is likely to stay with the host company. The chances are that if you like him and he likes the company he is working for well enough to stay there for some time, then you have a good fit.

(f) Finally, and perhaps most important of all, *examine your own motives* for seeking corporate venture capital with some care. The corporate venturer can have a significant influence on his portfolio companies in a number of ways, some of which are quite subtle and will not be immediately apparent. For example, the existence of a corporate venture backer may provide the entrepreneur with a greater sense of security. The stronger this feeling, however, the more inclined the entrepreneur may be to consider this company's current problems and future strategy from the host company's perspective, including key decisions such as new products to be developed, new markets to be attacked, etc. This may be exactly what the entrepreneur is looking for, but if not he may have consciously to fight against himself to preserve his independence.

Chapter 8

Other Methods of Raising Risk Capital

We have not yet, however, exhausted the potential sources of, or reasons for, the raising of risk capital. Significant amounts of money have been raised by other means or for other purposes, three of which are discussed in this chapter, viz:

(a) buying out existing shareholders, or replacement capital;
(b) the direct issue of shares to other members of the public;
(c) joint venture finance

REPLACEMENT CAPITAL

The distinguishing feature of replacement capital, as its name implies, is its role as a means of *substituting* one shareholder for another, rather than raising new capital. It is, however, increasingly common today for the two to be combined, ie, for the new investor to be prepared to inject new money into the investee company as well as buying-out existing shareholders, in which case the transaction will be very close in substance to a conventional venture or development capital financing (in fact, a management buy-out will typically be precisely this).

Replacement capital can provide the answer to the entrepreneur's problems in a number of circumstances, for example:

(a) In cases where one or more shareholders may need cash and may be forced to sell their shares. This in turn can arise for a number of reasons, including the burden of inheritance tax. This need for finance has been so important in the past that ICFC (now 3i) set up its own subsidiary, EDITH (Estate Duties Investment Trust), to buy-out minority shareholders in private companies which required finance for precisely this reason.
(b) Where there is a valid business reason for buying-out one or

more existing shareholders. A common example of this can occur in the case of mergers between two family companies, not all of whose shareholders may wish to continue to be involved in what for them would be a different business.

(c) In the case of companies facing succession problems, for example a family company where the proprietor is nearing retirement age and no successor has emerged within the family, the owner may be wary of selling his business to an outsider out of a sense of loyalty to his existing management team. In such cases, the most obvious alternative must be to sell the shares directly to existing management, funded by the replacement capitalist, or to a separate company formed for the purpose by management and finance from outside, ie, the family company management buy-out referred to in Chapter 5.

(d) In cases where existing shareholders have seriously fallen out amongst themselves, to the point where it may be difficult to carry on the existing business of the company without the replacement of at least one of the parties by an outsider.

A number of funds (concentrated among the development capitalists) have in the past invested significant amounts of money in such companies, taking on the role of minority shareholder. It is not unusual that the development capitalists have traditionally dominated this field, for most such companies will not be planning a Stock Exchange listing and in order to make such investments attractive the fund will require a running yield. In practice this means investing by way of cash-generating securities, in cash-generating companies. The fund will thus typically, after purchasing the share in question, insist on converting them into cash-generating instruments, usually by the addition of preferred dividend rights.

Replacement capital has attracted much less publicity in recent years than its headline-catching bedfellows such as management buy-outs or the BES. It has also suffered in recent years because of the increase of alternative exit routes for existing investors. These include the possibility of the company itself buying back the shares in question, which is discussed further in Chapter 15. Replacement capital is, however, likely to remain a mainstream activity of many of the funds in the foreseeable future, and as such represents an important financing alternative to be borne in mind by the entrepreneur.

Chapter 8 Other Methods of Raising Risk Capital 101

ISSUING SHARES TO OTHER MEMBERS OF THE PUBLIC

In addition to obtaining subscriptions from risk capital funds, there are a number of more traditional ways of obtaining permanent capital for businesses which still fall short of the requirements for a Stock Exchange listing or for their shares to be traded in the USM. These include:

(a) Informal arrangements for family and friends to subscribe for shares.
(b) Private placings of shares, by a broker or other intermediary with his institutional and private clients, of an unlisted company.
(c) Offers for subscription by the public (through a broker or other intermediary) for shares in unlisted companies.
(d) Raising capital on one of the 'alternative markets', such as the Over-The-Counter market or on the Third Market of the Stock Exchange.

Each of these routes are discussed below.

Informal arrangements

At its simplest, this can take the form of the entrepreneur taking a 'sleeping partner' solely in order to provide finance. This can be expected to include family, friends and contacts who in certain cases can raise surprisingly large sums of money. The major advantage of such arrangements for the entrepreneur usually lies in their informality which at best can provide patient, flexible money with no drain on cash resources and minimal issue costs.

Provided the entrepreneur can establish the right relationship with such investors, this can be the best way to raise money, especially at the start-up stage when investment is as much a matter of faith in the individual as in the project.

The main limitation of this form of finance is the limited amounts of money which can generally be raised. There are relatively few individuals able to invest large sums of money in a single project without it representing a disproportionate risk to them. On the other hand, to raise smaller amounts from a larger number of people takes the issue away from being an informal arrangement to one which will require issuing a prospectus complying with the Companies

Acts and compliance with the other laws dealing with the issue of securities (The laws relating to when a prospectus is required are complex, and are dealt with later in this chapter.)

Private placing

Private placings have raised significant amounts of money for unquoted companies for many years. They are so-called because the shares of the fund raising companies are not quoted on the Stock Exchange and the shares are *placed* with clients of the sponsor. The sponsor, generally a stockbroker or licensed dealer, places the shares with institutional clients, individual clients and funds under the sponsor's management by private arrangement, without advertising, and thus without public involvement.

Institutional private placings were for many years one of the main sources of venture capital. Today the majority (by number at least) of instances of institutional venture capital investment are through the funds described in Chapter 4. The institutional private placing does, however, play a significant role in financing unquoted companies, particularly where larger sums are required. The significant difference between such financings and the now more common venture or development capital funding is the absence of any significant involvement with the company by the investors. Partly because of the number of investors in these larger placings, and because of the nature of the institutions involved, institutional investors in private placings tend to be 'hands-off' in the extreme. In many cases they will regard the investment as speculative, not unlike locking away the odd case of claret for ten years in the hope that it will mature into something remarkable.

An advantage to the entrepreneur of raising funds in this way is that costs can be reduced if, as is the case with many placings to a limited number of investors, a prospectus complying with the Companies Acts is not required. In addition, generally fewer constraints are placed upon the company by its investors who, apart from perhaps appointing a representative director to the board, generally do not interfere with the management of the company. In addition it is sometimes said that a sponsor with a good reputation can raise money through a private placing at a price which more closely matches the entrepreneur's value of the company than is likely in a more routine venture or development capital financing. It is equally true that a reputable sponsor will be highly selective in deciding which companies to support.

The principal disadvantages of a private placing are that the sponsors are generally not interested in raising small sums of money and, if they are, the cost in relation to the funds raised can be high. Perhaps the biggest disadvantage of raising finance in this way, however, lies in the problem of raising any second round financing required. Many investors in the City still tend to view requests for subsequent financing rounds from unquoted companies as admissions of failure and this can either mean raising more money at the outset (with greater equity dilution) or the risk of returning for more money later when the investors may be unreceptive.

Offers for subscription

The Business Expansion Scheme has resulted in what, until relatively recently, was an almost unknown event — an offer to the public at large to subscribe for shares in a young, possibly start-up, unquoted company often involving heavy advertising. A number of brokers and licensed dealers have sponsored share issues to the public in companies whose activities have ranged from farming through property development, to a range of industrial and commercial enterprises. It is doubtful, however, how many of these issues would have gone ahead without the availability of BES tax relief.

From the company's viewpoint, raising finance in this way has both attractions and disadvantages. The principal attraction is the minimal degree of control which individual investors can exert upon the management of the company. The disadvantages include the need to prepare a prospectus. This involves significant cost to the company before there is any indication that the company will be successful in raising the money it is seeking. Other disadvantages include the difficulty of raising second round financing and the costs of administration involved with a large number of individual shareholders.

Prospectus requirements

Contrary to popular belief, the requirement to produce a statutory prospectus is not confined to quoted companies. It is a requirement of the Companies Acts that all offers of shares to the public by any company will require a prospectus, the contents of which must comply with the disclosure requirements of Schedule 3 of the Companies Act 1985. Although these are not typically as onerous as the disclosure requirements of a prospectus required by a new entrant on the Stock Exchange, to prepare a prospectus can still involve a significant amount of work, including the publication of audited historical financial information for the previous five years (if available). The standard of 'due diligence' required to verify all information appearing in a prospectus is also more than usually onerous as the publication of false or misleading information in that document can carry severe penalties.

Unfortunately, the definition of the phrase 'the public' is not specified in the Companies Acts. Subsequent case law has, however, defined it very widely — while approaching a small number of potential investors can generally be achieved without requiring a prospectus, in one case at least an invitation to six companies to subscribe for shares in a venture has been defined as an offer to the public requiring a prospectus. It is essential therefore that competent legal advice is obtained at the outset both to ensure compliance with the Companies Acts and the other complex regulations surrounding the issue of securities to the public.

Alternative markets

While companies which have a size and record which would support the admission of their shares to the Stock Exchange list or the Unlisted Securities Market would not generally require venture or development capital finance, and are therefore outside the scope of this book, there are alternative markets for less well established companies. These principally include the Over-The-Counter (OTC) market and the recently established Third Market. It is therefore a valid question for entrepreneurs to ask whether they should seek a quotation for the shares of their company in one of these markets and the effect this will have, both on the company's ability to raise funds and more generally on its activities.

Before commenting on the benefits and disadvantages of seeking a quotation in one or other of these markets, we will briefly outline their characteristics.

Over-The-Counter market

Unlike the Stock Exchange, the OTC is not a single market. It is a series of relatively small markets run by a number of dealers licensed to deal in securities. All dealing is done over the telephone and no formal central point exists for the dissemination of price information.

Over the last few years the OTC has grown in size and therefore in importance. Around 40 OTC houses trade in securities, dealing together in over 150 companies with a market value in excess of £600m. Harvard Securities is the largest of the licensed dealers with over 50 OTC quoted companies under its wing, roughly twice as many as its nearest competitor. Stocks traded by these dealers typically comprise companies which have raised money on entering the market under the sponsorship of one of the licensed dealers and whose shares are now traded by one or more of the market-makers. Many of these companies have raised money under the BES.

Typically, companies whose shares are traded in the OTC are small and young; no trading record is needed and many start-ups are quoted. As a result, investment in shares traded in the OTC generally involves a much higher degree of risk to the investor than, say, investing in a company whose shares are traded in the USM. Figure 14 on page 106 illustrates this point.

As the figure shows, a total of 23 out of 185 companies which have come to the OTC markets have either gone into receivership or are no longer traded, as against 19 out of 469 in the case of the USM. Although five OTC companies have graduated either to the USM or full Stock Exchange listing, this is much less than the 61 USM entrants who have since moved on to the official list.

Despite these figures, the OTC has firmly established itself as an alternative to the Stock Exchange as a place to invest in young companies carrying high risk but with a degree of up-side potential. It is the very success of this market that has led the Stock Exchange to open its own 'Third Market' for trading in the shares of companies which fall short of meeting the criteria for quotation on the USM.

The Third Market

Concurrent with other changes in the regulations for share dealing, the Third Market was to have been established by the Stock Exchange in October 1986. This was delayed until early 1987 and, although it appears to have got off to a slow start, it is as yet too early too comment on its success or effects. The aim of this market is to provide the opportunity, within the framework of the Stock Exchange, for the shares of young, and even start-up, companies to be traded. Companies that will qualify for this market include:

HISTORY OF OTC AND USM ENTRANTS TO JUNE 1986

FIGURE 14

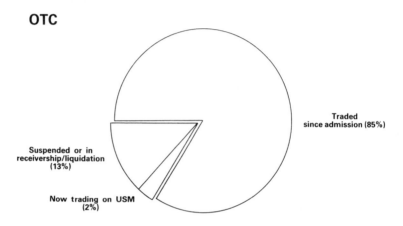

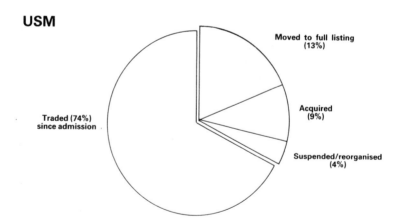

(a) companies demonstrating genuine trading activity with at least one year's audited accounts showing significant revenue flows;
(b) greenfield ventures, requiring development capital for a specific, fully researched and costed project or product, with the prospect of significant revenue flows within a reasonably short time scale;
(c) companies where securities are already traded off the Stock Exchange (eg, on the OTC market) but can be shown to be qualified for offering to the public on a Recognised Investment Exchange.

In addition, the following activities must not represent more than 10% of a company's profits, turnover or capital employed:

(a) holding of cash or 'near cash' assets;
(b) holding of minority interests in other companies.

The implications of the development of the Third Market for the OTC are as yet unclear. A number of the OTC market-makers are taking steps towards admission to the Stock Exchange which will allow them to sponsor companies entering the Third Market and make markets in their shares. Other OTC dealers are exploring ways of developing other regulated markets outside the Stock Exchange.

Obtaining an early quotation — advantages and disadvantages

Not all young and developing companies which are seeking venture or development capital finance are likely to be able to obtain a quotation for their shares in the OTC or Third Market. Many will not have the track record, management, prospects or other factors which the sponsors to such issues will feel are necessary in order for their shares to be traded in one of these markets. Nevertheless, for those that would qualify, the question arises as to the benefits and disadvantages of such a move.

The principal benefit of a quotation in one of these markets is the effect this has on attracting investors to the company. The opportunity to sell (or buy more) shares quickly on the market can significantly increase the attractiveness of an investment in the eyes of the potential investor. In addition some would say that the ability to obtain a quotation for its shares can enhance the reputation, visibility and possibly the trading prospects for a company.

On the other hand, these benefits have often historically proved difficult to obtain, at least in the case of the OTC. The majority of OTC market-makers have traditionally not been well capitalised and their ability to make an effective market in a company's shares has been constrained. As a result, the ability to buy and sell significant quantities of shares in many OTC companies has been very limited. In particular very few of the big City share-buying institutions have made significant investments in OTC companies and this has tended to inhibit the ability to raise further rounds of finance by way of rights issues through this market. In addition, due to the lack of overall regulation of this market and the questionable practices of one or two fringe members (including the 'hard-sell' methods by which shares are sometimes sold to customers, and the often wide dealing margins), the OTC has developed an uneven reputation.

As a result, the companies whose shares are traded in this market may not always reap the full benefits which are conventionally associated with a quotation. It remains to be seen whether the Third Market will have the liquidity and reputation which may make the quotation of shares of younger and developing companies more attractive.

JOINT VENTURES

The final significant risk financing alternatives for the growing company involves co-operation with outsiders in the form of joint ventures. These can take many forms, from collaborative agreements between companies covering research and development, marketing or manufacturing, to shared investments in jointly-owned companies. The latter represents a form of financing very close to corporate venturing, and the factors outlined in Chapter 7 which have increased interest in corporate venturing in recent years have also given rise to an increase in joint venture activity.

A number of institutions may also, however, be prepared to make joint venture finance available, most notably the British Technology Group, whose NRDC arm has invested significant sums in this form of finance over the last 30 years. This is *project finance* (usually in technology related ventures) by which the investor agrees to share the development costs of a particular project (and sometimes also fixed and working capital financing costs) which he expects to recover by way of a levy based on subsequent project sales. The finance is 'non-recourse', ie, the return to the investor depends solely on the success of the project, and the entrepreneur is not obliged to repay any money received in the event of failure.

Advantages and disadvantages

This form of joint venture finance can suit some companies very well. From the entrepreneur's point of view:

(a) No loss of control is involved.
(b) The servicing costs of the finance are automatically matched to the means to support it, ie, sales revenue.
(c) The risk to the entrepreneur is limited to his own contribution to project costs; it thus represents cheap finance in the event of failure.
(d) It is common practice among British companies in receipt of this type of funding to account for it as a reduction of operating costs, thus directly improving reported profit and loss in the early years of the project.

However, the following disadvantages should also seriously be considered:

(a) This form of finance can in practice be significantly limited in its application. This is especially the case where the project concerned is so material to the operations of the company that the investor may consider that its failure could bring down the company; in such a case he may decide that equity finance may be more appropriate for this form of risk.
(b) Perhaps most importantly, this form of joint venture finance can prove expensive if the project succeeds. Levies based on sales will automatically require royalty payments regardless of whether the company is making an overall profit. Faced with this possibility, the entrepreneur may be tempted to interpret the joint venture agreement unduly in his own favour by, for example, contriving to abort a project and use the technological expertise thus gained to develop a successful related product on which no royalties will be payable. This can lead in some cases to difficulties in negotiating the detailed terms of funding, and in some cases create undue suspicion between the partners even before the investment has been made.

Joint venture finance then can be a useful form of project finance for many companies. It is not, however, widely available or easy to obtain, and harmonious investor/investee relationships can be more difficult to maintain in practice than may appear at first sight; in this form of risk capital above all they need to be worked at.

PART 4
RAISING THE FINANCE

Chapter 9

Getting Started

Having looked at the alternative forms of risk capital at some length, we now return to the process of raising it. To do this we must go back to where we left our entrepreneur at the end of Chapter 2, asking:

IS RISK CAPITAL FOR ME?

Inevitable sacrifices

The entrepreneur who feels drawn to any of the types of risk capital discussed in the previous pages should first think carefully through the inevitable sacrifices this will involve whatever variety is sought. To recap what we said in Chapter 2, in particular:

(a) It will not be cheap. Venture capitalists often look for a 50%–60% internal rate of return (IRR) on investments they accept (roughly equivalent to a tenfold capital gain realised after five years) in order to achieve an overall fund return in excess of 25%, which may require significant dilution of the owner's equity. Development capitalists, although usually not as ambitious, still typically seek an IRR in excess of 25%, a large proportion of which will be received annually in cash from the company.
(b) Risk capital finance will in most cases involve some surrender of strategic flexibility on the part of the entrepreneur. This may be imposed directly in the form of restrictions imposed on owners by institutions as a precondition of their investments, a subject dealt with in more detail later. Less widely recognised, but just as important, however, are the more subtle pressures which may be placed on entrepreneurs by institutional backers to act in such a way as to fulfil their own original expectations rather than follow the long-term interests of the company.

Although all good risk capitalists try hard to avoid this, it is not always easy, and cases of venture capitalists pressing unwilling owners further along the treadmill of continuing growth, or development capitalists unreasonably insisting on excessive prudence, are sadly not unknown.

If such considerations represent sources of real concern to the entrepreneur, he should seriously consider whether a judicious package of commercial lending, project or specific asset-based finance would not be more appropriate, even though the price may be lower growth.

The task involved

For every company in this position however, there are many more who would like to raise risk capital but are unable to convince their hoped-for backers of their work. We will be dealing over the next three chapters with the key questions the risk capitalist will ask when evaluating investment proposes. In summary, however, to be successful, the entrepreneur will need to satisfy the potential investor that his company can pass the key tests of:

(a) *Establishing the potential of the venture.* To the development capitalist, this will mean the potential to generate required cash flow. In many cases this may not be too difficult to establish, if the proposition is underpinned by a good financial track record. The venture capitalist will often, however, have a much more difficult task in the absence of such information. His evaluation of potential will perforce almost always be concentrated around an examination of the current and future market for the company's products, which is one of the reasons why certain venture capital funds have a reputation for unusual thoroughness in their commercial evaluation of investment proposals.

(b) *The ability to exploit this potential.* No idea, however brilliantly conceived, will ever result in commercial success unless it is actively exploited and controlled. In practice, this requires the management ability to develop, execute and adapt strategies to achieve this in response to changing circumstances. All risk capital investors, without exception, acknowledge that the most critical element of their investment evaluation is their appraisal of management; in the long run, it is people, not products, they are investing in. Anyone considering raising risk capital, or advisers interested in entering the area, should ensure that, if their companies have not built up a competent, complete and rounded management team, appropriate plans have been set up to achieve this as soon as possible.

These are tough tests, met in practice by few applicants for risk capital funding.

The importance of commitment

The returns demanded by the risk capitalists, and the methods by which they evaluate and structure their investments to achieve them, will impose significant pressures on those companies which have not fallen by the wayside prior to investment. To survive these pressures requires more than a sound company with growth prospects; for risk capital investments fully to realise the expectations of their originators, both investor and investee need to be emotionally committed, not only to working for the success of the company but also to working with each other.

The entrepreneurs and his advisers will need to review carefully all the factors mentioned above to ensure that such a 'fit' is reasonably probable before starting the finance-raising process.

THE PRELIMINARIES

Once a company has decided to raise risk capital, however, and is convinced it has the ingredients for success, how does it go about it?

The first task on the agenda should be to put in place its professional advisory team.

CHOOSING PROFESSIONAL ADVISERS

We know of one or two cases where entrepreneurs have handled the whole process of raising equity finance entirely alone, without any professional assistance. This is unusual, however, as the process is complex and requires considerable specialist knowledge, particularly in the areas of accounting, property, pensions, and contract, tax and company law. As a result, most entrepreneurs seeking risk capital finance make use of professional advisers at some stage. These may include:

Accountants
Solicitors
Property Consultants
Pension Advisers
Marketing Consultants
Specialist Finance Brokers.

The entrepreneur will typically choose one of two approaches in using professional advisers:

(a) He may effectively sub-contract the leadership of the investment process in toto to an adviser, eg, a finance broker. In this case, the lead adviser or broker will himself typically draw on the service of some or all of the advisers noted above as necessary.
(b) Alternatively, the entrepreneur himself may take the lead, with appropriate assistance (often substantial) from his advisers. This line of action is becoming increasing popular, as many 'specialised' professional advisers are moving towards a more pro-active involvement in the finance-raising process, and can act as an integral part of the decision-making team rather than either a leader or a follower.

Accountants and solicitors in particular are devoting more and more time and resources to the provision of general advice to businessmen raising finance, as well as technical expertise on specific problems. The typical services they can provide, and the help they can bring to the process, are described below.

The role of the accountant

The accountant's role today is often many-faceted, embracing:

CONTINUING FINANCIAL ADVICE

This encompasses the 'traditional' accountant's role as tax planner and guide to accounting and reporting systems and controls. Increasingly, however, accountants are branching out. First, the accounting firms (and especially some of the larger ones) can bring to bear a wide range of skills in assisting their clients. It is becoming more common to see accountants (or their consulting divisions) presenting their capabilities not only in the areas of financial planning, management and control, but also in such fields as marketing, inventory and production management, computerisation, and executive selection.

In addition to these specific skills, the accountant also has an important continuing consultative role to play in acting as a sounding board and source of advice to his client on matters of overall financial and management strategy.

As a result, the presence on the professional team of a respected firm of accountants can significantly increase investor confidence from the outset, and help facilitate the smooth progress of the finance-raising.

ASSISTANCE IN RAISING FINANCE

In addition to the above, a number of accounting firms have set up teams with specific experience of risk capital raising. This can further oil the wheels of the entrepreneur's progress to the finance of his desire by assisting in:

(a) The preparation of the business plan, although we do not believe that the accountant should write the plan as, in the last resort, the investor wants to read about management's ideas, and not those of his consultant or accountant.

The accountant can, however, perform an invaluable role in advising in the overall structure and format of the plan, assisting in the validation of detailed information (eg, financial projections) and, most importantly, acting as a sounding board as management develops its thinking into concrete objectives, strategies and tactics.

(b) The choice of funds to be approached. The experienced accountant will be aware of the objectives, methods of operation, and current investment preferences of all significant potential sources of risk capital finance, and will be able to advise on the number and type of funds to be approached.

(c) The structure and pricing of the proposed deal, to optimise shareholders' return without placing an unreasonable financial burden on the company itself.

(d) Tax planning. Very few risk capital fundings do not raise important tax issues which need early consideration. One of the most frequently encountered is the need to ensure that any

future gains on the managers' shares attract capital gains rather than income tax treatment.
(e) Providing background information, and answering detailed investor queries, to assist management in the detailed investment negotiations.

COSTS AND BENEFITS

A major benefit which has historically been received from the involvement of the accountant as described above has been his demonstrable independence. This has arisen from his fee arrangements. The accountant has charged on a time basis, unlike many other advisers whose fees include a significant 'success' fee or similar arrangements. As a result, the accountant has been in no way financially interested in the financial outcome of his advice. While we are aware of a growing number of instances of reduced fees being agreed at the outset if the deal is unsuccessful, and they could to some extent be seen as challenging the principle of independence, the amount of the 'success' fee has rarely been so great as to challenge the principle of the accountants' independence.

More recently these historic principles have been challenged as accountants' professional rules have been changed to allow 'contingent fees' to be charged in certain circumstances. It is still too early to assess how widespread this practice will become or its likely effects.

The role of the solicitor

The entrepreneur will almost always require competent and experienced legal advice on the structure of the deal, and especially its detailed documentation. To do this the solicitor will need to have a full grasp of the nature of the business and the objectives of management. In the hands of a sufficiently able and experienced solicitor, such information could qualify him to take on the lead investor role described above.

In view of the above, it will be useful in most cases to introduce the solicitor onto the advisory team earlier rather than later. At this stage the solicitor can help reconcile the commercial objectives of the parties (eg, security for debt finance) with the legal constraints (eg, the general prohibitions contained in company law on a company giving any financial assistance in connection with the purchase of its shares). As one leading venture capital lawyer says, 'Those cases where entrepreneurs have found that introducing the lawyers at an early stage has not been constructive, probably indicate that the wrong lawyers have been chosen!'

Accountants and solicitors — overlapping roles

There are significant areas where accountants and solicitors hold themselves out as practising in the same areas. Some of these might include advice on:

(a) Specific taxation issues relating to investment documentation (eg, warranties, tax clearances, etc).
(b) Taxation implications for management and employees, eg, employee share schemes, pension arrangements, and specific anti-avoidance tax legislation.
(c) General advice on the structure and overall implications of the deal as a whole, depending on the experience and expertise of the particular accountants and lawyers concerned.

Whatever the split of work, it is vital that, where there are overlaps, the lawyers and accountants work together as a team and decide with the client which areas they will principally concentrate on.

Conflicts of interest

Once an investment has been completed, investors and management generally have common interests; at the stage of investment negotiation, however, they will invariably have different objectives in a number of areas. As such, it is not unusual to see separate solicitors and accountants advising investors and management.

ACCOUNTANTS

The investor may for example often instruct a separate firm of accountants to conduct an independent investigation of the company's affairs or to advise on the taxation implication of structuring the deal. In some cases this has been built up into a more formal relationship where funds will appoint a consultant accountant who will advise and investigate on behalf of the fund for all its potential investments.

The aim of such an arrangement is usually to build a relationship which allows the accountant's work to be discharged more efficiently, and, perhaps more importantly, to encourage the accountants to introduce deals to the fund.

In many cases, however, in order to reduce costs, if the investor is satisfied as to the reputation and ability of the entrepreneur's accountants, he may be happy for them to conduct any necessary investigation on his behalf. This is especially common if the accountant's main task is to report on facts or opinions designed to help the investor in his evaluation, rather than searching for ammunition for use against the company during negotiations.

SOLICITORS

The solicitor on the other hand is typically employed by the investor (as part of his duty of 'due diligence' to his own investors) to ensure as far as possible that his investment is adequately protected by all relevant legal safeguards. It is therefore more common than not for each side to take separate legal advice, especially at the negotiation stage.

Indeed, the investor's solicitor may be instructed to become involved in detail in other matters than the documentation of the deal itself. Where, for example, the financing required is specifically earmarked for a particular acquisition, the institution may wish to ensure that its solicitors act for the company in negotiating the purchase. This is often the case in management buy-outs, where:

(a) The overwhelming majority of funding may be provided by institutions.
(b) Management may have interpersonal problems in negotiating with their present employer.
(c) Management may be over-keen to do the deal at a higher price than can reasonably be supported.
(d) Management will normally be less experienced in acquisition negotiations than the institutions.

Separate legal representation is not, however, an invariable rule. Especially in the case of smaller transactions, the investor's solicitor may in practice take the lead in acting both for the risk capitalist and the management, who would only expect to be separately advised on likely points of potential conflict. Alternatively, two partners from the same firm will act — one for management and one for the investor — to minimise costs.

Costs

It is common practice for all professional costs incurred in risk capital financing to be borne by the investee company, including the fees of the investors' professional advisers.

This may not always be as draconian as it seems, as the investor will typically increase the amount of funding required to take account of such costs, although of course this will, directly or indirectly, have the effect of further diluting the existing owners' equity.

Although this practice may be common, however, it is not invariably followed. First, in a few cases, company law can stand in its way, in the form of section 151 of the Companies Act 1985. This generally prevents a company financing a subscription for or purchase of its own shares, and therefore can in certain circumstances prevent the company paying certain of the subscribers' costs. Expert legal advice is important to ensure this is not generally the case.

Secondly, it is occasionally agreed that all parties should pay their own costs, to encourage parsimony in the use of professional services, not least of all by the professionals themselves.

SETTING OUT THE STALL

With the advisory team in place, the entrepreneur can then begin to plan the first approach to potential backers.

The business plan

Before considering which sources of finance to approach, all companies seeking risk capital will need to prepare a business plan. This will be a fundamental document for any business. Not only will it serve internally as a road map for management, it will also, if soundly constructed, form the basis around which the venture or development capitalist will structure his evaluation of any funding request.

The successful business plan will sell the company persuasively, while at the same time presenting its current position and future prospects honestly. This is not always easy to do, but it is essential that it be done well to attract and retain the interest of the investor. We deal in more detail with the aims, content and techniques of writing a successful business plan in Chapter 10.

Approaching the funds

Armed with his business plan, the entrepreneur and his advisers can then consider which sources of finance to approach. If the plan has been written properly, the type of risk capital required should emerge clearly from its pages. Whom to chose from amongst the myriad of financial institutions offering risk capital funding can, however, be more difficult, not to say bewildering, for the uninitiated. Applicants will need to bear in mind not only the investment preferences and styles of the competing institutions, but also their market reputation and track record, commitment to the risk capital arena, availability of follow-on finance and many other factors. How can this information be obtained?

A wide range of brokers and other financial advisers have traditionally been active in this area. In addition, a number of accounting firms have set up specialist corporate finance, 'venture capital' (confusingly used in its widest sense here) or 'hi-tech' groups, to maintain close contact with the various sources of finance on offer in order better to advise their clients on their choice of fund. Alternatively, some helpful statistics on risk capital funds, together with summaries of their scope of operations, are published periodically by a number of trade journals, including *Investors Chronicle*. Finally, the British Venture Capital Associaton can help to put applicants for risk capital funds in touch with potential backers from amongst its members.

How many funds?

We do not believe that it is generally advisable for the entrepreneur to circulate his plan to a large number of institutions. Many potential investors may not be interested in a proposal if they feel they are in competition with a large number of other institutions. Equally important, the generation of significant interest from many sources is likely to involve management in much time-consuming processing of follow-up enquiries.

The well organised entrepreneur will research carefully the type of financiers he feels would react favourably to his proposal, and draw up a short list of three or four to circulate his plan to (or less if he has reason to believe that one or two funds would look especially favourably on his proposal). The professional adviser can obviously provide valuable input here, and, more importantly, can help ensure a sympathetic initial consideration of the proposal from any investors with whom he has previously established a working relationship.

Chapter 10

The Business Plan

'The time spent by the entrepreneur in preparing his business plan represents the best investment he can make. It will mean that he gets greater interest from a particular venture capital firm, if the business fits in with its investment criteria, and a quick "no" if it does not.'
(Ronald Cohen, Alan Patricof Associates Ltd, past Chairman of BVCA)

A business plan is a fundamental document for any business. Internally, it can help owners and managers to crystallise and focus their ideas, to set objectives and monitor performance against them. In one form or another, all successful businesses use them.

A good business plan is also vital when seeking outside finance, especially equity finance, for potential investors will invariable use a written business plan as the starting point of their evaluation of all investment prospects.

The institutions in the market of investing in unquoted companies are usually inundated by investment proposals from which they can choose only a few. One prominent investor has estimated that 85% of investment opportunities submitted to him are rejected at a very early stage, serious consideration is given to as few as 15%, and the negotiation stage is only reached by 5%. To a very great extent, the decision whether to proceed beyond an initial reading will turn on the quality of the business plan prepared by the entrepreneur to support his request for funding.

Thus the business plan is the first, and often best, chance for management to impress prospective investors with the quality of their proposal.

To discover how the plan achieves this, we have to go back again to the investor.

THE INVESTOR'S VIEW: A TWO-STAGE PROCESS

Institutional investors employ a wide variety of techniques and procedures to evaluate investment proposals before deciding whether or not to open detailed negotiations prior to making an investment. However, as noted in the previous chapter, before reaching this stage every investor needs to be convinced of two things:

(a) that the company has the potential to earn the investor the high return he demands; and
(b) that this potential can be exploited.

This in turn involves two distinct processes. First, the investor's interest and attention must be attracted, in order to persuade him as to the potential of the business; and, secondly, if this has been achieved, he will have to satisfy himself that the many risks inherent in the venture have been properly identified and can be acceptably minimised.

To achieve fully its aim, a business plan should strive to do both these things. It should forcefully stress the strengths of the company, especially in comparison with its competitors, while at the same time not hiding any of the real difficulties which any company is likely to face, but evaluating them realistically. This is not an easy thing to do. The remainder of this chapter, however, gives some guidance as to how it can be achieved, by setting out our thoughts on some of the more common practical issues faced by business plan authors, and highlighting some of the common themes running through all successful products.

In addition, we have included at the end of the chapter the typical contents of a business plan in outline. The accompanying commentary not only attempts to give some advice on matters of content, style and length, but also points out some of the key qualities the risk capitalist will be looking for in the venture and some of the specific critical business risks he will require to be addressed.

SOME COMMON QUESTIONS ANSWERED

The business plans received by institutional investors describe companies of all types and sizes. It is in some ways surprising, therefore, that so many entrepreneurs come across the same problems when drafting their plans. We have listed below some of the questions we are most often asked by managers writing business plans, and the answers we commonly give to them.

Who should write the plan?

Unless you have had considerable experience in writing proposals designed to influence financial institutions, it is quite possible that, given the required information, your advisers will be able to write a more professional-looking plan than you can.

We believe this temptation should be resisted. Any outsider will find it more difficult to capture the spontaneity and enthusiasm of management which in many cases will be critical to the success of the proposal, and, in the last resort, the investor wants to read management's plans, not his consultant's or accountant's. This is not to say that your advisers should not give you any help at all — in fact, far from it. They can be most useful in, for example:

(a) Helping to decide on the overall structure and format of the plan in advance, and acting as a sounding board in developing your ideas.
(b) Assisting in the validation of certain of its detailed contents (you should, for example, arrange for your accountant to review your financial projections, and check with your solicitor and tax adviser if your plan involves any corporate restructuring).
(c) Reading through the completed draft prior to submission.

This last step can be especially important, as it is here that the expertise of your advisers can pay off. Try if possible to arrange for a small number of carefully chosen contacts with experience in the field to review your plan for clarity, reasonableness and thoroughness. The views of any other entrepreneurs you may know who have raised capital successfully can be particularly useful in this exercise.

How long should it be?

This is one of the most common questions asked about business plans, and one of the most difficult to answer, because there are no set rules.

In many ways the answer we like best is that a business plan should be long enough to cover the subject adequately and short enough to maintain interest. This length will depend on individual circumstances — a £30m high technology start-up with sophisticated research and manufacturing elements may require a plan of well over

50 pages, including appendices, to include all the key points; on the other hand, a proposal for £65,000 to develop an existing product may be too long at ten pages.

Some commentators feel, however, that the current trend is to produce shorter business plans. This has some logic behind it, as the shorter the plan, the more impact it can be expected to have on the reader, if it is clearly written and covers all the essentials. Investors will also invariably follow up good plans with a detailed investigation of their own, and thus in most cases not necessarily expect to see every last detail covered at this stage.

The first essential here, then, should be to err on the side of brevity. As a tentative rule of thumb, for all projects requiring less than £1m, you should think carefully whether all of your material is absolutely necessary if the body of your plan is over 15 pages.

We discuss later in this chapter some techniques for keeping plans down to a manageable length.

What if I cannot forecast my results?

The problems associated with financial projections contained with business plans, and the uses made of them, have proved a constant source of friction in the field of financing proposals, both abortive and successful. Many entrepreneurs have felt uneasy or even bitter about having to forecast results three, four or even five years into the future, in circumstances where they may find it difficult to estimate what will be happening in 12 months' time. They may also fear that failure to meet these targets will be held against them by their investors. This has led to cases of ill-feeling and mistrust, and complaints by a number of entrepreneurs that 'our investors do not understand us.'

This is unfortunate, especially as in many cases such conflicts have resulted from a misunderstanding about the nature and purpose of financial projections. The purpose of financial projections in a business plan is in fact two-fold, viz:

(a) To set out the financial implications of the company's strategy.
(b) As a measure of performance.

Financial implications

The projections will set out the financial implications of the company's strategy which, in narrative form, will provide the core of the plan. The investor will here be looking at the overall shape of the company's expected financial performance as much as the exact estimate of profit in year 5, and trying to get some idea of:

(a) The growth potential of the company (and, by implication, the task its management faces in coping with it).
(b) The sensitivity of profitability to fluctuations in sales and margins, and the relationship between product contribution (which depends on sales) and fixed costs, which tend to rise more irregularly.
(c) The likely time lag between investment (eg, capital equipment, marketing, or research and development) and return through sales or licence income.
(d) Of special importance, the likely impact on cash flow, ie the major factors which will determine when the company will make the transition from a cash-consuming to a cash-generating business.

All the above trends can only become meaningful if analysed over time, and as the company's strategy set out in the plan will cover a number of years, so should its financial impact, embodied in its financial projections.

Thus financial projections, for all but short-term investment proposals, should be prepared for sufficient periods into the future to enable investors to identify and analyse these trends. This will usually mean at least three years, and longer in the case of projects with extended payback periods (a technology company with a heavy emphasis on long-term or basic research would be an example).

The content of the financial projections will also, however, depend critically on the second major purpose for which they are used, as a measure of performance.

Measure of performance

Most investors evaluate proposals principally upon their potential financial return on investment. This in turn will usually depend on financial performance. The accuracy of the figures in the financial projections will thus usually be of the utmost importance to them, and all companies should thus strive to ensure that they are as well thought-out and thoroughly prepared as possible.

There are, however, some key qualifications to this statement which need to be borne in mind when developing and commenting on the financial projections in the business plan:

(a) The value of some businesses at any point in time (as expressed by their worth to another buyer) may bear little relationship to current financial performance, especially if they have developed assets not disclosed in the accounts, such as saleable technology or established distribution networks and agreements. The business plans of such companies should make clear the importance of such non-financial factors in measuring performance.

(b) Some businesses operate in such volatile markets that even short-term forecasting is extremely difficult; in many other industries, while short-term forecasting within reasonable tolerance limits may be possible, long-term predictions may prove largely speculative. This is not a reason for omitting to forecast (for the reasons described above), but the uncertainties should be pointed out clearly in the plan. In some cases it may be advisable to prepare two sets of projections, on 'realistic' and 'pessimistic' assumptions, to give an indication of the possible variations involved. This is a form of sensitivity analysis, a technique to evaluate the impact of uncertainty which is discussed later in more detail.

(c) Some companies may not be able to forecast accurately in the medium-term because they will at some stage in the future have to decide between strategic alternatives with radically different financial effects. Examples of this can be seen where companies will in the future have to exploit new market sectors either by means of organic growth or acquisitions, or new projects through licensing or own-manufacture. Again, in such cases, this should be highlighted in the plan, and it may be advisable to show the financial effects of more than one alternative, if this can be done without adding excessively to its length. Sometimes these projections are called 'financial models' in order to emphasise the difference between them and more conventional forecasts.

In conclusion, then, it will be a rare occasion when financial projections covering at least three years will not be required in a business plan. These projections should be developed as carefully and thoroughly as possible, to the highest degree of detail and accuracy consistent with the uncertainties of each company's environment. At the same time, the plan should point out clearly the degree to which the projections may be relied on, or not, as the case may be. Some practical techniques to achieve this (eg, sensitivity analysis) are discussed below.

How much cushion should I put in my numbers?

Although we suggested above that the financial projections included in the plan should be as realistic as possible, many entrepreneurs feel more comfortable if their projections are conservative, to avoid potential problems with investors if their targets are not achieved. This is no bad thing, as no new venture ever goes exactly according to plan; the question is how to recognise this in the projections while at the same time remaining realistic.

The following suggestions may help here:

(a) If there are significant uncertainties over figures in the projections (eg, sales) it may be appropriate to produce two sets of figures, on a 'realistic' and 'pessimistic' basis.
(b) If only one set of projections is used, and anticipated revenues or expenses fall within a range of expected values (eg, sales), choose a figure at the lower end of the range.
(c) If you are looking for extra funds to take account of unexpected reverses, do not try and quantify this in the projections, which are only estimates anyway. Instead, add an appropriate modest percentage onto the amount of funding you are asking for, under the heading of 'contingency'.

Finally, remember that undue conservatism may prove self-defeating, if your projections are unrealistically modest to the point of materially reducing the value of your company in the eyes of the investor!

How specific should my plan be?

Many entrepreneurs are reluctant to commit themselves in writing to details of their future plans, preferring to leave themselves as much future operational flexibility as possible. Some plans may even ask for finance in excess of the requirements shown in the financial projections in order 'to take advantage of attractive business opportunities as they arise', or similar wording.

Such an opportunistic strategy may be appropriate, and indeed preferable, for some companies. This, however, throws more onus on the ability of management to identify and exploit these opportunities successfully; and indeed most successful financial proposals of this kind have tended to come from management teams of proven ability to achieve this. In cases where this may not be easy to demonstrate, all business plans should therefore include, as a minimum, specific mention of:

(a) How much funding is sought, and at what times.
(b) What detailed projects the money is to be used for.
(c) How the company plans to go about achieving its objectives.
(d) The expected financial impact of the proposed programmes.

It is, however, usually preferable not to be too specific about the form you would like your finance to take. This is because there will always be many alternative types of finance appropriate for any one project, singly or in combination, including various types of equity capital, joint venture finance or lending. Potential investors, however, may be limited by internal policies in the types of finance they can provide, and to demand any one financing package in a business plan may lose the chance of working with a suitable investor who might be very happy to invest in an alternative but acceptable form. It can also often pay dividends not to be too definite on the subject of price in the business plan, and leave this question also to be negotiated at a later stage.

What about inflation?

Problems always arise on the treatment of inflation in financial projections:

(a) If inflation is disregarded, and all financial figures are expressed at current prices, this may complicate the investor's calculation of return on investment, and prove misleading if prices of significant items in the projections rise faster or slower (eg, electronic components, computer equipment, etc) than the general level of inflation.
(b) On the other hand, if inflation is to be taken into account, an inflation rate must be assumed and this may well prove to be wrong unless the time span of the projections is very short.

There is no right answer to this question, and both bases described above are commonly used today. On balance, we would recommend that for the sake of clarity and simplicity constant prices are used, unless the distortive effect of differential inflation on historic-based revenues and expenses are expected to be significant. Otherwise, a reasonable rate of inflation which will give conservative results should be used.

Need I give away confidential information in my plan?

Many entrepreneurs have shown an understandable reluctance to divulge certain confidential information — details of a technological design, for example, or highly sensitive features of marketing strategy — even to prospective investors. This is to their credit, although it should be remembered that the institutional investment community in this country works to the highest professional standards, and its executives are trained to respect commercial confidences at all times.

There are, nevertheless, certain steps you can take, if you are still uneasy on the subject, to mitigate this problem, including:

(a) Ensuring prior to the submission of your plan that potential investors do not have any major conflicts of interest which would cause problems, eg a significant investment in or a close involvement with an unwelcome competitor. Your professional adviser should be able to elicit this information on your behalf.
(b) Marking the plan 'Commercial — in Confidence' or 'Private and Confidential', and issuing numbered copies only.
(c) If you are still worried, you can leave out the more confidential data and send potential investors what is in effect an extract of your business plan. Done judiciously, this can still be a highly effective document, presenting all the necessary data without compromising the truly confidential aspects of your business.

THE KEY POINTS

Every company requiring finance is different, and thus every business plan will be different. However, as we noted in the previous section, all business plans sent to institutions with the purpose of raising finance share the same two purposes — to convince the investor of the potential within the business, and to satisfy him of the ability of the company properly to exploit it. As such, although all business plans are different, the same themes can be found running through all good ones. Some of the more important of these themes are described below.

Selling management

Consider the following statements:
(a) 'I have seen many successful companies grown on the back of no

better than ordinary products by good management; I have never seen any product, however good, converted into a successful company by bad management' (practising American venture capitalist).

(b) 'In the final analysis, 91% of all business failures can be attributed to management' (a survey by a major financial services organisation on small company failures).

We said previously that one of the two key purposes of a business plan is to convince the reader of the company's ability to exploit its potential. In practice, this means management's ability to develop, execute and adapt appropriate strategies to achieve this in response to changing circumstances. In the last resort, investors are investing in management first and foremost, and a prime concern of all business plan authors should be to communicate management's abilities and competence, directly or indirectly, in the plan whenever possible.

This may not always be easy to do without turning the plan into too much of a selling document, which would be counter-productive. Nevertheless, the following suggestions may be of some use:

(a) Pay particular attention to those sections in the plan dealing with the management team. In the absence of any other information, the past track records of the company's key executives will be an important indicator of how they can be expected to cope with future challenges.

(b) Avoid over-optimism, of market potential, for example, or competitive advantages; this will only raise questions in the mind of the reader as to the judgement of the writer. Investors will use the plan as an important indicator of how realistic management are about their company's strengths and weaknesses.

(c) Try to ensure that all parts of the plan are put together as professionally as possible, even where they may be short in length or of only secondary importance. A good example of this can be seen in the financial projections of companies whose prime measures of performance may initially be non-financial, eg, a research-based bio-technology company. In such a case the projections will still play a key role, in the sense of demonstrating management's ability (or otherwise) to master this discipline, which will assume critical importance at a later stage of the company's development, as emphasis switches to technology exploitation.

What makes me so special?

Institutional investors are busy people, with full diaries and limited time to spend on each new business plan presented to them; as we have said before, few investors seriously follow up more than one in ten opportunities presented to them. In order to get past this stage, the entrepreneur has to convince the investor in his business plan that his proposal offers a higher-than-average chance of a better-than-average return.

To do this it is essential for the entrepreneur to focus clearly on those factors which set him apart from other applicants for the investor's funds, and to stress them clearly and forcefully in this plan. These factors could relate to market potential, product or production advantages, management strength or a number of other items. Ultimately, however, they will represent advantages relative to the other players (or products) in the company's target markets at that time.

As a result of this, the sections in the plan on competition (both at present and in their likely reactions in the future) will be critically important, to answer the basic investor questions of:

(a) 'Why should I invest in this, rather than any other market?'
(b) 'Does this company have a sufficient competitive edge to establish itself in the market?'
(c) 'Will this company be able to maintain its competitive edge?'

The question of risk

In the evaluation of target companies, investors place considerable importance on the risks inherent in these businesses and the ability of management to identify and minimise them. An essential attribute of a good business plan is, therefore, its success in establishing that management are aware of all major potential pitfalls and can react appropriately to minimise their effects.

One way of achieving this is to address the question directly by adding to the plan a specific section on risk stating all material identified risks and the steps taken by management either to prevent them or to minimise their effect. This is sometimes expanded into the heading of 'Risks and Rewards', by contrasting these with the anticipated rewards which can be expected from the investment, for example, by showing the likely future valuation of the company if the profits projected in the plan are realised in practice. Alternatively, risks can be contrasted with areas of upside potential not quantified in the financial projections.

This approach has provoked some controversy among readers and authors of business plans, with two conflicting schools of thought emerging. Opponents of this method of highlighting risk directly consider that in many cases this may lead to an undue concentration on the negative aspects of the business to the detriment of its true potential. Its adherents, on the other hand, argue that this approach can work positively by, first, demonstrating management foresight by its awareness of problems, and secondly, in cutting down investment time scales by reducing follow-up questions from the reader.

Whatever view is taken on this question, two factors must be borne in mind:

(a) If a specific section is devoted to risk assessment, it must be complete, not selective. If it is obvious that only those risks which can be adequately countered have been included in the plan, the mutual trust between investor and investee, so essential throughout the financial process, will prove significantly harder to establish.

(b) If the question of risk is not directly as outlined above, it must be done indirectly, at the appropriate place in the plan. For example, if a manufacturing company has to rely significantly on one or more components whose ready availability at reasonable prices may be a potential problem for the business, the plan should discuss alternative sources of supply and projected costs.

One useful technique often used to demonstrate that risk has been taken into account is *sensitivity analysis*. This is really a parallel set (or sets) of financial projections, setting out the likely financial effects if the outcome of certain key factors on which the plan were based (eg, product development time scales, sales, prices, etc) were to differ materially in practice from those assumed in the base forecast. These are often included in summary form, for example, a statement might be added to the narrative accompanying the financial projections noting the effect on profit and cash flow of, say, an annual sales growth of 20% against an original budget of 35%.

The availability and popularity of microcomputer-based spreadsheet packages has given many businessmen the facility to perform extensive sensitivity analysis with minimum effort, but it can be overdone. The figures derived from sensitivity analysis are meaningless in isolation, and must be analysed to have any point. In this context, too much sensitivity analysis can be as bad as too little, if the assumptions used have little chance of happening in real life. We recommend that where this technique is used, revised assumptions are applied, in limited number, to especially significant or volatile numbers or events, such as sales growth, or the impact of delays in product introduction schedules, capital expenditure, etc.

A particularly useful form of sensitivity analysis is *break-even analysis*, which calculates the minimum sales level necessary to cover all fixed costs, assuming anticipated margins. This is often included as part of the financial projections and the ratio of forecast sales: break-even sales can be a valuable performance indicator to an investor in the early years of a new project which is budgeting for initial losses.

Think of the reader!

For such an obvious piece of advice, it is surprising how often this is disregarded by writers of business plans. Too many plans are still over-long, indigestible, badly structured and designed, or just plain incomprehensible. It is important to remember that, in many cases, the investor will not have the relevant specialist industry knowledge, especially in any area of high technology. This may mean that the reader will not only be unaware of much of the terminology used in the plan, but also of some of the basic technological or marketing concepts taken for granted by management.

How much knowledge to assume the reader has may not prove a straightforward question, and it is here that the worth of using outside reviewers should begin to show. Nevertheless, as a minimum, discussions of new products or production processes should always be amplified by comparing them with current proprietary or competitive products. In the case of more specialised or unusual industries, a glossary of technical terms, included as an appendix, may also prove useful.

Keep it short!

If the business plans should be as clear as possible, and if brevity aids clarity, then they should also be as short as possible.

A useful way of achieving this without losing any important points of detail is to stratify the plan by confining all details, where possible, to an appendix, leaving only the overall message in the body of the document. This will enable the reader to master the basic points of your proposal more quickly, without having to digest any undue detail, which he can then refer to in the appendices as a separate exercise.

It is not uncommon to see this device used in the drafting of business plans to such an extent that, in a number of plans, over 50% of their length has been accounted for by appendices. The outline business plan in the Appendix to this chapter gives some idea of the types of detail which can suitably be relegated to the appendices.

The executive summary

Another way of enhancing the clarity of the business plan is to begin it with a brief summary of the proposal, the so-called 'executive summary'.

Any sort of summary will be a key element, and one should be included in every business plan. Its purpose is to attract the attention of the reader, and encourage him to read on (remember the competition for his time!). As such, the summary should first of all be short, preferably on one page, and certainly not more than two. It must also convey concisely yet clearly what unique factors will enable the business to succeed in a competitive marketplace. As a minimum, we suggest the summary should include:

(a) A statement of how much finance is required, and when.
(b) A brief (one paragraph) description of the business, and markets it plans to operate in.
(c) A summary of the highlights included in the financial projections — usually anticipated sales and pre-tax profits for the next three to five years.

In certain cases where it will be immediately apparent that the calibre of management will be a critical factor (eg, in start-up companies, or in the case of new projects with new management teams), a brief description of the background or attributes of the key managers may also need to be included.

Setting benchmarks

All companies planning ahead must set themselves objectives, both as targets to aim for and as benchmarks against which to monitor and evaluate current performance. Not all of these objectives will be financial as, to at least some degree, financial performance is merely the monetary result of a given course of action. Examples of such non-financial objectives include time schedules for: the introduction of new products to the market; patents to be applied for; the build-up of staffing levels in key departments; the construction of critical production facilities, and many more.

Those objectives and time scales need to be included in the plan, either together in one section or separately in the relevant section of the plan to which each will apply. Where their completion will take some time, it may help management to split down the tasks to be attempted into 'milestones', to serve as more frequent gauges of progress and performance. Such milestones will normally be specified in some detail in the company's internal business plan for the use of management; it may not, however, in all cases be necessary to include all of them in any extract of the plan to be sent to outsiders, unless by way of an appendix.

This will be especially important for those companies whose performance at any one point in time cannot primarily be measured in purely financial terms. In such cases, it may be advisable to emphasise, in the narrative financial section of the plan, that the financial projections on which the proposal is based provided only a long-term measure of performance, noting where within the document (eg, an appendix) the key non-financial performance monitors, or milestones, can be found.

The importance of presentation

Physical presentation can also be important in determining the impact of the business plan. This is not to advocate elaborate or expensively produced proposals, which may prove counter-productive. However, a document which does not fall into the trap of ostentation, but which gives the impression that some care has gone into its production, will help distinguish the plan. Among the techniques which may prove useful in this area are:

(a) Providing a table of contents, and 'tabbing' each section for easy reference. This will enable investors more easily to identify and concentrate on those areas they are most interested in.
(b) If the financial projections are likely to prove a critical part of the plan, and they are to be included as an appendix, the use of a double page layout for the key information, typed on the right hand page only. This will enable the reader, by opening out this page, easily to refer to this data at any time while reading through the body of the plan.
(c) The use of a looseleaf binder to package the plan will facilitate any subsequent revisions or insertions.

(d) The use of charts, graphs and diagrams (especially if they can be produced easily on a microcomputer) can add interest and improve comprehension. The inclusion of any available photographs of products, production facilities, etc, may also both inform and add life to the proposal.

APPENDIX — OUTLINE BUSINESS PLAN

The following pages set out an outline of a business plan designed for use in connection with a proposed equity financing, together with commentary on its contents.

The enclosed outline gives general guidance only. The entrepreneur seeking to use it as the basis of his own business plan should not apply it mechanistically; its order can be altered or its suggested sections combined or split up if it is felt appropriate. In particular, not all of the items mentioned here will be of sufficient importance or relevance to warrant inclusion in every plan — indeed, in some cases it may be difficult to include every detail contained in the form set out included here and still follow one of the key principles of business plan writing ('keep it short!'). Nevertheless, all the areas included here should represent questions which management will need to consider, and be able to answer at some stage, as they will all represent key concerns of the risk capitalist.

The outline plan is designed primarily to be applied to a manufacturing company. It will also be relevant, however, with relatively minor amendment, to distribution, service or other companies, and, of course, the principles set out earlier in the chapter will apply, in the drafting of the plan, to any company, of whatever type.

ABCO BUSINESS PLAN

Contents	Comments
Section one — Summary Section two — History Section three — Products Section four — Markets and marketing — The market — The competition — Marketing and sales Section five — Manufacturing and operations Section six — Management Section seven — Financial analysis Section eight — Risks and rewards Section nine — Objectives and milestones Appendices	A contents page will be essential for all plans of any length, to aid the comprehension of the reader, and enable anyone who is interested in certain sections of the document only to identify and access them easily.
Section one — Summary	**Comments**
Purpose of the plan How much finance is required, and what for? Brief description of the company, and its marketplace Highlights of financial projections	The summary should provide a concise overview of the whole plan — it may be the only part of the document some investors will read. Keep it short!
Section two — History	**Comments**
Date and form of incorporation Brief summary of progress since incorporation Relevance to current funding application Previous and current involvement of outside shareholders (if any)	This section is intended to summarise the history of the business for prospective investors. It is important because a common way of evaluating future potential is to look first at past performance. It should be brief, but should point out any past successes or otherwise of the

	company, in terms of products or services developed and marketed which will help enhance its future. If, however, there are good reasons to believe that past performance may not be a reliable indicator of future potential, they should be noted briefly here, and developed elsewhere in the plan.
Section three — Products	**Comments**
Description of principal — products or services — markets — applications	This section should define precisely what is to be developed and marketed. Its length will vary according to the number and complexity of products which are planned and it should be written in layman's language.
Significant distinctive competence	Although the competitive environment will be dealt with specifically at a later stage, it is important to establish clearly, as early as possible in the plan, the distinctive advantages of the products or services to be sold. These could take many forms — low production cost, for example, or superior product technology; ease of use and versatility or the ability to react quickly to customer needs — but all successful businesses will have some distinctive features.
Current technology: — essential features (eg, similarities/differences from competitors) — detailed specifications, diagrams or technical documents — status (eg, development, prototype, pre-production, etc) — intellectual property (eg, patents applied for, etc) — regulatory constraints (eg, product approval procedures, if necessary or significant)	This information should be analytical rather than descriptive (eg, patent applications can be attached as appendices, or omitted entirely and produced at a later stage). Its purpose is to give the prospective investor an idea of the complexity and difficulties inherent in the company's technological environment in relation to other key operating areas (eg, marketing, production, etc).

Future developments: — need for replacement products — possibility of emergence of competitive technologies — research and development: objectives; new products; resources required	This area will be especially important in industries where technological change is typically rapid. Where this is true it will also be vital to avoid the common mistake of comparing the product it is hoped to launch in 18 months' time with what is on the market now, instead of addressing the likely competition of that time.
Section four — Markets and marketing	**Comments**
	Markets and marketing will be critical to all companies. The business plan should recognise this, and ensure that appropriate weight is given to all the factors mentioned in this section which are relevant to an understanding of the company's operations. If this would result in a statement of excessive length in the body of the plan, parts or even the whole of this section should be included as an appendix. Many institutional investors agree that this is also an area where major mistakes are made. The following comments point out a number of the more obvious pitfalls.
A The market Description and outlook — Description of industry — Current size and projected growth — Major business applications — Major customers and users	This section is designed to familiarise the reader with the nature and potential of the general market areas in which the company is operating. It should be brief. In the case of generically new products, market research (possibly detailed in an appendix) may be required to give meaning to the size and nature of the expected initial and future market.

Segmentation

— What target market segments are to be penetrated?

— Location (regional, national, international?)

— What are their current sizes and projected growth rates?

Characteristics (of each target segment)

— Critical product characteristics (performance, reliability, durability, availability, price, service, other)

— Customer buying patterns: position of key decision-makers
typical order sizes
other factors (eg, approved supplier lists, single-sourcing, competitive tender policies, etc)

— Special characteristics: seasonal; cyclical; other.

One of the biggest traps which entrepreneurs can fall into is the failure to define precisely enough the market segments they can reasonably hope to penetrate. The more common errors include:

* The use of statistics of market size which in reality relate to a wider market than the target.

* The assumption that all market segments contain a standard mix of large, medium and small companies. For example, if acceptable margins can only be earned through sales to smaller-than-average customers and 80% of current industry sales are purchased by five major corporations, the company's target customer base will represent less than 20% of the market.

* The failure to identify any significant unusual market characteristics. In the above example, failure to recognise any obstacles to the penetration of these large corporations could cripple the company's marketing strategy, if its target were the total market.

Such errors can readily result in over-optimistic sales targets which can rapidly lead to financial difficulties. This is particularly applicable where such targets are used to justify the creation of a fixed overhead structure which is not sufficiently flexible to cope with the failure to achieve budgeted sales.

B The competition

— Identity of current competitors

— Size and potential of current competitors

The nature, intensity and ability of the competition will prove critical to the prospects of any company, and thus should feature prominently in every plan. This will be especially important in the case of small or start-up companies entering markets dominated by large and

— Comparison of products/ services with current competitors — Likely responses of competitors — Danger of future market entry by new competitors	powerful competitors. Common mistakes have included: — The failure to consider the response of potential new entrants and existing competitors to the planned strategy. This can be especially costly if new products directly threaten the existence of a major competitor. — The over-estimation of competitive strengths, and the under-estimation of weaknesses. In the end, this will be self-defeating, as management will base its future actions on the course charted in the business plan. Prospective investors are unlikely to choose to back an entrepreneur who lacks a realistic view of his competition.

C Marketing and sales
 	
Marketing
 	
— Market positioning — how will products/services be positioned in relation to competitors (in terms of quality, price, customer service, image, etc)
 	
— Pricing policy (cost-based or demand-based? volume discounts, etc)
 	
— Field service and product support policy
 	
— Promotion and advertising
 	
Sales
 	
— Distribution channels:
    agents
    franchises
    in-house sales force
    exports
	Most companies at some stage will need to develop a separate detailed marketing plan to guide their own executives in this critical function on both an annual and a long-term basis. If such a guide has already been developed, it (or extracts from it) could be included as an appendix to the business plan, enabling the marketing and sales section to summarise overall goals in this area. These goals should be realistic and consistent with the market analysis described above.
	
	It may not be necessary to mention all the details of the company's sales plan set out opposite, unless the efficiency with which the selling effort is managed is of critical importance. Nevertheless, it will be essential to analyse all these factors in detail when formulating sales projections. These projections should be

— Size and geographical coverage of sales force — Anticipated productivity of sales force (eg, calls per salesman, sales per call, average order size) — Sales force compensation policy (commission structure, salary/commission mix)	built up in as much detail as is practicable, to act as a cross-check against the sales targets developed from the market analysis process outlined above. Failure to go through this process is a mistake made by many companies who try to predict sales by assuming a certain share of an assumed market size. For example, a company selling a specialised electronic component for use in solar heaters might assume the European solar heater market at £100m, growing at 5% per annum, of which 10% by value was represented by the particular part in question. 'On the basis of a 50% distributor margin', the argument might run, 'we are attacking a market of £5m this year, £5.25m next year, and so on up to £6.08m in year 5. If we capture 1% of this market this year, rising to 25% in year 5, our sales will rise from £50,000 to £1.5m over that period'. Unless this process is backed up by careful definition of the market, and the answers to the sort of questions posed previously, the projections will be unconvincing, and may be seriously wrong.
Interest shown by prospective customers — Extent (enquiries, orders, contracts signed, etc) — Basis (were they given prototypes, demonstration models, etc?)	This section again should be sketched out in summary only, with all details shown by way of appendix.
Section five — Manufacturing and operations	**Comments**
Sources of supply: — significant dependence on key materials, skilled labour, etc	Efficient production (or supply of goods or services) will be a major factor in any company's success — or lack of it. This section of the business plan should summarise the nature and extent of operating facilities and procedures, emphasising those areas which will be critical to future success.

Manufacturing: — in-house capability/use of sub-contractors — nature of productive process, critical points — importance of plant and machinery Facilities: — description of premises — production capacity (current and future, compared to growth plans)	Any distinctive competitive edge the company may have in this area should be brought out here, along with any potential significant problems and how it is planned to counteract them.
Section six — Management	**Comments**
  Owners/directors — Degree of control held by managers — Experience and role of non-executive directors (if any) Managers — Summary of planned staff numbers (broken down by key functions) — Brief details of experience and expertise of key management — Future recruitment plans (if strengthening of management team is required) — Strategies to develop and retain staff (eg, share option schemes, etc)	The importance of this area cannot be over-emphasised. Special care should be taken when writing this section. This should comprise a summary only — analysis of shareholdings and details of non-executive shareholders (if any) can be left to an appendix. Again, this should be a summary only — a detailed organisation chart will usually form an essential appendix in every plan. Detailed CV's of all key management should be included as an appendix. The summary opposite should concentrate on the achievements and experience of each key individual which will be relevant in meeting the company's future success requirements. For example, in the case of a head of research, an ability to manage people may be at least as important as academic qualifications.

Chapter 10 The Business Plan

Section seven — Financial analysis	Comments

Summary of key data in forecasts (sales, profit before tax)
 	
Commentary on forecasts
 	
— profit and loss
    trend of sales and product contribution
    fixed cost patterns (eg, R & D, marketing expenses)
    impact on profitability
 	
— cash flow
    peak cash equipment
    impact of capital expenditure, working capital investment, on cash generation
 	
— sensitivity/break-even analysis
 	
Funds required — timing and uses
 	
Anticipated gearing (if any)
 	
Possible exit routes for investors, eg:
 	
— public offering (Stock Exchange listing, USM, etc)
 	
— take-over by third party
 	
— purchase by the company of institutional shareholdings
	In most cases it is appropriate to file the financial projections themselves as an appendix. In such cases, the financial analysis contained in the body of the plan can most usefully contain a summary commenting briefly on the overall shape of the company revealed by the financial projections. Examples of this might include (if appropriate) statements along the lines of:
	
	* 'High initial fixed costs necessary to establish volume production and an efficient sales force will lead to losses until year W. Thereafter, the impact of rapidly increasing sales levels on relatively static fixed overheads is expected to lead to fast-growing profits, reaching a budgeted £Xm (on sales of £Ym) by year Z.'
	
	* 'The need to maintain R & D expenditure at high levels to secure the company's competitive future, even after its first products are on the market, is expected to delay the advent of break-even until year X.'
	
	* 'The impact of the new factory construction in year A, together with the increased working capital investment caused by expected sales growth of the manufacturing division in the same year, is anticipated to result in a peaking of the net cash requirement at £8m.'
	
	* 'At this point, the company is expected to be cash-rich, with its major products fully established in the market. The directors plan to seek further growth through diversification, either organically or through acquisition.'

Section eight — Risks and rewards	Comments
Risks — and how management plans to minimise them Rewards — possible worth of the company if forecast results are achieved	There are three ways to deal with these questions, either: — by dealing with each one in a separate section of the plan (the course adopted here); — by discussing each of them in an appendix; — by dealing with the relevant issues as they arise in the body of the document. Remember, whichever route you choose, these points should be dealt with somewhere in your plan!
Section nine — Objectives and milestones	**Comments**
Objectives — description by department Milestones — timetable, detailed key deadlines, for each major segment of the plan (products, marketing, manufacturing/facilities, management, etc)	Financial achievements are the results of successful operations. By setting out the key objectives, tasks and time-scales, the investor can begin to assess whether management is likely to be able to translate its plans into successful achievement.
Appendices (as applicable)	**Comments**
1 Glossary of terms 2 Summary — technical data, new products (including patent specifications, etc)	A note on financial projections: We have assumed opposite that it will be possible to project profits and cash flows for a period of up to five years ahead.

3	Market entry report — XY Marketing Consultants Ltd	In developing the projections, management will almost certainly need to forecast profits on a monthly basis for at least the first year, and also to prepare a cash flow forecast in order to determine projected cash surplus or requirements. The cash flow forecast will also provide the basis for the balance sheets and source and application of funds statements. It will not always be necessary to include such detail in the business plan, although it may be required at a later stage of any investors' investigations. It will also be vital to set out alongside the forecast a statement of assumptions on which they are based. These should be as detailed and comprehensive as possible and should cover the cash flow as well as the profit projections.
4	Marketing plan	
5	Order and enquiry status — new product	
6	Current shareholders	
7	Organisation chart — current — year 2 — year 5	
8	CV of senior management	
9	Financial projections (years 1–5): — profit and loss account, years 1–5 — source and application of funds statement, years 1–5 — balance sheet, years 1–5 — assumptions used — sensitivity/break-even analysis	
10	Audited accounts (latest available)	

Chapter 11

Obtaining Offers

'There is no question that irrespective of the horse (product), horse race (market), or odds (financial criteria), it is the jockey (entrepreneur) who fundamentally determines whether the venture capitalist will place a bet at all' (*Journal of Business Venturing*, Winter 1985).

SURVIVING THE EVALUATION

Once the financing proposals have been sent to the target institutions, the entrepreneur may well find that, at least initially, things start moving quickly. If a fund is interested in the proposal, an initial meeting (or even a telephone call) soon after receipt should serve to confirm this and set up a schedule for a more formal evaluation. Alternatively the fund manager should be able to say 'no' quickly if the proposal is not of interest. (In this case, the entrepreneur or his advisers should quickly attempt to discover the reasons for the rejection, in case any re-formulation of the proposal is necessary.)

As a general rule, if one risk capitalist is interested in a proposal, others will be too. Serious potential investors will then want to spend a significant number of man-days evaluating the target business, much of it on the company's premises. The entrepreneur will need to prepare carefully for these visits, in order to minimise the calls on his time, as well as to create a good impression on his potential backers.

Evaluation approaches

The process of evaluation will not differ greatly whether the applicant is seeking venture or development capital. Although every fund will have its own evaluation routines, refined and validated from practical experience, they will all be attempting to satisfy themselves that the two tests we mentioned previously when discussing the suitability of companies for risk capital investment have been successfully met, ie, that the company has potential which management have the requisite ability to exploit and control.

Hopefully, much of the groundwork here will have been prepared, and many of the investor's questions answered, by reading the business plan. If the entrepreneur has, however, followed key point number five in the preceding chapter ('keep it short!'), the investor will have many supplementary questions, and may wish to examine management personally in greater depth on issues which he regards as particularly critical. The performance of the management team in responding to these enquiries will be a major determinant in the investor's eventual decision.

Validating the business plan

As we said before, if the business plan has been well-written, all investors will tend to use it as their jumping-off point, and many will structure their subsequent evaluation to 'fill in the gaps' identified on first reading.

Where the various types of funds will tend to differ in their evaluation procedures, however, is in the depth of their examination of the various assumptions behind different areas of the plan. The venture capitalist, for example, looking at small companies with substantial growth prospects, is likely to be particularly concerned about the market in which the company is operating, especially its position in relation to its competitors, both current and potential. This part of the evaluation process may involve less work for the development capitalist looking at companies in more mature markets, who will often be able to use other information (eg, the company's historic track record) to support his analysis in this area. He can, however, be expected to cast an especially careful eye over the plan's financial projections, to assess the risk of the venture failing to generate the cash necessary to provide him with his running yield.

In a number of venture capital propositions on the other hand, some managers have been surprised when the financial projections which they have painstakingly prepared over many weeks or months have been given seemingly only a cursory glance by the venture capitalist.

This should not be too surprising in cases where financial matters may not represent the most immediate critical success factors in the early stages of a business, eg, a new bio-technology venture which will initially stand or fall on its ability to develop saleable technology. In addition, venture capitalists conventionally consider that the earlier stage the project, the less important will be the exact quantum of their return — at the extreme, a start-up investment will either fail, in which case they will lose their money, or it will succeed, in which case they will reap handsome rewards, whether the return is 30, 40 or 50% per annum. The development capitalist's return, on the other hand, from a portfolio of investments with a typically lower risk/reward profile, is usually far more sensitive to small fluctuations in the financial results of his portfolio companies.

Evaluating management

However well the business plan has been prepared, it is almost inevitable that the investor will want to know more about management, and that he will therefore see this as one of the prime aims of his subsequent evaluation. In his questions, he will not only be looking to find out how well the management team (and especially the Chief Executive or Team Leader) know their business, but also, critically, forming his view of their personal qualities. This invariably requires an extensive degree of personal contact, as many of the key factors the investor will be looking for will be intangible and difficult to boil down into standard questions and answers.

In the last resort, all judgements about what constitutes the key to managerial success will be subjective. The current consensus among risk capitalists, both in the USA and the UK today, however, suggests that, in addition to a good knowledge of his chosen market, it is vital for the entrepreneur to have a highly developed capacity for:

(a) *Effort.* When asked to what he attributed his phenomenal success, the film director Alfred Hitchcock was accustomed to quote his own amendment of his favourite saying, 'all work and no play makes Jack . . .!' The successful entrepreneur has to be capable of sustained intense effort over a long period. Just as importantly, he will need to be able to demonstrate what the risk capitalist calls 'staying power' — the ability to press ahead with his plans undaunted in the face of all the reverses and disappointments which are inevitably strewn in the path of the new, the revolutionary, and the threatening.

(b) *Risk Taking.* The entrepreneur will need, first, to be able to evaluate risk well when formulating his plans. This will apply equally to product, market and management risk. Even more importantly, he will need to be able to react appropriately as

these risk profiles change in response to market forces. This is often particularly difficult to achieve successfully when it effectively involves admitting past mistakes, requiring both a high degree of intellectual honesty and the capacity to deal effectively with self doubt.
(c) *Leadership*. If the entrepreneur does not himself possess all these qualities, he will need to be able to recruit a management team which does, and prove that he will be capable of leading it successfully. This in turn demands much of both the entrepreneur himself and of his team. The entrepreneur needs to be a combination of both 'achiever' — persuasive, articulate, action-oriented — and 'receptor' — emollient, concerned, conciliatory — in order to ensure that his team works efficiently together, and that their decisions are clearly communicated to the rest of the employees.

Now the risk capitalist would be the first to admit that this paragon outlined above is more often met in books such as this than in real life. Nevertheless, he will look for evidence that all the qualities mentioned previously are present in at least some degree; if he has serious doubts about management's ability in any one of these areas, he will think very seriously indeed before going any further.

Evaluating the funds

While he is under the microscope, however, the entrepreneur can take comfort from the knowledge that this is part of a two-way process. For he in his turn should at the same time always take the opportunity to evaluate the risk capitalist. Risk capital invetsment, especially in its hands-on mode, is very much a partnership between investor and investee, involving close and regular contact over many years. Identifying incompatible corporate aims or investment styles at this early stage can not only save everyone's time, but also avoid the aggravation and bitterness which is often the by-product of negotiations which break down at an advanced stage because of the late emergence of irreconcilable differences.

THE INITIAL OFFER

In dealing with risk capital institutions, it is sometimes difficult to know exactly when negotiations have started in earnest. At some stage, however, if all goes well, the company seeking finance will receive some form of offer from an interested backer. This can come at a surprisingly early stage in the process — if the investor is especially interested, it may even arrive before his evaluation is complete.

The offer letter

Precisely what form such an offer should take is a matter of some conjecture. It is usual, however, for the interested institution to set out the general terms of the offer it would like to make, in writing, subject to the satisfactory conclusion of detailed negotiations and enquiries. this list of 'subject to's' can be important — the offer will usually be subject to contract, to the results of any outside investigation to be undertaken, and even in some cases the approval of the fund's own board or investment committee — and, as we will see, it requires careful consideration by management.

We would encourage all companies to obtain such an 'in principle' offer in writing at an early stage, covering all major features of the proposed investment. This will not only have the effect of providing a firm and agreed base from which detailed negotiations can begin, but it will also demonstrate in a tangible form a significant degree of investor commitment. In particular, it is likely that, in order to reach this stage, the fund's investment executives dealing with the project will have had to make their own proposal internally to justify the investment, and will therefore be psychologically attuned to sympathise with and defend the company's viewpoint.

By the same token, however, we would not in general recommend to the entrepreneur that he seek a detailed offer covering every factor to be included in the final investment documentation. Not only does this run the risk of pre-empting those detailed negotiations better left until a later stage, but it may also unnecessarily limit the flexibility of the executives of the investing institutions, if they have to obtain specific approval from a higher authority to sanction every subsequent change to their initial offer.

What does the offer letter mean?

The initial offer letter (sometimes known as a 'heads of agreement') is an important document, as it typically forms the basis of subsequent negotiations, and can, in certain circumstances, bind one or both parties to its terms and conditions. It is vital, therefore, for the entrepreneur to consult his legal advisers at an early stage after receiving such a document before acting on it.

An example of a preliminary offer letter is set out in Figure 15 on pages 156–157 and illustrates some of the issues commonly encountered at this stage of the capital raising process. These may include:

(a) *What does 'subject to contract' mean?* This phrase means that the offer letter is an indication of intent in good faith but is not legally binding on either the risk capitalists or upon the investee company.

(b) *Are all of the key issues identified and the way in which they are to be resolved set out sufficiently clearly?* We are not advocating here that the letter should be drafted with the sort of absolute precision which will characterise the final legal documentation. It is quite appropriate for example in paragraph 3 to defer consideration of the mechanism by which the investors' share stake will be increased to account for under-performance as long as the eventual position is clear and agreed by both sides. Similarly, in paragraph 2, it should not be necessary at this stage to specify the rate of dividend to be paid in 1991, as this clearly represents no more than a contingency plan of which both sides hope will never become an issue; consideration of such details which do not fundamentally effect the shape of the deal can in most cases safely be left until later.

This is not true, however, of a number of points in the letter which directly impact on what for the entrepreneur will represent the 'core' of the deal, ie the price. Here, ambiguities of detail can be of vital importance. For example:

(i) In paragraph 1, will the investors be paying their £0.5m for 20% of the shares currently in issue, or for that number of shares which will represent 20% of the enlarged share capital after investment? ie, if the current share capital is 1,000, will they be buying an extra 200 or 250? This is of more than academic interest for, as will quickly be apparent, the former approach values the existing company at £2.5m, but the latter only at £2m.

(ii) Paragraph 4 is not at all clear on how much is to be paid, to whom, and under what circumstances, or alternatively whether a re-adjustment of their relative shareholdings is envisaged. As this directly impacts on price, and also could have significant impact on the tax position of existing management, further details should be sought.

Figure 15

Illustrative Offer Letter

14 April 1988

The Directors
AB Technology Company Limited
132 South Street
Oxbridge
OX3 4JS

Dear Sirs

SUBJECT TO CONTRACT

Following our various recent discussions with you, the Beta Fund and Go-go Ventures ('the Investors') are prepared, subject to contract and Board and/or Trustee approval, to subscribe for ordinary shares in AB Technology Company Limited ('AB') under the following principal terms and conditions:

1. The Investors will invest initially a total of £500,000 for 20% of the ordinary shares, divided equally between them.

2. The Investors' shares will be 'B' ordinary shares which will be preferred as to capital in the event of a sale and will have the right to a dividend after 31 March 1991. The 'B' ordinary shares will convert to ordinary shares prior to a flotation.

3. AB forecasts aggregate profits before tax for the two financial years ending 31 March 1988 and 1989 of £1.75m. In the event that the actual aggregate profits are below £1.75m, the Investors' percentage equity holding will increase up to a maximum of 50% of the share capital, according to a mechanism to be agreed, to protect the Investors' valuation of AB

4. In the event that AB shares are traded in the USM or listed on the Stock Exchange before 31 March 1991 at a market valuation of the ordinary share capital in excess of £15m, the Investors will, according to a mechanism to be agreed, make a further payment of 5p for every £1 that the market capitalisation of AB exceeds £15m, up to a maximum to be agreed to secure the Investors' valuation of AB.

5. The Investors will require normal warranties, indemnities, and minority protections including the following:

    (a) The Investors will require the right to appoint a director to the Board of AB.

(b) All Investors will receive regular management information and will have the right to meet regularly with the senior management of AB.

(c) The company will prepare an annual business plan which will require the approval of the Investors as will any subsequent variations.

(d) Mr I. Movit and Mr B. Careful will enter into service contracts with AB, who will provide 'key man' insurance for Mr Movit and Mr Careful.

6. It is the intention of all parties to seek admission, placing or introduction of the shares of AB to either the official list of the Stock Exchange or the Unlisted Securities Market before 31 March 1991.

   If a listing is not achieved by March 1991, a dividend policy will be adopted for the Investors' shares.

7. Prior to completion, AB shall arrange an overdraft facility sufficient to meet the working capital requirement forecast in its business plan.

8. Investment is subject to a report satisfactory to the Investors from Quill, Pen and Co (Chartered Accountants).

9. The Investors will require reasonable access to AB to complete their further investigation of the company, and will require the company to produce additional documents related to its organisation and future plans and strategy. The Investors will also require to inspect and be satisfied with key contracts between AB and third parties.

10. AB will meet in any event the costs of the accountants' report, and legal fees and disbursements of all Investors in connection with the transaction.

11. It is the intention of the parties to complete the above transaction before 15 June 1988.

Yours faithfully
for Beta Fund

John Smith

(c) *What do 'normal warranties and indemnities' mean?* It would be unusual for risk capital investors not to expect and obtain warranties as to the completeness and accuracy of specified information provided to them and typically they will expect indemnities to be given to the company by key shareholders or directors in relation to identified contingencies (typically relating to taxation issues). It is impractical to resolve all the issues which will inevitably arise and have to be negotiated in relation to warranties and indemnities at this stage. It is, however, worthwhile seeking a general statement as to the key elements of information which will need to be warranted, the investor's attitude to accepting disclosure of uncertainties, and an identification of indemnities expected.

(d) *Is there a deadline for acceptance?* Paragraph 11 of the illustrative offer letter refers to an intention to complete the transaction by a specified date. In practice, in the absence of other information, this is not regarded as a deadline but a target date which should provide a basis for co-ordinating and planning of other steps in the investment process.

(e) *What would be the scope of the accountant's investigation?* Particularly as the company seeking the funds is to be responsible for costs, it is important to get clear at this stage the proposed scope of the accountant's investigation. If left unchallenged, there is a tendency for the scope (and therefore the cost of the accountant's work) to expand as time progresses. A summary of the particular concerns of the investor should be obtained if at all possible, as well as an estimate of the likely fees involved. Fee estimates from both sides' solicitors should also be requested, although as they will be more dependent on the length of subsequent negotiations, this may not be easy to achieve.

(f) *Is there anything missing?* The entrepreneur and his advisers should always carefully examine the offer letter for possible omissions, as it is not safe to assume that if an issue not mentioned, then the investor is unconcerned about it. In this case, the offer is silent on the subject of any fees payable to the investors. This is somewhat surprising, as the deal in prospect appears to involve a possible syndication and investor board representation.

These issues are important, and in this case should be clarified immediately to avoid confusion in the next stage of the process — optimising the offer.

Chapter 12

Optimising the Offer

Once an offer is on the table, what for many entrepreneurs will constitute 'the real negotiations' can begin — the process of optimising his offer (or offers) and, in particular, increasing the price.

There is more to it than this of course, and, as we will see, some of the details commonly left until the end of the negotiations are important and can be time-consuming. The entire negotiation process deserves careful attention and planning on the part of the entrepreneur and his advisers. Nevertheless, for most risk capital investments, the entrepreneur will want to agree on who will be his backers, and on the overall shape of the deal, before going on to the final stages of drafting the detailed completion documents.

MANAGEMENT OBJECTIVES

To optimise the offer requires a clear understanding of the owner's objectives. These may include:

(a) *The cheapest deal.* This in turn can be broken down into the aims of giving away the least amount of equity; deceasing the gearing; and minimising restrictions on control. These aims themselves may be mutually incompatible — for example, decreasing the gearing may require equity dilution — and their attainment may require an element of trade-off.

Other objectives, however, may be as or more important to existing management, for example:

(b) *A quality backer.* The prestige of the institutional backer can be important, especially when the investor has an established reputation in the relevant industry.

(c) *Access to second round finance.* This will be especially critical in the case of many early stage companies, which will tend to be cash-consuming for many years if growth targets are met. In such cases, the entrepreneur will need to satisfy himself that sufficient follow-up funding will be available when required.

(d) *Management and operational support*, using the industrial expertise and contacts of the investor.

Understanding which of these is most important may affect not only which offer to choose, but also in which areas the entrepreneur should concentrate when trying to negotiate improvements in the offer.

Ideally, the proposition will generate two or more preliminary offers. Competitive offers significantly improve the scope for negotiation. The entrepreneur will wish to analyse and compare the offers in the light of his objectives. He will also try to identify the aims and minimum requirements of each fund, in preparation for discussions on overall structure and pricing of the deal. Appendix I gives an example of how this approach was followed to the advantage of the owners of an electronics company seeking risk capital funding.

SHAPING THE DEAL

The entrepreneur will be concerned about two major issues at this stage:

(a) the type of capital structure needed to support the required funding; and
(b) the percentage of equity capital (which in this case means voting capital) to be given to the institutions as part of the package, ie, fixing the price.

Creating the structure

As a general rule, no single venture or development capital investor will seek to take a controlling interest in investee companies. As they will often, however, be injecting the bulk of any new finance required, they will commonly be forced to invest via a package of securities, many of which will not carry ordinary equity voting rights. The risk capitalist will therefore require the right to both his desired income flow, and the protection of the capital value of his investment, by conversion or redemption rights, or other provisions. This is typically achieved by the use of special types of loan stock or preference shares.

DEBT VERSUS EQUITY

The issues involved in the choice of loan stock and/or preference shares as a form of finance are complex, and can be important. The entrepreneur should always ensure he takes appropriate professional advice if this question is raised. It is not within the scope of this book to discuss these issues in detail; two points, however, should be mentioned:

(a) The tax treatment of loan stock interest and preference share dividends is different, both in the hands of the payer and the recipient. Again, specialist advice should be sought to ensure the optimum benefit to the entrepreneur.
(b) Of perhaps more wide-ranging importance, however, the holder of loan stock will be a creditor of the company, which could create conflicts of interest in cases where he is also an equity investor. In addition, other sources of finance will typically regard loan stock, even if subordinated to the other creditors of the company, as part of borrowings, unlike preference shares, which are usually regarded as capital of the company. This may inhibit the company's ability to raise further debt finance.

FLEXIBILITY

Both debt and preferred equity can be extremely flexible. In order to satisfy the varying requirements of the risk capital investor, debt can carry a variable interest rate, be repayable by reference to time or some measure of performance and/or convertible into equity of various types.

Preference shares can offer similar flexibility and, as they typically form part of the capital of the company without involving the entrepreneur in equity dilution, are very widely used in risk capital investments. With some ingenuity, they can be structured so as to satisfy almost all of an investor's objectives, whether it is venture or development capital funding which is required. Sometimes known by the acronym CREEPS ('Cumulative Redeemable and Everything Else Preference Shares'!), such shares can carry any or all of the following titles:

(a) *Cumulative.* Providing for a cumulative fixed dividend, ie, where any arrears of preference share dividends have to be paid before any other distributions to shareholders. The dividend

coupon on such shares is commonly set at a market rate or better.
(b) *Participating.* The holders of participating preferred shares also carry the right, ahead of ordinary equity holders, to a cumulative participating dividend, usually expressed as a percentage of annual pre-tax profits, appropriately adjusted (eg, to disregard interest expense, directors' emoluments, etc).

This is one of the most commonly used vehicles for the development capitalist to secure the required running yield on his investment. A variation of this approach is for the investor to attach such participating rights to his ordinary shares, sometimes known as CPPOS (or 'Cumulative Preferred Participating Ordinary Shares'), giving him the additional advantage of increased voting powers.

(c) *Redeemable.* The preference share capital can be redeemed at an agreed date (or dates) or in the event of a subsequent Stock Exchange listing or third party takeover. This can give the investor an easy way to recover his investment without falling foul of the many pitfalls inherent in the process of selling ordinary shares back to the company.

The venture capitalist, backing cash-consuming companies, may also use redemption provisions to secure part of his investment return, while at the same time deferring the cash drain on the investee company. This is typically achieved by negotiating a premium to be paid on redemption, usually increasing with the passage of time.

Unlike debt, the redemption of which only requires available funds, redemption of preference shares is subject to the restrictions of company law. In summary, a company may only redeem its shares out of distributable profits or the proceeds of a new issue of shares.

(d) *Convertible.* Both venture and development capital investors commonly seek to protect the value of their investments by providing for the right to convert preference shares (or loan finance) into ordinary equity (with normal or enhanced voting rights) in the event of default, eg, a failure to pay dividends or interest, or redeem the securities, on the due date.

The conversion of preference shares into ordinary shares in accordance with a predetermined formula is also often used as a mechanism to maintain the value of the total equity stake of the investor at a constant level. Known as a *ratchet* (or sometimes an *earn-out*) this is usually structured so as to increase the investing institution's equity stake on a sliding scale if the company fails to achieve pre-set performance targets (eg, pre-tax profit over the next three years) by the conversion of an appropriate amount of preference or loan capital. This can also work in reverse, ie, a proportion of the investor's equity will be surrendered in cases where the company exceeds the fund's expectations.

In recent years such ratchet arrangements have become an increasingly popular feature of risk capital investments, and now often form an integral part of overall deal pricing.

Concluding on structure before passing on to pricing, however, it should be apparent that there is an almost limitless number of combinations of various types of finance which should be able to fit any individual case. If the entrepreneur has been competently advised, and has sensibly formulated his own objectives, which he has communicated to the funds, the structuring of any risk capital investment should not prove a major problem. If such problems are encountered, it is more than likely that either the potential investors are not convinced of the worth of the company they are being asked to invest in, or that the entrepreneur has chosen the wrong fund!

Fixing the price

If agreeing on an appropriate form of finance should not prove too much of a problem, the same certainly cannot be said for the question of fixing the price!

The entrepreneur has fewer ground rules to help him here. As in all such negotiations, the only right price is that which a willing buyer is prepared to pay, and a willing seller is prepared to receive. Nevertheless, the following points will be relevant:

(a) In general terms, the earlier stage the investment, the less sensitive the price is likely to be. The early stage venture capitalist will often be more concerned about the survival of his portfolio companies rather than the price of his investments — any price will be too high in the case of a failed investment, whereas his unqualified successes will almost certainly earn him exceptional rates of return, whatever their exact amount. The development capitalist investor, however, who should be investing in more secure companies but who will be more dependent on an annual running yield for his return, is likely to be much more concerned about the precise terms of his investments, both as regards the percentage of equity required and the coupon on cash-generating securities.

(b) Having said this, most institutional investors, venture as well as development capitalists, use in essence the same method to calculate the equity and cash flow they require for the funds provided, based on their own internally-generated target rates of return. Appendix IV gives an example of how this might work in practice. The entrepreneur should be able to look to the experience and expertise of his professional advisers here for guidance as to the procedures and preferences of the institutions in play at this point.

(c) As noted above, the use of ratchets is increasing as a means of attempting to reconcile the aims of both investor and entrepreneur. Their value is, however, currently the topic of some controversy among risk capital executives, and strong views are held on both sides. The 'in favour' camp can point to two major advantages of their use, both to the funds and to the company:

(i) Their value in effectively by-passing what might be otherwise acrimonious price negotiations. The essence of a ratchet is to defer the final determination of price (ie, of money subscribed or equity surrendered) until subsequent performance is known — the 'proof of the pudding is in the eating' argument.

(ii) The importance of the 'carrot and stick' approach implicit in the ratchet as a motivator of management.

Its opponents, however, can point to some equally damaging side-effects, including:

(i) The problem of establishing a valid measure of performance. The difficulty here arises because the most objective measure of performance from the point of view of the company — ie, profit — does not of itself mean anything to the investor, whose return will solely depend on his cash proceeds when he realises his investment. He will therefore be as much if not more concerned with subsequent profit trends as with absolute amounts, a point which he may not always find easy to address in the final legal documentation. In attempts to get round this, we are now beginning to see ratchets which are flexed according to the increase in the value of the fund's original investment in the company should it be sold or floated within a certain time scale, or even according to the investor's internal rate of return (IRR) at the time of such an event. Unfortunately, these can be even more difficult to understand as finally drafted without the advantage of giving management a clearly defined performance target (such as a profit figure) to aim at.

(ii) The danger of short-termism. The period of time over which ratchets operate today is typically short — three years is common. In many cases this does not sit easily with the concept of the risk capitalist as a long-term investor, and can lead to post-investment performance by management designed to boost short-term profits at the expense of long-term prospects.

(iii) The taxation position of management. Ratchets can easily, in the words of the one noted British practitioner, become 'a tax minefield'. In particular, despite recent moves by the Inland Revenue to ease some of these problems, there is widespread concern among a number of tax accountants that many ratchets as presently drafted will result in shareholders/managers falling liable to income tax on subsequent capital gains. It is imperative that specialised tax advice should be sought on this specific issue whenever a ratchet or earn-out arrangement, of whatever type, is in contemplation.

(iv) Dealing with 'supervening' events. What would happen, for example, where the investor equity stake is to be varied on the basis of profits earned three years after investment, but after two years a third party offers to buy the company, or, alternatively, if further finance is required?

(v) Complexity. Most of the above problems can to some extent be 'drafted away' by specifically dealing with them in the final completion documentation. Too often, however, this will result in ratchet documentation of such complexity that in future years both management and investors will be spending a disproportionate amount of valuable time in an attempt merely to understand its terms, rather than attending to more pressing problems of the business.

This is a difficult question, and one where we often find it is not possible to give any more than the obvious advice that ratchets are good in theory but can be difficult to operate in practice. It is, however, part of human nature, especially in our experience among entrepreneurs, to underestimate these practical difficulties at the outset, which should be thought through clearly before proposing or agreeing to any such arrangements. It is also vitally important that any complexities in agreeing ratchet terms which will impact the key question of price should be settled at this stage, and certainly not left until the final act of the investment process, the detailed negotiations surrounding the final legal documentation.

Chapter 13

Detailed Negotiations

When both sides are agreed on the overall shape of the deal, the solicitors of either the risk capitalist or the company will usually be asked to begin drafting the legal documents. The entrepreneur at this stage, however, may still be spending most of his time dealing with the final stages of the evaluation routines of the investor, or his specialist investigators, and often substantive progress on the legal stages will await their completion.

SPECIALISTS' INVESTIGATIONS AND REPORTS

In addition to his own investigations, the risk capital investor will often require formal investigations by outside specialists. This is less likely to be the case where the risk capitalist relies on a more intuitive evaluation approach; where the investee is well known to the investor; or where time or cost constraints are agreed to be of overriding importance by both parties. However, in most cases the risk capitalist will rely, to some extent at least, on work performed by outsiders as part of his investment evaluation.

Types of investigation

Most investors require an accountant's investigation, the aims and typical content of which are described below. Several other types of investigation are also, however, often undertaken, to provide the investor with:

(a) Marketing reports (from marketing consultants) to comment on the assumptions behind the marketing plan.

(b) Technical reports to assess the status and capability of any technological innovation on which the project will rely.
(c) Real estate valuations by surveyors (and possibly structural surveys of properties, premises, plans, etc).
(d) Other expert reports depending on the nature of the business. It has, for example, in recent years become common in the case of investments in hotels to obtain a professional opinion on the likelihood of projected room occupancy rates being realised in practice by a firm of specialist hotel consultants.

There is also on occasions a requirement for investigation of areas of legal importance at this stage, such as intellectual property rights, licensing and distribution agreements, or the investigation of a particular piece of litigation or other 'skeletons in the cupboard', eg, Inland Revenue disputes. The lawyers would not normally be asked at this stage to investigate titles to properties and assets, and other matters which would normally be subject to warranties at a later date.

Solicitors for financial institutions are also sometimes instructed at this preliminary stage to advise on potential areas of conflict of interests which might give rise to claims after completion. This is common in cases where employees of one company propose to leave and set up their own in competition with their former employer. Financial institutions have to be careful to ensure that they are not attacked for inducing or conspiring to induce a breach of contract or other breach of duty by any of the parties concerned.

Investigations — the need

It is rare for all the above types of investigation to be required for any single investment. Investigations are not cheap and have to be paid for, if the deal goes ahead, by the investor, either directly or indirectly by increasing the size of funding required or, if the investment is not made, usually by the company seeking finance. The investor tends generally to confine his investigations to areas:

(a) Where he does not have the expertise to evaluate a particular issue.
(b) Where he does not have the time to examine a particular area in the desired depth. This is often true in respect of the financial evaluation of the target company, where the manpower resources required for the investigation may not be available to the risk capitalist.

Very few institutions can afford to tie up significant amounts of time of a team of executives to review the financial status and prospects of the target company in the required detail, and write up their results into the 'document of record' required by the fund and its backers to ensure that its own standards of 'due diligence' have been met.

(c) Where the area or issue in question is so critical to the success of the proposed investment that a second opinion is felt necessary.

The accountant's investigation

The extent of the accountant's investigation can vary dramatically according to the objectives of the investing institution and the circumstances of the investee company, from a full audit plus a 'long form' financial commentary, to a one or two day review of strictly limited scope.

The conventional accountant's investigation, undertaken typically for 'hand-off' investors, often provided the investor with his major source of detailed information (both financial and non-financial) about the affairs of the target company. It was consequently extensive and thorough, with the principal financial information being formally reported on, sometimes in the form of an audit opinion. Today's venture and development capitalists, however, have the ability to perform much of the commercial evaluation of the target company themselves, especially in the case of the venture capital funds staffed by executives with relevant industry experience. These funds in particular are beginning to use investigating accountants for a somewhat different purpose — of 'filling in gaps' in their own knowledge. This is especially true where the proposed investment is an early-stage venture with a limited track record, the key to whose success lies in its future potential, which may itself critically depend on non-financial factors. In such a case, an extended investigation of the type described above may prove of little use to the investor, as it is likely to be out of date on completion, and of limited relevance to his major concerns.

Scope of work

The investigation will usually, however, include, as a minimum, a review of:

(a) *The latest audited accounts.* The investor will be especially

interested in the company's accounting policies, and any problems which the company's auditors encountered in interpreting them.
(b) *Systems and procedures.* Investors generally do not look for an exhaustive review or testing of systems but an assessment of the degree to which they will need to be improved to cope with anticipated growth.
(c) *The latest management accounts.* Although the accountant will not be able to verify the results they contain, in the absence of the performance of any audit procedures (eg, attending the stock count, confirming debtor balances, etc), he will be able, after discussions with management, to analyse the various key components of the financial statements (eg, gross margin percentages, stock and debtor turn, etc) in comparison with budget and prior year results, and identify any unusual items or trends which may cause the investors to require the performance of further work.
(d) *Profit and cash projections.* This will be of critical concern to many investors, especially where the existing asset backing of the target company is small, and the institution will very much be investing in the future. The accountant will not always be able to say whether he believes the results assumed in the projections will be realised in practice, as these will almost certainly require evaluation (eg, of market factors) of issues outside his specific competence and are often based upon one set of assumptions concerning future events or actions chosen from a number of credible alternatives. The investor will, however, be interested in the method and degree of detail with which the projections were constructed; whether the figures represent management targets, as opposed to best or conservative estimates; and the accuracy of the company's previous forecasting history.
(e) *Tax status.* The investor here will be seeking an indication of the status of the company's tax computations, the magnitude and nature of any open items, and the history or existence of any disputes or other unusual items.

As noted above, the investors may require the investigating accountant to perform additional work, either by extending his areas of enquiry (transactions between the company and its directors is a common example of this) or the depth of his work (eg, a specific description and evaluation of production and inventory controls). Whatever the agreed scope of work, however, it will be in the interests of all parties (including management, who will probably have to bear the cost of this exercise) to ensure that the precise terms of reference for the investigation are clearly set out, preferably in writing, before work starts, to facilitate an efficient review at minimum cost. It is also common (although not invariable) practice for the company to receive a copy of the accountant's final report, or at least to discuss its contents prior to release.

The entrepreneur should also be aware that many investors may well ask for the informal views of their investigating accountants on the quality of company management. These may well not be submitted in writing, but in some cases they will be as important to the investor as the overt results of the work performed.

Reporting to the institutions

The investigating accountant can report to his instructing institutions in a number of ways. If the investigation is running to a tight timetable, the accountant may report informally as the work progresses, particularly where problems are encountered. The institution may also request an oral presentation of the accountant's findings as soon as the work is completed, to speed up the process. The subsequent written report will then serve to confirm them, and provide the investor with a document of record, to comply with his own standards of due diligence.

COMPLETION DOCUMENTATION

Despite the trend towards shorter and more focused investigations, however, in many cases, by the time they are complete the parties will be fully involved in hammering out the detailed terms and conditions of the deal via the legal documentation.

This stage of the finance-raising process commonly takes up significantly more time than originally envisaged, especially by inexperienced entrepreneurs. Risk capital investments tend to involve somewhat more complex documentation than that typically found in a standard sale and purchase agreement. The main reason for this lies in the often complex capital structures (and related issues) which characterise venture and development capital investments.

Final documentation — contents

As an example of this, consider a development capital investment including ordinary equity, preference shares and loan stock. This will generate, inter alia, the following documents on completion:

(a) A *shareholders' agreement* (or *subscription agreement*) documenting the terms of the investment. This will include any continuing obligations of existing management sought by the investor and any warranties and indemnities by the company's owners on which he will rely.
(b) The force of the warranties and indemnities given by management may be qualified by the effect of any items previously disclosed to the investor. This is typically accomplished by drawing up a *disclosure letter*, which will be filed as part of the completion documents.
(c) If funding is required for the acquisition of another business, the *acquisition agreement* setting out its detailed terms, together with its own warranties, indemnities and disclosure letter, will also typically be included in the package.
(d) It is common for any specific rights and duties attaching to the ordinary or preference shares invested to be incorporated in the *articles of association* of the investee company.
(e) The terms and conditions of any *loan stock or debenture finance* will also be evidenced in a form of written agreement.
(f) Finally, as all risk capital investments are made primarily on the strength of management, both the investor and the key executives of the company will be anxious to formalise the ties between them by the agreement of *service contracts*.

What is the purpose of all these documents? Some will be relatively obvious, but others will be different from or more complex in form than the documentation of many corporate legal agreements. Some of these issues are discussed below.

1 THE SUBSCRIPTION AGREEMENT

The subscription agreement is a contract between the investors, the company, and its existing shareholders. Its purpose is to document the terms of the funding to be provided by the investor, and the related rights and duties to be imposed on both sides. This, of course, involves much more than setting out the number of shares to be acquired and the price to be paid for them; the agreement will also deal, inter alia, with:

(a) Additional rights to protect the minority risk capital investor, sometimes known as negative covenants.
(b) Other obligations of the company to the investors, such as board representation, access to operating information, etc.
(c) Management warranties and indemnities.
(d) Other items, such as transferability of shares, etc.

Negative covenants

Despite some recent changes in company law, the power of a minority shareholder to influence the operations of an unquoted company is extremely limited. It would therefore be imprudent of the risk capital investor merely to 'walk away' from his investment once the funds had been subscribed, leaving the company to use the proceeds for an entirely different purpose from that originally intended. The investor will therefore seek to ensure as far as possible that the business in which he has invested bears more than a passing resemblance to the company portrayed in the business plan on which he based his evaluation. In addition, he will wish to ensure that the size and influence of his stake in the company will not be diluted by subsequent changes in the company's structure or internal constitution.

The investor will apply these safeguards by including in the subscription agreement a list of actions which the company will undertake (or 'covenant') not to enter into without his prior permission. Common examples of such negative covenants can be found in Appendix III. They will almost always include a right of veto on major changes in corporate direction (eg, acquisitions, divestitures, etc) and capital structure (eg, subsequent dilution of the powers of investor-held shares), but are often extended into more detailed operational matters, eg, establishing permitted levels of borrowing or leasing, and the appointment, remuneration and removal of directors, etc.

Negative covenants are often the cause of a great deal of friction at the negotiating stage, especially in cases where they are first introduced late in the day. The entrepreneur will be well advised to enquire as to the extent and type of such covenants as the investor will require, before the first draft of the subscription agreement is drawn up, in order to minimise this.

This will not of course solve all the problems in every case; the list given in Appendix III may look somewhat fearsome to the entrepreneur, and he may disagree profoundly with much of its contents. Management should, however, bear in mind the following:

(a) Negative covenants are essentially defensive in purpose — the investor is employing them as a right of veto in certain defined circumstances rather than as a tool to enjoy active day-to-day control. A good fund manager will view his investments as partnerships between himself and his portfolio companies; in this context, many of the negative covenants which investors ask their portfolio companies to enter into are not dissimilar to normal partnership rights.

(b) The investor may not feel as strongly about some covenants as he will about others. For example, the investor in a management buy-out of a well-established and managed company with the expectation of a Stock Exchange listing in the near future may feel much more relaxed about its future direction than a comparable investor in a small, earlier-stage investment where the funds are to be earmarked for the development of a specific new product. In the case of the former, it may be possible for management to negotiate less onerous restrictions on changes in the direction of the business, or remove them altogether. Whatever the circumstances however, the entrepreneur should not hesitate to find out from the investor the reasons behind each of the proposed negative covenants, and how strongly he feels about them, in order properly to prepare his negotiating strategy.

(c) Finally, as or more important to the entrepreneur than the contents of the negative covenants will be the character of the people who will interpret them, usually an executive of the venture or development capital fund or a nominee. The 'partnership' concept mentioned above will in practice be a partnership between the board of the directors of the company and the relevant fund executive. If the relationship of mutual trust has been established between the two sides by this stage, the entrepreneur should be able to judge how flexible the investor is likely to be in practice; if not, he should be asking himself whether he is talking to the right fund!

Continuing company obligations

In addition to the negative covenants of the type described above, the investor will often ask for other rights from the company of a continuing nature. A common example of this is the entitlement to a seat on the board, and for the board of the company to meet at regular intervals. The fund will generally charge a fee for such non-executive directors, especially if the fund's nominee is not one of its own employees.

The investor will also commonly ask to be sent certain management information on a regular and timely basis, eg, monthly management accounts and audited annual financial statements. In some cases, they may also reserve the right to approve the format of the management accounts, in consultation with the company's or the fund's auditors. Additionally, the fund may ask to see annual operating budgets or corporate plans, and even sometimes to approve them in advance, although it is not always clear exactly what purpose their approval is designed to serve.

The above obligations do not in practice tend to cause as much friction as in the case of negative covenants — indeed many entrepreneurs will welcome them if they have developed the right relationship with the investor. The risk capital partnership starts rather than ends with the act of investment, and the experienced and sympathetic investor can prove an indispensable source of expertise and advice to the entrepreneur trying to grapple with his company's growing pains.

Warranties

As part of the subscription agreement the investor will invariably ask the directors and/or key shareholders to confirm or 'warrant' specified information provided to the investor. Further, the agreement typically acknowledges that the investor has relied upon this information as the basis for his investment and accordingly if this information subsequently proves to be inaccurate the investor will be able to make a claim against the persons giving the warranties for any damage the investor has suffered. Damage will typically relate to any effect the inaccuracy has upon the value of the investment. In many cases, errors or omissions in relation to warranted information will have no effect upon the value of the investment and accordingly no claim will arise; in other cases the effect of the inaccuracy will cause a loss and a claim will arise. It is also common to place monetary limits on warranty claims, for example, a claim may not arise until the aggregate of all claims exceeds a fixed amount and there may well be an upper limit on the value of all claims.

A sadly large number of risk capital negotiations, especially those already in choppy waters, have finally foundered on the rock of warranties. To many entrepreneurs, the warranties they are asked to give are individually petty, insulting, irrelevant, superfluous, duplicated or unnecessary, and cumulatively far too detailed and time-consuming to consider properly. A similarly intransigent response from the investor will not only raise the negotiating temperature to an often unhealthy level, but may also permanently damage the post-investment relationship between the parties to the extent that neither can benefit fully from it.

This is sad, for warranties serve two essential purposes for the investor, of which the entrepreneur should be aware, viz:

(a) The investor does not want to assume the role of bloodhound in his investigation of the company. He will thus rely significantly on written representation from management as to the accuracy and completeness of the information he has been given in order significantly to cut down the scope of his investigation.
(b) All warranties will to some extent be superfluous once the warrantor has represented that the investor has been given all the facts relevant to his decision to invest, and that, so far as he is aware, these facts are accurate. Nevertheless, warranties in writing given by management on specific areas of critical concern to the investor will often give him the necessary comfort that the company and its management have considered each of these areas fully, and properly disclosed to him all significant related facts. This process of forcing the entrepreneur to concentrate his mind on such areas in order to give the appropriate warranty is one of the final but by no means the least important of the steps in the investor's evaluation process.

Nevertheless, in some cases at least, the entrepreneur's frustrations detailed above may in some part be justified. The management team and their advisers should carefully examine each area to be warranted, and discuss with the investor any they feel to be irrelevant, misguided, or unduly onerous. As noted previously, the ability of each side to ascertain the aims (and thus the concerns) of the other, will be critical to ensuring that the final warranties are of minimum length consistent with their function as an adequate response to the concerns of the investor.

Appendix III sets out some of the more common types of warranties sought in risk capital investments, with an accompanying commentary.

Indemnities

Indemnities are similar to warranties in that they are typically given by directors and/or key shareholders. They differ from warranties, however, in that in relation to the specified matters to which indemnities are given, the directors or key shareholders typically agree to reimburse on a pound-for-pound basis the investor or the company seeking to raise funds for any loss it suffers in relation to the specified events. In almost all risk capital investments, the investor will seek indemnities in relation to tax matters. This means that if the company raising funds has any tax liabilities (corporation tax, income tax, VAT, etc) arising in the period prior to the investment for which provision has not been made in the company's financial statements in the ordinary way, the directors or key shareholders will indemnify the company for the additional unprovided liability. Other areas where indemnities might be required are in relation to specified contingent liabilities, for example, in relation to the outcome of a known claim or litigation.

Other items

Other matters which may be dealt with in the subscription agreement include:

(a) Agreement by any directors or key shareholders not to compete with the company in certain specified business areas (either currently, or for a specified period after they leave employment).
(b) Arrangements for the transfer or pre-emption of shares. This will more typically be dealt with in the articles of association.
(c) Agreement to change, either currently or within a specified period of time, certain key professional advisers, for example, auditors or solicitors.
(d) An undertaking by the company to secure 'key man' insurance policies on the critical members of the management team.

2 DISCLOSURE LETTER

In the event of a breach of warranties given by management, the investor will be able to claim damages against the warrantors to recoup any losses he may have suffered as a result of his investment. The management will therefore be anxious to ensure that any exposure of this nature is minimised by limiting warranties to items not previously disclosed to the investor. This disclosure is conventionally made by what is known as a disclosure letter. This can be an extremely bulky document, and it is in management's interest to ensure that it is as comprehensive as possible. This will require the inclusion of all the relevant information on the items disclosed, including, for example, copies of material contracts with suppliers and customers, property leases and other unusual contracts, etc.

By the same token, however, the disclosure letter may well take a considerable time to prepare and finalise, and some time also for the investor to examine. It is advisable therefore for the entrepreneur to have sight at the earliest possible opportunity of the warranties desired by the investor so that, in conjunction with his advisers, he can begin the task of preparing the disclosure letter at the same time as the final details of the investment are being agreed.

3 ARTICLES OF ASSOCIATION

The articles of association are the internal rules by which a company operates. A general framework for the rules is established in the Companies Act but is generally modified to meet the specific requirements of each company. Invariably when a risk investor provides funds to a company, changes in the articles of association are required. These changes will typically reflect the protection which the investor requires as a minority shareholder. Areas where the investor typically requires modification of the articles of association will include:

(a) Voting rights, dividends and conversion rights of the various classes of shares. Most risk investments involve creation of new classes of shares carrying special rights, and these need to be reflected in the articles of association.
(b) Composition of the board of directors. Typically this will provide for the risk capital investor holding a certain class of shares to be able to appoint a specified number of directors to the board.
(c) Restrictions on the borrowing powers of the company without the prior consent of members.
(d) Arrangements for the transfer of shares either at the wish of a member or on his death or leaving the company's employment. Typically a key employee is required to sell his shares on leaving employment. If at that or any other time he wishes to sell his shares, he is usually first required to offer them to the other shareholders, and the articles will establish the order in which they will be offered to other shareholders and at what price.

4 SERVICE CONTRACTS

The formalisation of the conditions of employment of existing key management by way of formal service contracts can be of great benefit to both sides. The investor, who will after all primarily be investing in management, will want to feel that he has 'tied in' the company's key executives after the deal has been struck, and also to protect himself against any manager who subsequently leaves the company from unfairly using the knowledge gained by virtue of his employment on behalf of a competitor.

The individual manager on the other hand, even in cases where he may still hold a controlling interest in the company after a refinancing, will be open to the scrutiny of new investors, and possible pressures to change the management structure in a way he may not like. He therefore may also value the increased sense of security given by a formal service contract.

Typical contents of a service contract include:

(a) A statement of the job/responsibility.
(b) The period of the contract and the notice of termination required of the company and employee.
(c) The benefits receivable by the employee, including salary, bonus, share options, benefits in kind, etc.
(d) A statement as to the time commitment required of the employee and whether this is to be his exclusive employment.
(e) A statement concerning the restriction or otherwise of the employee's other business interests.
(f) An agreement not to compete with the company after the completion of the contract for a specified period of time.

NEGOTIATIONS — DO'S AND DONT'S

Do

(a) Understand your own objectives and anticipate the likely objectives of the investor. To achieve an agreement which will provide the basis for an effective future partnership between investor and investee requires *both* to achieve their objectives.
(b) Be flexible in negotiation. Provided your own key objectives are met, be flexible in the structuring of the deal so as to allow the investor to reach his objectives.
(c) Seek guidance from experienced advisers. They will be able to

tell you whether what the risk capitalist is asking for is reasonable and normal (and therefore should generally be accepted), or whether what is being requested is abnormal and unreasonable (and therefore should be resisted).

(d) Use the offer letter as a guiding framework for the negotiations. This is only possible if the offer letter dealt with all the key issues.

(e) Expect some areas of dispute and problems. Be reasonable in the process of 'give and take'.

Do not

(a) Do not negotiate for ever. If every point, however trivial, is fought to the end, it is not unusual for the risk investors to feel that they are dealing with management who lack vision and who will be too time consuming in their future relationship.

(b) On the other hand do not set unrealistically tight negotiating deadlines. The negotiation process outlined in this and preceding chapters will typically raise many complex issues which will require mature consideration before they can be satisfactorily resolved. Remember also that you will be dealing with professional negotiators who, by and large, will find it easier to walk away from the deal at this late stage than you will — especially if you are paying the costs! As a tentative rule of thumb, allow at least two months from your acceptance of the letter to completion, given the maximum co-operation by all parties — more if you can think of potential time bottlenecks on major negotiating problems. Finally, always bear in mind the old maxim that a quick deal is a bad deal.

(c) Do not over-complicate. You will be surprised how quickly the details of your negotiations will fade from memory after investment, and how difficult it can be to remember the purpose of any particularly obscurely drafted part of your agreement after the event. If the detailed terms of your agreement with the risk capitalist ever subsequently become a real issue, you will certainly have better things to do with your time than trying to work out what they meant when they were drafted. Keeping it simple may sacrifice some fine tuning at investment, but it will save time and help avoid irritation and distrust in the long run.

PART 5
AFTER INVESTMENT

Chapter 14

Aftercare

In contrast to the considerable body of literature which is now building up on the subject of making venture capital investments, comparatively little has been written about the post-investment period, and the question of the *aftercare* which all risk capitalists would say characterises their investments.

This picture is at last, however, beginning to change as more funds become fully invested and the focus of attention begins to shift towards the question of subsequent performance. The subject is also important, however, in its own right — indeed, some would say it is far more important than the process of investment itself. One successful American entrepreneur with a wealth of experience in dealing with many venture capitalists has been quoted as saying, 'it is far more important whose money you get than how much you get or how much you pay for it'. Others would say that if, as the venture capitalists maintain, the risk capital relationship is like a marriage, then it is reasonable to suppose that married life is more important than the preceding courtship or the investment process itself.

The aftercare period can also bring in its train some major problems between investor and management. To take the marriage analogy a stage further, another American practitioner with experience on both sides of the venture capital fence once remarked, 'getting venture capital is like getting married — you wake up the next morning and the honeymoon is over. In a venture backed situation the honeymoon is generally a very short period — it usually ends at the closing.'

TYPES OF AFTERCARE

The entrepreneur should by the time he receives his risk capital funding have a good idea of the type of relationship his investor will expect, and the degree of contact between them. Much of detail here will be apparent from the negative covenants and company undertakings included in the subscription agreement; on a more general level, however, the company ought to be able to form a view at a very early stage as to the fund's general stance on this matter.

Venture and development capital fund post-investment styles fall into two basic categories: 'hands-off' and 'hands-on'. In practice, however, things tend to be more complicated. Although venture capitalists will generally be hands-on investors, and development capitalists more hands-off, there are many examples where this will work in reverse. Many venture capital 'hands-on' funds will for example take very much a back seat in syndicated investments where they are not the leader. Likewise, 'hands-off' funds investing in companies which have subsequently experienced significant problems may find themselves acting in a more or less hands-on way until they have been satisfactorily sorted out. In addition, many funds in the UK today, including some of the largest, are general funds in the widest sense of the word, not only with no industry specialisation but also embracing both hands-on and hands-off management styles. This has given rise to a situation where a number of funds have adopted for many of their companies a monitoring style which is not really either hand-on or hands-off but somewhere in between. This is the *reactive* management style mentioned in Chapter 3, characterised graphically by one British practitioner as 'not quite hands-on, but certainly jackets off!'

The question of which type of monitoring is most appropriate to which company should be addressed by each entrepreneur from the outset, and should be at the heart of the finance raising process. What does each of these styles involve, and how are they put into practice?

Hands-off

As implied above, hands-off investors cover a wide spectrum, from the remarkably active to the almost comatose. Towards the passive end of this scale will in many cases come the sponsors of the type of direct share issues to the public described in Chapter 8, including direct Business Expansion Scheme (BES) financings. The sponsor here may have earned the bulk of his remuneration on the transaction by way of a financing fee, in which case his continuing interest in the company's progress is as likely to be concerned with what he perceives to be his responsibility to the market as it is in the degree of future commercial success. In such cases, the sponsor will typically be most concerned to ensure that the directors of the company act in such a way as to conform to the standards of behaviour expected by investors in a public company, and to ensure that shareholders are kept informed of the company's affairs. In the specific case of BES financings, the sponsor may additionally maintain a continuing role with the company to ensure that its future activities do not prejudice the tax relief previously obtained by the investors by engaging in non-qualifying activities.

The inclination to keep an especially close eye on the affairs of portfolio companies may be similarly diminished in the case of those development capital investors who have structured their investments so as to rely for their return preponderantly upon a running yield, and thus have a less immediate motive to concentrate on enhancing the value of their equity holding through extensive input. This is not to say that they will not help their companies with post-investment assistance and advice in any way they can, merely that they will not insist on it, unless asked. 3i's for example, the largest British development capital investor, although its post-investment management styles embrace the whole spectrum discussed in this chapter, typically insists as a minimum on regular information and what might be called 'visiting rights'. This regular information is usually financial in nature, and can vary in regularity from monthly to semi-annually or even annually. The hands-off investor will not usually himself sit on the board of directors of all of his investee companies, although he may reserve the right to do so, and in many cases will insist on the company appointing a non-executive director known to or nominated by the investor as a pre-condition of investment in order to strengthen the sources of expertise which the management team will be expected to call on regularly. For the same reasons, the investor may require the company to choose other professional advisors (eg, accountants or solicitors) approved by his executives.

In many cases, the main difference between the post-investment styles of hands-off investors will lie in the degree of interest they pay to the information systems of their portfolio companies. As a minimum, every investor, whether hands-on or hands-off, will want to be sure that the financial information presented to them by their portfolio companies is as accurate and reliable as warranted by the circumstances, whether the information relates to interim or audited figures. They will also want to be sure that the company is capable of acting appropriately on the information contained within the figures. Other investors will, however, go further. They may for example take much more interest in the format and content of the company's management information systems, including its methods of budgeting and forecasting. Some will ask to see the budgets on a regular basis. At this stage the monitoring style begins to approach the reactive, which can best be described as active monitoring of the company's progress on a regular basis by executives of the fund, usually sitting as directors on the board. Such monitoring could include, at a high level, all the critical areas of the company's operations, but is often confined to financial review and analysis (where their specific expertise often lies) in cases where the financial results provide a sound indicator of financial success.

Hands-on

Some commentators would define a hands-on investment as one where the invetor takes a seat on the board of the portfolio company. We would prefer to define the term more narrowly, to distinguish the hands-on investor from his reactive counterpart by moving closer to the mode of operation of most of the hands-on investors in the USA. Our hands-on investor earns his title by the *proactive* role he takes within his companies. His role will be active and forward looking — not unlike an active non-executive chairman in some ways — involving the initiation of debate and discussion, full consultation in all major corporate decisions, and sometimes practical help in implementing significant transactions. To do this the relevant executive will usually require first hand knowledge of the industry of his portfolio company, in addition to considerable broad-based industrial experience. He will also spend a great deal of time with each of his companies — two or three days a month on site and several hours a week on the telephone is not unusual.

As such, executives in truly hands-on funds cannot handle many companies at the same time — a portfolio of half a dozen or so is the conventional industry norm in the USA. This is in sharp contrast with 3i, a largely hands-off or reactive investor, where 100 executives together control over 4,000 existing investments, and make over 700 new investments each year.

To some entrepreneurs, this hands-on involvement may seem somewhat excessive, and border on interference. If, however, it were correct at the outset for the entrepreneur to choose a hands-on fund for his finance, this should not be the case, as:

(a) Hands-on investors are typically attracted to the fastest-growing companies. All companies which have experienced significant growth over a sustained period have been faced by numerous issues, problems and crises which management had not previously experienced and which had not previously been anticipated. In such cases expert advice and guidance from a

trusted sources should therefore be welcomed rather than resented by the entrepreneur.
(b) The hands-on investor will not typically seek executive (ie, day-to-day) control, although he will be involved in all non-recurring major corporate decisions. Thus the freedom of existing management to make day-to-day operating decisions should not be impaired.

The areas of input provided by the hands-on investor commonly include:

POLICY INPUT

This can and often does take place before the financing is completed in the form of amending the business plan to take account of any changes in direction advised by the investor and agreed by management.

In some cases this can be carried to the extreme by the investor himself providing the spark for the original business idea and writing the original business plan, before assembling the management team. His role will certainly, however, continue after the original financing, where the investor will expect to play an integral part in the regular planning process of the company, including key areas of:

(a) *Marketing:* which markets a company should be attacking, and how (ie, what distribution channels it should be using); how the company can best compete in its chosen markets, and in particular how it should set its pricing policies to achieve this.
(b) *Research and development:* how much should be spent, and in what areas; the degree of focus and concentration of the R & D spent; and the technology profile of the company, including the issues of whether the company should be an incremental improver or technology leader in high technology or low technology markets.
(c) *Risk management:* including the question of the optimum pace of growth for the company; preferred methods of growth (organic growth as against expansion via acquisition, etc); and the timing of the investment in fixed overheads necessary to service anticipated expansion.
(d) *Information systems:* the degree of detail and focus of concentration required of the company's information systems (non financial as well as financial), and the regularity and speed with which the information is produced.

Throughout this process the investor will act as a sounding board for the views of management, using persuasion rather than threats as the tools of his trade. While this may at first glance appear to be 'second guessing' of management's abilities, in fact this can be one of the greatest services the venture capitalist can be to his investee, for, unlike large companies who will often have formalised procedures to ensure this, it is often extremely difficult for the managing director of a smaller business to have access to a sufficiently experienced and respected colleague to test the reasonableness of his ideas and plans as they are formed and before he becomes emotionally attached to them.

EXECUTIVE ASSISTANCE

The hands-on investor can also be called upon by his portfolio company to assist directly in major non-recurring business transactions. These could include the identification and negotiation of acquisitions, licensing arrangements, or the selection of distributors, especially overseas. He may also be of assistance in fostering or securing valued suppliers and customers — a quick 'phone call to a major potential customer to convince him of the faith the venture capital fund has in the management team can, for example, play a key role in persuading an otherwise sceptical buyer of the stability and standing of the seller.

In this, as in so much of his advice, the investor should be able to rely on a wide range of contacts built up by himself and his fund. Such contact networks, especially overseas, represent one of the venture capitalist's major assets, which investee companies will need to use increasingly as they grow. The importance of a network of international contacts has been recognised by the European Venture Capital Association which has established a database for participating member firms to record and exchange information on their portfolio companies which might then trade or enter into joint ventures with each other.

MANAGEMENT STRUCTURE

One of the biggest problems faced by all fast-growing companies is to staff their ventures appropriately, with management of the calibre which will be required to support future expansion. The venture capitalist can help here, particularly on:

(a) Advising on the crucial question of *when* it becomes necessary, as opposed to merely advisable, to expand the management

structure (eg, when to bring in a specialist quality assurance or information systems controller).
(b) The identification of suitable candidates for key management posts, either via personal knowledge, or by the choice and proper briefing of appropriate executive search or recruitment consultants and assisting in the resulting interview process. This is felt by many management groups of venture backed companies in the USA to be one of the most valuable services provided by the hands-on investor.
(c) Using his experience to help in the design of appropriate executive remuneration structures, including the key question for fast-growing companies of equity participation via share option schemes, etc.

Finally, on a more negative but no less useful note, the investor can often effectively act as an arbitrator in the case of disputes within the management team, and may be the appropriate person to take the unpopular but necessary decision of getting rid of an unsatisfactory but key director, a point to which we will return later.

FURTHER FINANCING

If is argued by some hands-on investors in the USA that they are likely to be more effective than their hands-off contemporaries in raising subsequent rounds of finance for their portfolio companies because of their greater knowledge of the business. This is perhaps less true in the UK, in view of the exceptionally close links between the City and the risk capital community. It is true nevertheless in a number of cases that the presence on the board of a venture-backed company seeking further finance of a risk capitalist with proven financial and industrial expertise can significantly 'oil the wheels' of the finance raising process. In this context, those hands-on funds with especially close connections with City institutions can be expected to come into their own.

COPING WITH GROWTH

All fast-growing companies are characterised to some extent by confusion, and an apparent lack of control — everything and everyone seems stretched to the limit, as activity is constantly outgrowing the company's existing personnel and systems base. This can be a frightening experience for all concerned, and advice and reassurance from someone who has seen it all before, such as the experienced hands-on investor, can be welcome. In particular, the venture capitalist can be a real help to management in identifying the challenges it will face, considering the alternative ways of responding to them and establishing priorities for their implementation. These issues may include the organisation and management structure of the business; the nature and timing of diversification; the need to invest in new information systems; and the need to hire or train new people.

PROBLEMS AND FLASHPOINTS

This approach is not, however, without its problems in practice. The hands-on investor may for example become too involved in the affairs of the company. This will not only diminish his usefulness as an independent sounding board (if he cannot see the wood for the trees) but unless he is careful he may find it difficult to avoid encroaching on executive decision-making which is properly the preserve of the management team.

In addition to or as a result of the above, the investor may lose the trust of management, or move into an antagonistic relationship with them. Once this has happened, his value to the company will often diminish virtually to nil since he is likely to find it extremely difficult to force his views on an unwilling management, and must rely on his persuasive powers. In such conditions it is seldom profitable for the investor/management relationship to resemble a constant state of seige; often the only solution is either for the fund to change executives (which may be difficult in a small fund) or for the investor to sell out.

Common flashpoints

Such a breakdown of trust can arise from an almost infinite array of causes. Some of the more common flashpoints which can, however, lead to such disagreements are listed below.

(a) The time, type and pricing of *new finance*. For the most part, once the risk investor has completed his investment, the management and investor have common goals. However, when new money is required, conflicts of interest can soon arise. Management and investors may have differing views as to when it is advisable to raise additional funds. Further, if the additional funds are to be provided by the existing investor, there is considerable scope for disagreement over the price of the new investment. This can be a particularly difficult negotiation where the previous financing was at a price dependent on future performance (eg, through a ratchet mechanism) for a period which has not yet been completed. On this basis, the price for the previous round has typically to be re-negotiated as well as agreeing a price for the new money. The most difficult of these negotiations arise where additional funding is required to meet an unexpectedly poor performance. Management often feels that the additional funding required is only of a temporary nature and should carry little or no equity participation; the risk investor on the other hand feels that if he is required to provide the money (as opposed to a bank or other sources of finance) it should carry the normal risk rate of return.

(b) The amount and timing of *long-term investment decisions*. The management of a company may favour investments which in their view will favour the long-term profitable development of the business, even though these may incur short-term costs. The risk investor may feel that this delays or jeopardises the realisation of his investment. For example, if the investment strategy results in operating losses, a proposed stockmarket flotation of an investee company may have to be delayed by a number of years until the benefits of this strategy have been reflected in improved profits.

(c) *Divestment*, or decisions whether to cut back on problematical operations. These can be especially painful when management is emotionally committed to a project or venture which is failing to perform.

(d) *Removal of non-performing management*. This can be a particularly critical problem to many companies, and is specifically dealt with below.

There are no magic ways round these difficulties — as always, each side will need to be aware of the other's point of view if such problems are to be resolved. In particular, the entrepreneur should be aware that the investor must have a fiduciary duty to his own subscribers prudently to safeguard their (ie, his) investment in the company.

'Bad management'

The most difficult aftercare issue for all concerned typically arises when the risk capitalist loses confidence in the top management of the company, and most acutely when the executive concerned is the managing director who was also the previous controlling shareholder. This is not an uncommon occurrence (although most risk capitalists, both hands-on and hands-off investors, would not consider it usual) which has in many cases led to the removal of the executive concerned by the investor.

This may appear to confirm the worst fears of the entrepreneur at the time of the investment. In one sense, however, this should in many cases be seen as an entirely normal and indeed desirable development for the qualities required to manage a large company successfully are quite different from those required to grow a venture from scratch. In very few managers is this range of qualities equally developed, and the faster a company is growing, the less time there will be to acquire them through experience. Indeed, in the case of particularly fast-growing companies, it is sometimes difficult to see how any single executive could possibly rise successfully to the succession of challenges which such growth would create.

The entrepreneur should also, before deciding to seek risk capital, have carefully considered his own personal objectives and strengths and weaknesses, as well as those of his company. If this appraisal were done honestly, he should have a realistic view of the likelihood of his now being able to meet these challenges, and he should be able to respond logically rather than emotionally to any concerns the risk capitalist may have on this point. For as with the decision to go for growth rather than control which we discussed in Chapter 2, as long as the entrepreneur retains a stake in the business it should be in his interest to relinquish management control if the net effect of doing so would be to increase the value of his equity stake. Finally, in many cases it will be in the interest of both risk capitalist and entrepreneur for the latter to retain a working relationship with the company after he has stepped down from day-to-day control in order to retain the strengths and competitive advantage which he originally brought to the venture. This can be done in a number of ways, including promoting the executive in question to chairman, leaving him on the board as a specialist (eg, technical director, marketing director, head of administration, etc) or negotiating a continuing consultancy contract.

DO'S AND DON'TS

It is difficult to give any specific advice to the entrepreneur on how best to work with the risk capital investor, whether hands-on or hands-off, after first-round financing, as every investment is different. In general, however:

(a) *Know your investor.* Ensure you have researched how much time your chosen fund expects to spend with you, and whether the executive you are dealing with is likely to be able to achieve this.
(b) Use your investor to the maximum, but *do not ask too much.* Although the hands-on investor will want to spend a considerable time with you, his time is not unlimited, and there will be a point beyond which your constant telephone calls will not receive the cream of his attention (and therefore you will not receive the cream of his advice).
(c) *Build confidence.* Any worthwhile long-term relationship has to be worked at, and this is no exception. The best way in our experience to impress your risk capitalist is to *do what you say you are going to.* Not only will this avoid unpleasant surprises (the most effective destroyer of investor/investee confidence we know of), but it will also positively enhance his opinion of your managerial ability — and mutual respect is the soundest foundation for a successful post-investment relationship.

Chapter 15

Exit Routes

Some companies will be fortunate enough to view the question of how the venture capitalist is to realise his investment as a matter of less than primary importance. This will certainly be true of companies financed by way of loan stock or preference share capital where, barring untoward circumstances, the capital will be repaid to its holders over an agreed period of time. This may also be true for some companies who have financed their growth through ordinary equity finance. Where shares have already for example been issued directly to the public, the exchange of shares from one sector of the public to another may not have an unduly traumatic effect on management. Likewise, the investments of certain development capitalists may be structured so as to ensure that their target rate of return is met almost entirely from a running yield. It may thus be a matter of some indifference to such investors whether their equity stake is cashed in this year, next year, or never.

In the vast majority of cases, however, the timing and manner in which the risk capital investor realises his equity investment — his so-called *exit route* — will be of critical importance to the entrepreneur, who, unlike the risk capitalist, may well want to stay with his company beyond this point. The entrepreneur and the risk capitalist together will therefore want to agree the alternative exit routes envisaged, and their impact on the current operations and development of business.

TYPES OF EXIT ROUTE

Disregarding replacement capital, which in effect merely substitutes one institution for another and defers rather than completes the exit process, and liquidation (a somewhat extreme solution), there are, broadly speaking, three types of exit routes available to the risk capitalist, viz:

(a) *market quotation*, giving the risk capitalist the ability to sell his shares when he wishes;
(b) *acquisition* of the company by a third party; and
(c) *re-purchase by the company* itself of the shares held by the fund.

These are described briefly below.

Market quotation

This is the most well-publicised form of exit route for the venture capitalist, and the ultimate aim (and indeed dream) of many entrepreneurs. It has in the past in the UK been the most popular form of exit route for risk capitalists, with well over 100 examples to date.

Despite some well-publicised exceptions (for example, Rodime, which was originally quoted in the USA), listings of venture backed companies have taken place overwhelmingly in the UK. The companies concerned have been principally quoted on the Stock Exchange, which in turn is subdivided into the Official List (a so-called full quotation), the Unlisted Securities Market (USM) and the Third Market. In addition there is the possibility of quotation on various Over-the-Counter (OTC) markets.

The choice of which of these public markets to choose, and how to achieve a quotation, is complex and requires specialist professional advice; the main points only are summarised below. As noted before, this is one of the main areas where the venture capitalist can be of assistance to his portfolio companies; this is especially true of those funds which are closely linked with a merchant bank or a stockbroker.

When thinking of going public, the entrepreneur will need to decide:

(a) *Whether the business is suitable for flotation*. For a flotation by way of admission to the Stock Exchange official list or USM to be successful, or indeed possible, in addition to meeting the technical requirements for admission to the respective markets, the company must meet the commercial tests of the market. These include:

Demonstrated sound trading record
Good financial control
Good management
An effective board of directors
Good prospects
No major uncertainties or risks in the foreseeable future.

Whether the Third Market will be more flexible in its demands, it is too early to say.

(b) *What market* to be quoted on. Many issues will typically impact this decision, and in many cases the answer will involve fine judgement. Certainly, there is little difference between the standards of conduct expected of USM and fully-listed companies once on the market.

The main difference in entry requirements between the USM and the Official List is in the minimum amount of shares which have to be in public hands immediately after the issue — 10% for USM companies as against 25% on the Official List. In general, however, the main test is usually one of size, with few companies capitalised at under £15m making their market debut directly on the 'Big Board'.

The main factors affecting the choice of market are summarised in Figure 16.

Figure 16

Main Factors Affecting the Choice of Market for Flotation

	Official list	*USM*	*Third Market*
Minimum trading record (generally with unqualified audit reports)	5 years	3 years	Nil
Minimum shares to be in public hands post flotation	25%	10%	?
Level of institutional interest in share trading	High	Variable	?
Business property relief available on shares for inheritance tax purposes?	No	No	Yes

(c) *Whether to raise further finance* as part of the flotation, by issuing new shares, as opposed to selling a percentage of the shareholdings of existing owners. It is usually considered desirable to raise some new money to reinforce the impression that the company expects growth to continue. This is not always

the case, however, and indeed it would serve little purpose to raise new money if it were not needed, in view of the dilutive effect this could be expected to have on earnings per share.
(d) *How much control to surrender.* This is usually a delicate balancing act between the desire of the entrepreneur to surrender as little equity as possible, and the need to ensure that sufficient shares remain in public hands to create a market in the shares which is not unduly volatile. On average, 23% of shares of American companies have been sold to the public on flotation between 1979 and 1985.
(e) *What method* of flotation to use. With the exception of companies whose shares are already in public hands, this will involve the choice between an *offer for sale* of shares direct to the public, and a *placing*, where the majority of shares will be sold privately to contacts of the sponsor.

The method of flotation will not generally affect the process of going public; it will, however, affect issue costs. These will be typically significantly greater in the case of offers for sale, in view of the heavy advertising and underwriting costs, which are not usually necessary in the case of a placing. Most companies have therefore in the past chosen a placing of shares with clients of a stockbroker, thus avoiding significant advertising costs. This method of entry to the market is limited to issues of £5m (or £15m in the case of a full listing).

Acquisition

Alternatively, the venture capitalist can be 'taken out' by selling his shares to someone else, either through a replacement capital transaction or, more usually, by selling the whole company to a third party, usually a larger company looking to grow by acquisition.

In the USA the main form of exit route for venture capitalists has for many years been by way of third party sale. In recent years, this has also increased in popularity in the UK, as Figure 17 shows.

The reasons for this changing trend in the UK include:

(a) Decreased investor enthusiasm for shares in a number of sectors heavily populated by venture backed companies, including electronics and a large number of USM stocks. This has had the effect of depressing share prices and causing more companies to question the worth of a Stock Exchange quotation.
(b) In the case of venture backed companies in financial difficulty, the pressures on both management and investor to sell out as an

VENTURE-BACKED NEW ISSUES AND ACQUISITIONS

FIGURE 17

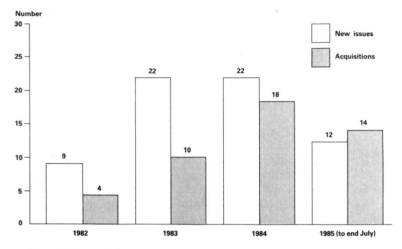

(Source: UK Venture Capital Journal, September 1985)

alternative to receivership. This can be expected to increase as more venture and development capital investments are made, and the inevitable failures begin to come to the surface.

(c) The difficulty of growing many venture backed companies beyond a certain size (often related to the potential of the British market) without the help of the resources of a major corporation.

As a result of the above, many commentators believe that acquisitions will continue to play an increasingly important part in the exit calculations of venture and development capitalists.

Company share re-purchase

In recent years, a third alternative exit route has opened for the venture capitalist. With some exceptions, it is now possible for a company to buy back, for cash, its own shares, which are then cancelled.

In past years this was not allowed by company law, which has always set great store by maintaining the capital base of a company. In 1981, however, the Companies Act was changed to allow companies to repurchase their own share capital if permitted to do so by their articles of association and subject to shareholder approval by way of a special resolution (ie, requiring the consent of 75% of votes cast). Assuming redemption is not by way of a new issue of shares, it must be made from distributable profits, unless they are not available, in which case approval of the court is required by way of a somewhat complex process which embraces the right of shareholders and creditors to petition the court to have the resolution cancelled.

It is critical, however, for any company considering this method of exit route to consider carefully the tax consequences. As a general principle, the purchase by a company of its own shares will be treated for tax purposes as a distribution (ie, a dividend). As such, the company will have to pay advance corporation tax (ACT) currently at the rate of 27/73rds of the redemption profits, which it may or may not be able to offset against its normal corporation tax payments, depending on circumstances. Furthermore, if the cash is received by an individual, he will be potentially subject to income tax at higher rates on the gross amount received. It is, however, possible, if certain complex conditions embodied in the Finance Act 1982 are complied with, to structure the purchase so that it does not constitute a distribution for tax purposes. The transaction is then treated as a disposal for capital gains tax purposes. The Inland Revenue has helpfully given companies the option to apply for advance clearance as to the availability of this relief, which it is almost always advisable to seek, preferably under the supervision of a competent professional advisor.

CHOICE OF ALTERNATIVES

In well-executed risk capital financings, both sides should have a clear idea of the type and timing of exit route envisaged at the outset. Circumstances change, however, and what may have been appropriate at the time of the initial investment may not always hold true. So what factors should the entrepreneur bear in mind when considering how his risk capitalist can realise his investment to their maximum mutual advantage?

To take the three alternative forms of potential exit in turn:

Market quotation

This will usually be an attractive exit alternative to the risk capitalist, for not only will he often find it financially rewarding, it can also add usefully to his own prestige and reputation. In the absence of other 'hard' evidence of venture and development capital fund performance (ie, at any time other than the closing of the fund) the number of flotations is widely used as a leading indicator of the success of the fund and the acumen of its managers, especially where a management group is trying to raise money for a new fund before any of its existing funds have come to the end of their lives, as is currently common in the UK.

The picture is typically, however, not so clear from the point of view of the company. The following are usually listed as the major advantages and disadvantages of any company going public.

ADVANTAGES

(a) *Control.* The entrepreneur does not need to lose control on flotation, and in practice seldom does. Indeed, many sponsors would seek actively to dissuade existing management teams from relinquishing control at this stage, because of the risk that the market may doubt their continuing commitment to the venture.

(b) *Liquidity.* The realisation of wealth locked up in shares is difficult when there is no public market for them, and their value is commonly reduced as a result. Flotation will enable the share price to reflect properly the company's performance and can, subject to certain restrictions, allow the entrepreneur to decide on the timing as well as the extent of his share sales.

(c) *Acquisitions.* The acquisition of other businesses either for cash via a rights issue or (more tax efficiently) in exchange for new shares in the company is very much easier when there is a public market in the shares of the acquiror.

(d) *Prestige,* will be enhanced by public company status and this, together with increased publicity, can create new marketing opportunities and improved borrowing and purchasing power.

(e) *Employees.* The motivation, recruitment and retention of staff can be improved dramatically once the company is floated. This is especially true if employee share option schemes can be introduced, when public marketability will enable holdings to be valued and realised with ease.

(f) *Share structure.* A specific advantage to the venture backed company on flotation is the dislike by the market of complex share structures. It is thus common as a pre-condition of flotation for the complex capital structures common in risk capital financings to be dismantled and all non-ordinary equity shares held by outside investors to be either converted into ordinary shares immediately prior to the flotation, or redeemed out of the proceeds of the issue.

DISADVANTAGES

(a) *Dividend pressure.* All quoted companies will be under pressure to pay some dividends each year. The magnitude of this pressure should not, however, be exaggerated, especially in the case of fast-growing companies which typically need to retain the bulk of their profits for future expansion, in which case investors will typically be attracted to the company's shares by the prospect of capital growth rather than dividend potential. In addition, in certain respects, the payment of dividends can compare favourably with other available alternatives. For example, faced with a choice of raising new money by way of debt or equity, the continuing cash cost of servicing newly issued share capital by way of dividend, typically around 5%, is almost cheaper than bank borrowing.

(b) *Pressure for results.* A much more important disadvantage of going public in the eyes of many entrepreneurs is what may appear to be constant interest on the part of the financial press and investment community in the company's current results and future prospects. Management interested in maintaining its share price will need to devote considerable time to the task of keeping journalists and investment analysts informed about the company's progress, and critically, not misleading them about the expected current year profit outturn. This puts a premium not only on the company's management accounting system, but also its ability to forecast future profits, which may not always be easy. In addition, although this is not a universally held proposition, it is considered by many that the investment community sets unreasonably high store on a company's ability to produce uninterrupted profit growth once it is on the market, on pain of seeing its share price fall significantly. As all entrepreneurs will know, this is not always easy to achieve, especially in the case of smaller quoted companies for whom the price of profitable long-term investment programmes may be reduced current income.

(c) *Public scrutiny.* These pressures from the investment community can also work in a more general sense, with increasing press and public interest in and comment on everything the company does. Some will enjoy this limelight, but others may resent unwelcome public interference in what has hitherto been a private company.

(d) *Rules and regulations.* The standards of conduct and operations of quoted companies expected by the investment community are buttressed by the regulations of the Stock Exchange, whose requirements extend beyond those of the Companies Act. As a condition of quotation on the Stock Exchange, all companies are required to sign a formal agreement with the Exchange whose various conditions are designed overall to ensure the maintenance of an orderly market in the company's shares. Under these provisions, the company is required to disclose a wide range of commercial and financial detail on a regular basis, including an overriding requirement to notify the Exchange of all items which could materially affect the share price. The directors of the company will also be expected to abide by a 'Model Code' of directors' dealings in the company's shares, again to guidelines set by the Exchange.

The cumulative impact of these external forces on the time and energy of every quoted company's top management team is significant, and should not be under-estimated.

(e) *Taxation.* This will be an important consideration if any gifts of shares are contemplated. A higher post-flotation market share price will result in a higher charge for inheritance tax, although the effect of this can be reduced by early tax planning.

(f) *Liquidity.* Although the existence of a market in the company's shares as a means to facilitate the realisation of the owner's investment is an oft-quoted (and real) advantage of going public, this is not always easy to achieve in practice.

First, at the time of the investment, existing shareholders (whether management or outside investors) will often come under severe pressure from the sponsors of the issue to agree not to sell any shares for a prescribed period following flotation, in order both to enhance investor confidence and maintain an orderly market. This can prove a source of significant friction, as many risk capital funds have a policy of refusing to be bound by many of the restrictions which sponsors of Stock Exchange flotations typically attempt to place on the new entrant company and all its directors and selling shareholders.

It may also be easier said than done for directors to sell shares after this date, for in addition to the general company law on share dealings by those with 'inside knowledge', the Model Code prohibits directors' share sales in the two months immediately preceding the announcement of half-year and full-year results, thus limiting the time frame in which shares can be sold to eight months in the year. In addition, directors' share sales at any time are coming under increasing market scrutiny, and some would say that in recent years it is becoming increasingly common for the market as a whole to regard such sales with disfavour as a matter of principle.

Finally, despite the care taken by many companies to ensure that a proper market exists in their shares, it is still not uncommon to find many USM shares in which there is at best an extremely thin market, where sales or purchases of small parcels of shares can be expected to move the market price significantly. It is this factor, accompanied by the unwillingness of some large institutions to deal or restrict their dealings in USM shares, which perhaps provides the biggest single incentive for quoted companies to make their debut on the Official List, or graduate to it from the USM as quickly as possible.

(g) *Pre-launch dislocation.* One of the biggest problems for companies coming to the market is the significant amount of management time involved in satisfying the sponsor's due diligence work to ensure that the company is fit to come to market. This commonly takes in excess of three months, and in some cases can extend to over a year. Costs too can sometimes be unpleasantly high, although the average percentage of issue costs to total capital raised (usually between 6% and 9%) is not out of line with other countries, and many would say is not an unreasonable price to pay for the benefits granted.

COMMENT

The above disadvantages are real, and to some will be a major headache. A number of owners who have taken their companies public have discovered that the flotation process has merely resulted in changing one partner (the venture capitalist) for another less congenial master in the form of the City institutions and other impersonal forces which set share prices.

To the management team who are truly determined to grow their company into a major industrial corporation, this should not matter, as it will rightly be seen as another price to be paid for success, but to other entrepreneurs with less singleminded objectives, including the many who live primarily to control their own companies, other exit routes may be more attractive.

Selling out

The most obvious disadvantage to the entrepreneur of selling out to another company is the resulting loss of control. In some cases this could even be followed by dismissal by his new employers, and in all cases he will have to learn to adapt to new styles and procedures imposed from outside.

This can be mitigated, however, by choosing the acquiror carefully, and obtaining a service contract to provide a measure of protection. Many buyers will themselves insist on this if they believe that the existing manager shareholders are critical to the success of the business at the time of acquisition. In addition, there will be many entrepreneurs who believe that their prime skill is in building businesses from scratch, to whom the chance to 'sell out and start again' may be welcome. Although there are as yet few well-known examples of this in the UK, this phenomenon is common in the USA.

A third party acquisition can also have its own advantages. The most obvious of these lies in the security of the 'money in the bank' to the entrepreneur from the sales proceeds. Less obvious but also important is the fact that, as a generalisation, in more cases than not, other companies will be prepared to pay a higher price for a company than it could achieve on flotation.

This may seem somewhat surprising in view of the high stock market prices still commanded by many growing companies. The stock market will, however, tend to discount the price of any publicly quoted stock to take account of products it does not understand, markets it is not familiar with, and management it does not know. An industrial company, however, with the appropriate expertise, ought to be able to form a judgement on all of these critical determinants of performance, and, when it sees what it considers a good company, to be prepared to pay a price more in line with the entrepreneur's expectations.

For the above reasons, this form of exit may in many cases be more attractive to the venture capitalist. It should also certainly be given serious consideration by all owners and managers of companies for whom this is a 'live' issue.

Share re-purchase

The major advantage of the share re-purchase route to the entrepreneur is that he will retain, and indeed strengthen, his control of the company. It may, however, be difficult to finance, even if net assets will permit it, for if the company has to borrow money to fund the re-purchase, its debt:equity ratio will suffer a 'double hit', ie, its debt will increase and its net assets (ie equity) will decrease simultaneously, thus doubly straining its debt capacity. As such, most examples of private companies who have re-purchased their own shares have involved relatively small amounts of money.

As a result, share re-purchases have not proved as important an exit route in practice as the other two alternatives described above. We are, however, seeing an increasing number of examples of such transactions in practice, and their popularity can be expected to increase, especially if and when the recent buoyancy of the stock markets should come to an end. Activity in this field can also be expected to increase dramatically after 1988, when the first BES investors will have held their shares for the full five year qualifying period and will be looking for an exit route.

PART 6
THE FUTURE

Chapter 16

The Future

We began this book in what for the small businessman were the dark days of 1977 as the Wilson Committee began its work. If a similar body were set up today, how would they analyse the present problems of and opportunities for the financing of small firms? What would their analysis of the present lead them to conclude would be the prospects for the future? Finally, would its conclusions be of any relevance to the entrepreneur and, if so, how much reliance should he place on them?

There should be no doubt that this issue is of more than passing relevance to the entrepreneur seeking finance. The small business sector in general would be significantly the poorer if we were to return to the 1977 position. This can perhaps be seen most obviously in the area of financing activity.

THE PRESENT — ISSUES AND OPPORTUNITIES

The Report on Investment Activity by the British Venture Capital Association (BVCA) for 1986 (referred to in Appendix II) shows investment by the risk capital funds (excluding 3i) running at a rate of around £300m per annum. By any measure these are significant sums in the context of the British economy and indicate a continuing level of investment activity by institutions. Interestingly enough, it has been pointed out that this represents a higher percentage of gross domestic product than is the case in the USA, so often quoted as the apotheosis of the venture capital industry and culture.

It can also be persuasively argued that the volume of risk capital investment throughout the 1980s has had a more significant and widespread impact on our lives. A survey, sponsored by Arthur Andersen & Co, produced by Venture Economics Limited for the BVCA in 1987 on the economic impact of venture capital in the UK revealed that, in the case of 92 companies chosen as successful examples of risk capital investment, turnover in the four year period prior to flotation increased by an average compound rate of 12% per annum, profits by 35%, and number of employees by 16%. The publicity given to such examples has contributed greatly to a major resurgence in political and social status of the entrepreneur, and policies to encourage further growth of the small business sector currently enjoy a wide measure of bi-partisan political support.

Too much can, however, be made of this. The investment figures noted above, for example, are significantly distorted by the sums of money invested in management buy-outs of mature businesses. Excluding these amounts indicates a risk capital sector significantly smaller than it is often currently perceived. In addition, some would say that closer examination reveals an industry which is only to a limited extent willing and able to support technical innovation, particularly through financing start-up and early stage high technology businesses.

It would similarly be easy to over-estimate the significance of the wider impact of the risk capital boom. Even the crude figures quoted above lose some of their bloom when seen against, for example, the annual investment in research and development of a single company such as IBM, which is currently running in the region of $5 billion. The results of the BVCA Impact Survey should also be viewed with some caution, based solely as they are on a study of the successes of the risk capitalists, rather than a representative sample. Finally, social and political infrastructures are not changed overnight, and the bloom of the 'enterprise culture' could still prove vulnerable to any prolonged frost following a change of government.

Turning to specifics, the risk capital industry is still struggling to find an answer to at least two major problems of immediate practical impact:

(a) How can the industry meet the 'equity gap'? It can be extremely difficult to obtain equity finance for projects requiring less than £100,000 of venture finance and the majority of investors prefer to invest in excess of £250,000. As a result an 'equity gap' has developed. This absence of seed finance has implications for the longer term development of the industry: will there be a sufficient flow of new projects demanding larger scale venture funding? More immediately, however, the failure of the industry to respond to this gap has become a political issue and a test of the industry's resolve to support innovation.

(b) Are the resources available for the *support of earlier stage technology projects*? These requirements include not only the finance but also the necessary technical expertise, especially on the part of the venture capital funds. The risk capital community is increasingly focusing on management buy-out financings and later stage investments with only a minority of the funds (albeit including some distinguished names) making significant investments in technology. Unless the industry can effectively move 'upstream' and fund earlier stage deals, it is an open question as to whether, in the long term, acceptable rates of return on venture investment can be obtained.

Will it last?

The latter point begs what, for the entrepreneur, is likely to be the all important question of whether the pool of money available for investment by the funds will be allowed to drain away in the future. For, as we have noted in previous chapters, the risk capital relationship is a long term process, and the availability of second round finance will be as vital a requirement of many existing venture backed companies as that of first round finance will be to the potential new market entrant.

The availability of future financing will depend on the answers to a number of key questions, all of which are related. In summary, however, they can be boiled down to two:

(a) *Will demand expand to meet supply?* This is a key question, in view of the vast amounts of money currently awaiting investment by the risk capital funds (which has been recently estimated at approximately £1 billion). Unless the flow of soundly-based financing proposals continues to grow, there is a real danger that the market will become overheated, and suppliers of finance to the risk capitalists, especially the pension funds, will invest their money elsewhere. To a significant extent the risk capitalists are banking on a repetition of the expansion of demand, which has characterised the American risk capital scene, in the UK over the next few years. As such, much of the prestige of the industry as a whole, as well as its money, is riding on this belief.

It is almost impossible, however, to state with any certainty whether this is likely to happen, or even whether it is currently happening. The most we can say is that the view of many funds would be that historically the answer to this question has been Yes, but that currently there is widespread concern that supply and demand are becoming significantly unbalanced, with too much money chasing too few high quality proposals, and consequently high prices. If true, this would be good news for the entrepreneur in the short term, but less good in the long term. How much of this, however, merely reflects exaggerated concern by the funds at the impact of normal healthy competition is open to debate — more than one seasoned observer has noted that this has been a constant complaint within the industry throughout the 1980s.

The more important underlying question, however, is probably whether growing companies will be able to attract more experienced entrepreneurs who should be able to manage these ventures better and give them a greater chance of successfully raising finance. This will in turn depend critically on how individual managers perceive the potential rewards available from risk capital backing, and in practical terms on the continuing flow of venture backed success stories to reinforce the role models already available. This issue will in turn be significantly influenced by the political climate, which will affect in so many ways the attitudes and aspirations of experienced managers thinking of becoming entrepreneurs.

(b) *How committed are the suppliers of risk capital?* Unlike the risk capitalists themselves, there is no reason why the City institutions who provide most of their money should be automatically committed to the risk capital business. Their function is to maximise the financial return on the money under their control. As such, the risk capital funds represent merely one of a number of alternative investment sources whose relative attractiveness will fluctuate in response to an often complex combination of specific and general economic, political and fiscal factors.

An analysis of the detailed impact of the interaction of these factors and their implications for the entrepreneur would take us deep into the workings of the City, and well beyond the scope of this book. It is worth pointing out in this context, however, how fragile the popularity of risk capital has been among the investment community in the USA, where the industry has been well established since the 1960s. Investment in risk capital funds in the USA has shown a pronounced cyclical trend, where peak years such as 1983 (when nearly $3.5 billion was invested by institutions in private venture capital) have been matched by troughs such as 1975, when the comparable figure shrank to $15m. Investment activity has also been heavily influenced by federal government policies, with sharply increased risk capital

Chapter 16 The Future 213

funding following hot on the heels of a relaxation in the capital gains taxation environment in the late 1970s. The British risk capital industry, by comparison still in its infancy, has as yet by and large only been exposed to those factors characteristic of a cyclical upswing; how it will react to the other side of the coin remains to be seen.

A case in point, and one currently much discussed both within the industry and in the press, is the potential impact of any sustained downturn in the stock market. This could be expected, the argument runs, to decrease the returns of the funds who would be deprived of exit routes by way of flotation, and thereby make the going more difficult when raising new money. This argument also, however, cannot be validated historically, for the last bear market in the UK was before the advent of the USM or the Third Market, although events on the Stock Market in and after October 1987 are now putting this thesis sternly to the test! And although the fallout from 'Black Monday' has reduced the prices at which some market newcomers have been quoted, it is another thing entirely to argue that this will prevent any small company with a good track record and prospects from obtaining a quote at any price. Finally, a bear market could conversely be expected to help the risk capital industry in one important sense, by discouraging quoted companies from using their own shares to fund acquisitions, thus reducing competition in the management buy-out market.

The fact that the risk capital industry has not lived through a sustained bear market does, however, in one respect lie at the route of what we believe is perhaps the biggest danger to the future supply of risk capital finance, in the sense of creating unrealistic expectations. The continuing bull market of the mid-1980s has led to increased demand in the City for new equity issues, including those by companies who have only recently been backed by risk capital finance — the 'MBO' flotations referred to in Chapter 5 are perhaps the most obvious, but not the only examples of this. There is a real risk that the high returns earned by many of the funds as a result of such realisations will be seen as the norm, rather than the product of a temporary aberration caused by favourable market conditions. Any focusing on short term results in what is essentially a long term business could cause problems for fund managers in the future when the stock market boom runs out of steam.

Conclusion

Overall, the risk capital industry is now entering a phase of maturity. The number of fund managers has begun to stabilise, and most of the major City institutions have dipped their toes in the risk capital water, either as fund investors or managers. Past successes have established the attractiveness of the industry both in the eyes of suppliers and seekers of finance. The continuing availability and popularity of risk capital investment, however, although buttressed to some extent by its past reputation, will be dependent on how the industry reacts to the various pressures outlined above, both internal and external. The future success is not assured; as with their portfolio companies, the risk capitalists will have to work at it.

THE FUTURE

How will the funds respond to try to safeguard their own future? What impact can this be expected to have on the entrepreneur seeking finance?

At the heart of the strategies of all risk capital investors will lie the necessity of attracting a high quality deal flow, although in a fast-changing marketplace it is perhaps foolhardy to predict how they will try to achieve this. Nevertheless, we envisage the following trends developing or continuing over the course of the next few years, all of which can be expected to be of benefit to the seeker of finance:

(a) *Concentration of fund raising.* Funds for later-stage transactions (development capital investments and management buy-outs) will increasingly be concentrated in funds associated with larger financial institutions, such as the development capital arms of the clearing banks or specialist funds linked to merchant banks. These will either be open-ended vehicles with funds continuously supplied by the parent bank or increasingly large funds provided by institutions. Funds to finance earlier-stage transactions will become concentrated in the hands of a relatively small number of venture managers who have established a good track record. The emergence of a core of powerful and experienced funds can be expected to increase the confidence of potential portfolio companies that their backers possess the same staying power as they will demand of management.

(b) *Specialist funds.* As the management of funds for investment in early-stage transactions become concentrated in fewer hands, the fund managers will increasingly specialise in particular sectors. For example, one organisation may attract under its wing a range of separately managed funds investing in a particular industry, eg, biotechnology or communications equipment. The fund will then have a better chance of attracting the required specialist staff and a deal flow relevant to a particular sector and be better equipped to support the companies in which it invests. This expertise will be particularly relevant where the fund is specialising in high technology investment. This type of specialisation is already emerging in the British venture capital industry and we believe that it will develop further and as a result increase the proportion of true venture capital available to support the development and application of technology.

(c) *Regional funds.* We foresee continuing growth of regional funds, and especially their role as providers of seed capital for earlier-stage ventures with which the risk capitalist will wish to keep in close contact and for which the cost of doing so can be significantly reduced by being located nearby. The regional funds will probably be associated with one or more major funds or fund mangers based in London who will continue to provide the funds for more substantial financings.

(d) *Internationalisation.* Although the British venture capital industry is still some years ahead of that in any other European country, the interest in and growth of risk capital activity is increasing rapidly in several countries, including West Germany, France, Holland and Spain. Many of the managers of British risk capital funds have either established their own funds or are associated with fund managers in other European countries. This could be of significant benefit to the British entrepreneur, for in practice the greatest benefit which many risk capitalists bring to their investee companies is the introduction to a network of contacts. As risk capital managers become more experienced and broaden their own network of contacts, this will directly benefit their investee companies in terms of introductions to customers, suppliers, university and research establishments throughout Europe.

Finally, and underlying all the above activity, the risk capitalists will actively be courting the entrepreneurs. At a national political level they will be lobbying for government legislation or other action to encourage more experienced managers to leave secure, well-paid, pensionable employment to start their own businesses. More parochially, in publicising their own achievements and those of their portfolio companies, they will be aiming also to enhance the status of the entrepreneur in the public eye.

Most fundamentally, they will be attempting to convince the seeker of finance that he can achieve lasting benefits from a long-term risk capital relationship, for all its attendant irritations and problems. We hope that, while stressing in the preceding pages of this book the practical issues typically faced by the entrepreneur in his dealings with the risk capitalist from inception to exit, we have not totally obscured this crucial message. Given clear objectives, good communications, common goals and a great deal of hard work, the risk capital relationship can yield significant real gains to the entrepreneur, to the risk capitalist, and to society as a whole.

Appendix I

A Practical Example — Leader Electronics Limited

CASE STUDY

The case study summarises the background and subsequent financing of Leader Electronics. The case, which is based on a practical example with only minor changes, illustrates the approach, some of the difficulties, and the elements of success in venture financing which is described in this book.

Background

Leader Electronics Limited was founded in 1978 by six shareholders/directors to manufacture and distribute quality hi-fi products. They had identified an opening for a British manufacturer producing a high quality and reliable product line at a reasonable price, marketed and sold professionally and aggressively. There appeared to be considerable export potential, particularly in view of the high regard in other countries of the world for British hi-fi.

Starting from a small warehouse in London, the company expanded from sales of £87,000 in 1978 to just under £3m in 1983. During that period the company moved its base from London to Cambridge. Initially in Cambridge it operated out of an old factory/warehouse but moved into a brand new purpose built factory of 22,000 sq ft in the summer of 1983. It adopted a very aggressive export policy early on and set up an associated company with a parallel manufacturing base in the USA from which to serve the North American market. Another associated company was set up in the Netherlands, but purely as a distribution rather than a manufacturing base.

During the latter part of 1983 certain teething problems were encountered with a new range of products, while the North American market placed a far greater strain on resources than had initially been anticipated. In particular the costs of opening up the North American market were much greater than had been thought and it was found that much greater credit had to be given to dealers in North America than was the pattern in Europe, resulting largely from Japanese marketing practices with dealer payment terms in excess of six months.

Financing development

The company was initially financed by its own shareholders/directors who raised some £125,000 from their own resources during the first four years of operation. This was augmented by accumulated profits of some £400,000 by the end of 1982 and a bank overdraft facility of £350,000. The company was, however, under-capitalised for its current and anticipated volume of business, particularly if there were any temporary hiccups in supply of components, demand from the market, etc.

A summary of the company's actual and projected results and financial position is shown on pages 226–227.

To that end the directors resolved in the first half of 1984 to seek £1m of new finance in order to provide working capital for the expansion of its business. The directors concluded that they would seek equity finance to support their ambitious growth plans and to avoid the pressures recently experienced by the business through its dependence on bank overdraft facilities. Based upon their own assessment of the value of the business, the directors felt that £1m of new money should give the new investor not more than 40% of the enlarged share capital. In order to support approaches to various sources of funds, the directors put together a comprehensive business plan, summarising its history, its profile in the market place, the kind of products it was producing and proposed to produce, its research and development activities, its manufacturing processes, the CV of the senior management, and how the proceeds of the issue were to be used. This was accompanied by detailed statistics of the company's trading record, its profits forecasts and its future strategy and prospects.

The company tackled the fund raising on three fronts:

(a) It approached a large firm of stockbrokers with a view to gaining

introductions to possible institutional investors, such as pension funds.
(b) It approached the development capital arm of its clearing bank, via an introduction from its bank manager.
(c) It approached its auditors for any recommendations that they might put forward.

Fund raising

INVESTMENT EVALUATION

The company attracted significant interest on all fronts, as described below.

(a) *The Stockbroker.* One particular pension fund approached by the stockbrokers expressed an interest in Leader. Preliminary discussions were followed by a site visit by the investment manager of the fund.

He knew that the hi-fi industry had, if anything, been contracting over the previous years in view of the competing demands on consumer resources from video, home computers, etc. He was persuaded, however, that this was a relatively stable market, in which Leader had established a strong reputation with a 'BMW/Porsche' quality image. He was convinced that they were likely to be able to carve out an increased market share in future years, and had adequately safeguarded themselves against any larger company 'muscling in' on their market segment.

He concluded that this might be an interesting investment for the fund particularly as Leader had plans to diversify away from hi-fi into a broader base of consumer electronics activities and that, if successful, they would be requiring further finance in due course. In this regard, the fund's policy was to support a limited number of established unquoted companies with development capital finance, and in due course to realise their investment through a Stock Exchange listing.

Towards the end of 1984 the board of the fund had accepted the manager's recommendation in principle that an investment in Leader was worthy of serious consideration and appointed an independent investigator to make a detailed report on the company and, if appropriate, to put together an investment package that would suit the institution and would be acceptable to Leader's shareholders.

(b) *Development Capital Fund.* Parallel negotiations were proceeding with the development capital fund associated with the company's clearing bank. It became apparent, however, that while the main fund was not prepared to take a direct stake in Leader, an investment in Leader might be considered by their BES fund.

(c) *The Accountant.* In the meantime, the company had been taking advice from its auditors as to what other avenues might be pursued and a number of introductions were made to risk capital funds. One of these was managed by a small but aggressive finance house, which had heard of Leader, knew that its products were well-regarded and acted very promptly.

OBTAINING THE PRELIMINARY OFFER

Intensive discussions were pursued with all these three separate entities.

(a) *The pension fund.* The fund's advisers concluded their investigations and, subject to agreeing a satisfactory investment package, they would recommend that the institution proceed. However, the initial target of raising £1m of finance in return for 40% of the company was regarded as somewhat unrealistic and a figure of £500,000 was considered to be more realistic. The institution's advisers indicated that for this size of investment they would be looking at a shareholding of between some 40–50%. The company indicated that because the amount of £1m had been reduced to some £500,000 their view was that a 20% equity stake was appropriate.

One of the problems was then 'engineering' a package which satisfied the needs of the institution but which did not demotivate the director shareholders — there were then ten shareholders, many of whom held rather low stakes in the company.

Management proposed that part of the means of enabling the institution to increase its shareholding would be to buy-out a sleeping shareholder who had indicated that he would be happy to sell his shares in Leader provided the price was right. After a long series of negotiations, the following package was agreed in principle, and subject to the approval of the institution's board.

Pension fund's offer

(i) The fund would acquire the shares of the sleeping

shareholder, who owned 11% of the equity of the company, for £110,000 (thus valuing the company at £1m).
(ii) The institution would lend Leader £500,000 by way of a medium-term loan, part of which would be convertible into an additional 15% shareholding in the company, the price to be on a 'ratchet basis' depending on average profits for 1985, 1986 and 1987.
(iii) The loan would carry an interest rate of 8%. However, after the conversion option had been exercised, the balance of any loan would carry interest at 12% until repayment.
(iv) There would be a shareholders' agreement which would place the usual kind of protections for a minority shareholder and which would give the institution some control over major business decisions.

(b) *BES fund offer.* Negotiations which had been continuing with the development capital fund led to their BES fund offer as follows:

(i) A sum of £400,000 for between 20-25% of the share capital as enlarged by the issue of new shares, the exact percentages to be agreed between the parties on the basis of further discussions (this would value the company at between £1.2m and £1.6m).
(ii) There was to be an accountants' investigation into the affairs of the company, although the fund was agreeable to Leader's auditors undertaking this work.
(iii) Satisfactory arrangements had to be made to accommodate the rules of the BES, in relation to Leader's associated companies in Europe and North America.

In the meantime the company had received the offer from the pension fund and reported back to the BES fund that their offer would increase the dilution of the equity shareholders and inject £100,000 less extra finance (ie, £400,000). The BES fund came back with a revised package proposal for an investment in conjunction with the main development capital fund as follows:

I The BES fund would invest £450,000 in Leader — this being the maximum permissible sum they were allowed to invest in one company under the rules of their scheme — for 18% of the equity.
II The main fund would purchase the 11% minority shareholder for £110,000.

(c) *Offer by smaller finance house.* In the knowledge that packages of such kind had been offered to the company, the smaller finance house then made an offer on behalf of its fund as follows:

  (i) Its fund would invest £450,000 by way of cumulative redeemable partially convertible participating preference shares at par. Subject to the group's performance over the ensuing three years, this would be convertible into between 18% and 35% of the company's ordinary share capital. For the conversion rate of 18% to be applicable, the company's average pre-tax profits over the three year period would have to be at least £500,000.
  (ii) Total fees and costs payable were estimated at £50,000, plus an option to the finance house to take up to a 5% equity shareholding in Leader at any time within ten years at a price per share which would value the Leader Group at 2.5 times pre-tax profits of Leader for the year ended 31 December 1985.

EVALUATING THE OFFERS

It was thought that the third offer from funds managed by the smaller finance house was the least attractive, not least because of the costs involved, including the option. This was therefore rejected.

The decision then whether to accept the offer from the pension fund or from the BES fund was extremely difficult. The matter was discussed at some length with Leader's auditors and other advisers before a final decision was taken. On the face of it, the BES offer was the more attractive since it achieved the original objective of strengthening the company's balance sheet considerably and involved no continuing interest costs. It also valued the company at a higher price.

However, it was thought that there were a number of disadvantages with the BES fund offer:

(a) It might be difficult to raise any additional money in the future from the fund. This could set a limit on future expansion possibilities, or at the very least lead to the complexities involved in negotiating with a different investment arm of the 'parent' bank.
(b) The BES fund investors would be likely to wish to realise their investment as soon as possible after the five year initial period was up and this could conflict with the best interests of the company and its remaining shareholders.

(c) It was felt that the BES fund managers were interested in short-term objectives rather than long-term growth. This, it was feared, could lead to future conflicts over the management of the company, especially in view of the negative covenants demanded by the fund as a pre-condition of its involvement.

The pension fund investment had the disadvantages that it would involve a continuing interest burden and did little to strengthen the company's balance sheet, but it appeared to have the following advantages:

(a) The fund had indicated that, subject to satisfactory performance, additional funds for expansion would be available without the fund increasing its own equity share.
(b) The fund had stated that it was prepared to support its investment in future periods and this was felt to provide a degree of security.
(c) The fund had indicated that they would welcome a diversification programme in future, and it was evident that they had the resources to enable this to be accomplished.
(d) The fund was interested in long-term growth rather than short-term profit.
(e) The institution operated a 'hands-off' approach towards the management of the company, so long as budgets and other agreed targets were being achieved.

After considerable analysis and deliberation, the directors decided to proceed with the offer from the pension fund. Up to this point the directors of Leader had been spending time in discussions with representatives of all three potential investors and been providing each of them with additional information they had requested. From this point the activity changed from both parties working towards an initial overall decision to work with each other to the detailed and painstaking task of finalising and documenting the detailed terms and completing all of the due diligence work required by the pension fund.

CONCLUDING THE FORMALITIES

The conclusion of the formalities took rather longer than expected and involved the senior management of the company, particularly the financial director, in a considerable amount of work. Although the basic parameters of the offer had been made and accepted in principle, there remained a considerable amount of detail to be thrashed out between the parties and their respective lawyers. There was considerable amount of debate and hard talking on such matters as warranties, and detailed restrictions on the directors' activities and management decisions. This stage was more complicated than normal for two reasons. First, at the same time as making its investment in the company, the fund was acquiring shares from existing shareholders with whom negotiations had to be completed and an agreement drawn up. Secondly, the Leader Group had a number of overseas associated companies and the fund, not surprisingly, required the arrangements for operation of these activities to be formalised such that all transactions were on arms-length basis and the management of Leader did not devote undue attention to the affairs of the associates in which the fund had no financial interest.

Furthermore, the sheer amount of information that was requested by the lawyers for the institution took much longer to assemble than had been realised. Thus the board of the institution approved in principle the deal in February 1985 but contracts were not exchanged and the money paid over until towards the end of May 1985.

Postscript

Events which followed the completion of the deal served to reinforce the belief of directors of the company that they had made the right decision. First of all, closer personal ties developed between the directors of the company and the institution's investment manager and other senior executives. These very much confirmed the initial view that Leader was dealing with people of absolute integrity. Furthermore, by the beginning of 1986, the institution had formally approved the injection of a further £250,000 of loan finance on similar terms to enable an accelerated expansion plan for its hi-fi activities, in particular the introduction, financing and marketing of a new state-of-the-art system.

COMMENTARY

The experience of Leader illustrates a number of common features of risk capital financing, many of which have been noted in the preceding pages. Some of the more important points as they apply to Leader are as follows:

(a) *Timetable.* It invariably takes longer than anticipated to complete the process of raising risk capital. This is in part due to the time the risk capital investors feel they need to take in order to get to know the management of the company. It is also influenced by the number of potential investors with which the company is negotiating. In the first instance, the Leader financing took longer than might have been the case as a result of the time taken by the directors in meeting several potential investors and deciding which offer to accept. What had not been anticipated by them was the length of time taken in the legal stages completing the agreement with the vendor shareholders and settling the arrangements for the overseas associates.

(b) *Price.* Risk capital money can often seem expensive to the entrepreneur. In the case of Leader, the investors valued the company at little more than half the valuation anticipated by the directors. The price is, however, negotiable and, if they think the investment is attractive, the risk capitalists will compete with each other on price to secure the investment.

(c) *Choice of investor.* It was significant, and not uncommon in such situations, for the directors of Leader to choose an investor who did not offer initially the best financial terms. With hindsight it is perhaps surprising, in view of Leader's intention to develop international export business, that greater emphasis was not placed upon identifying an investor who had extensive overseas contacts and could help in this regard.

(d) *Advisers.* The directors of Leader consulted and involved advisers — their auditors, stockbrokers, solicitors — at various stages in the transaction. As a result they had the benefit of independent advice in identifying sources of finance and evaluating the offers received. It is possible that the investment process would have been speeded up somewhat if either one of the advisers had been asked to lead and co-ordinate the effort or if there had been meetings of the advisers at which they could keep up to date with the progress of negotiations and co-ordinate their advice to the company.

LEADER ELECTRONICS LIMITED

BALANCE SHEETS

£000's	Actual		Projected	
	1983	1984	1985	1986
CURRENT ASSETS				
Stock	613	700	1,150	1,500
Debtors	434	560	1,000	1,400
Cash	19	—	—	172
	1,066	1,260	2,150	3,072
CURRENT LIABILITIES				
Bank overdraft	343	247	78	—
Creditors	859	725	900	1,200
	1,202	972	978	1,200
Net current assets	(136)	288	1,172	1,872
Due from associates	507	334	183	83
Net fixed assets	238	220	300	400
Deferred R & D	100	90	30	—
Long-term liabilities	(52)	(382)	(300)	(600)
	657	550	1,385	1,755
CAPITAL EMPLOYED				
Share capital	102	102	102	102
Retained earnings	400	268	683	1,153
	502	370	785	1,255
Shareholders' loans	155	180	600	500
	657	550	1,385	1,755

LEADER ELECTRONICS LIMITED

PROFIT AND LOSS ACCOUNTS (TO 31 DECEMBER)

£000's	1982	Actual 1983	1984	Projected 1985	1986
Sales	2,919	2,841	2,239	5,000	7,000
Cost of sales	2,045	1,903	1,667	3,550	4,970
Gross profit	874	938	572	1,450	2,030
General expenses	592	819	516	755	995
Profit before capital charges	282	119	56	695	1,035
Capital charges					
Depreciation & amortisation	35	48	57	50	50
R & D	12	26	51	80	50
Interest & finance charges	14	48	80	50	90
Profit from operations	221	(3)	(132)	515	845
Tax charge	(18)	—	—	(100)	(350)
Net profit	203	(3)	(132)	415	495

Appendix II

Extracts from 'British Venture Capital Association Report on Investment Activity (1986)'

The following pages comprise extracts from a report written by Venture Economics Limited, which was commissioned by the British Venture Capital Association (BVCA) to collect and analyse data on the investment activity of BVCA members in 1986. The report contains an analysis of the investments made by the 77 full members as at 31 December 1986.

AGGREGATE INVESTMENT

BVCA members invested £426m in 708 companies in 1986, an increase of 31% over the £325m invested by the 67 full members in 1985. A total of 1,105 investments were made.

Table 1

Investment Activity of BVCA Members

	1985	1986	% Change
Total Amount Invested (£m)	324.6	425.9	+31%
Number of Individual Investments	1,021	1,105	+ 8%
Number of Companies Financed	635	708	+11%

The difference between the number of investments and the number of companies financed arises principally because of investments which were syndicated between two or more investment vehicles managed by BVCA members. In addition, some companies received more than one round of finance during the year.

The following table shows 1986 investments by country:

Table 2

Investments by Country — 1986

Country	No. of Cos.	% of Cos.	Amount Invested (£m)	% of Amount
UK	600	84.7	384.0	90.2
USA	95	13.4	36.8	8.6
Eire	2	0.3	0.8	0.2
Continental Europe	9	1.3	4.2	1.0
Other Overseas	2	0.3	0.1	0.0
TOTAL	708	100%	425.9	100%

The proportion of the total amount invested accounted for by investment in the UK increased to 90% from 86% in 1985. Investment in the USA, on the other hand, decreased from 12% of the total investment amount in 1985 to 9% in 1986. After having increased slightly in 1985, investment in Continental Europe fell back to only 1% of the total investment amount in 1986.

Investments in British companies were on average larger than investments in American companies, so the UK accounted for a higher proportion of the total investment amount (90%) than of the total number of companies backed (85%).

UK INVESTMENT PATTERNS

This section contains a more detailed analysis of investments in the UK.

In 1986 BVCA members invested a total of £384m in 600 British companies. This represented an increase of 38% over the £278m invested in the UK in 1985.

Of the £384m invested in 1986, £300m (78%) was invested in companies which had not previously received venture capital finance. The remaining £84m (22%) was invested in follow-on financings. A total of 962 individual investments were made. The average size of investment was therefore £399,000. Investments in new financings were on average larger than follow-on investments, £459,000 compared with £272,000.

The average number of investments per British financing fell slightly to 1.52, from 1.56 in 1985.

Investment by financing stage

Investments have been categorised by five different financing stages: start-up, other early-stage, expansion, buy-out and acquisition, and secondary purchase. These stages are defined in greater detail at the end of this appendix.

Expansion financings continued to account for the largest proportion of total financings, though their share of the total was down slightly in 1986 to 45% of all financings, from 48% in 1985.

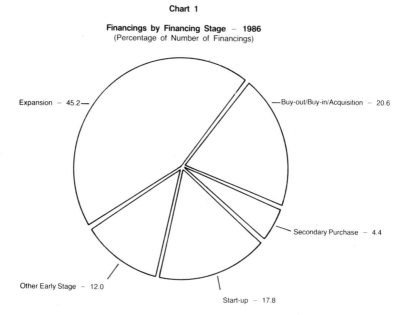

Chart 1

Financings by Financing Stage – 1986
(Percentage of Number of Financings)

Expansion – 45.2
Buy-out/Buy-in/Acquisition – 20.6
Secondary Purchase – 4.4
Start-up – 17.8
Other Early Stage – 12.0

Management buy-outs, buy-ins and acquisitions showed the greatest increase in 1986, their share of total financings rising to 21% from 17% in 1985.

The table below shows the detailed breakdown of financings and amount invested by financing stage:

Table 3

Investment by Financing Stage — 1986

Stage	No. of Fins.	% of Fins.	Amount Invested (£m)	% of Amount
Start-up	113	17.8	57.9	15.1
Other Early-Stage	76	12.0	28.2	7.3
Expansion	287	45.2	104.0	27.1
Buy-out/Buy-in/Acq.	131	20.6	173.6	45.2
Secondary Purchase	28	4.4	20.3	5.3
TOTAL	635	100%	384.0	100%

Companies at an early stage of development, including 113 start-ups, accounted for almost 30% of financings and 22% of the total amount invested.

Management buy-outs, buy-ins and acquisitions accounted for over 45% of the total amount invested, a much higher percentage than their share of total financings (21%). This difference is explained by the higher average size of financing in this category.

The following table shows the average size of financing and the average number of investments per financing for the different financing stages:

Table 4

Number and Average Size of Investments by Stage — 1986

Stage	No. of Fins.	% of Fins.	Ave. No of Invs. per Fin.	Ave. Size of Fin. (£000's)
Start-up	116	17.3	1.5	512
Other Early-Stage	108	11.2	1.4	371
Expansion	359	37.3	1.3	362
Buy-out/Buy-in/Acq.	284	39.5	2.2	1,325
Secondary Purchase	45	4.7	1.6	725
TOTAL	962	100%	1.5	605

As in 1985, the average number of investments per financing and the average size of financing are significantly higher for buy-outs than any other category. The average size of start-up financings, £512,000, was significantly higher than the 1985 average of £343,000. The average size of expansion financings fell to £362,000 in 1986 from £402,000 in the previous year.

Investment by industry sector

Venture Economics has carried out an analysis of investments by industry sector, first by major industry sector and then by sub-sectors within these categories. Buy-outs, buy-ins, acquisitions and secondary purchases have been excluded from the analysis.

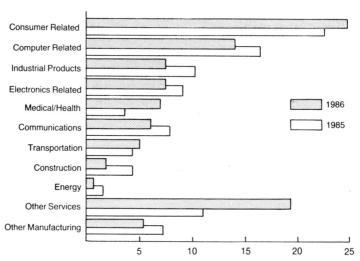

Chart 2

Investments by Industry Sector – 1986
(Percentage of Companies Financed)

Almost a quarter of all companies financed were in the consumer related sector, making this sector dominant in terms of number of companies financed for the third successive year. The sectors showing the greater relative increases in 1986 were 'other services', which includes financial services, and medical/health related businesses. The proportion of all companies financed in the other services sector rose from 11% to 19% while the number of companies in the medical/health sector doubled from 16 in 1985 to 32 in 1986 to reach 7% of the total.

The combined share of companies in the computer and electronics related sectors dropped to 22% of all companies financed in 1986 from 26% in 1985. The industrial products and 'other manufacturing' sectors also declined in importance from 18% in 1985 to 13% in 1986.

The following table shows a more detailed breakdown of 1986 investments by industry sub-sector:

Table 5

Investments by Industry Sector — 1986

Sector	No of Cos.	% of Cos.	Amount Invested (£m)	% of Amount
Consumer Related	112	24.7	38.8	20.4
Leisure	23		9.1	
Retailing	16		5.6	
Food	11		3.0	
Products	32		10.0	
Services	24		9.6	
Other	6		1.5	
Computer Related	64	14.1	21.5	11.3
Computers	6		1.4	
Graphics	6		2.1	
Peripherals	12		8.1	
Services	6		0.9	
Software	27		8.1	
Other	7		0.9	
Electronics Related	35	7.7	14.9	7.8
Components	7		5.4	
Instrumentation	9		1.7	
Other	19		7.8	
Industrial Products	35	7.7	13.2	6.9
Chemicals	8		1.1	
Automation	6		1.7	
Equipment & Machinery	10		3.0	
Other	11		7.4	
Medical/Health	32	7.1	17.5	9.2
Communications	28	6.2	14.4	7.6
Energy	3	0.7	0.6	0.3
Transportation	23	5.1	15.5	8.2
Construction	9	2.0	3.5	1.9
Financial Services	24	5.3	18.6	9.8
Other Services	64	14.1	25.4	13.4
Other Manufacturing	24	5.3	6.2	3.2
TOTAL	453	100%	190.1	100%

The average size of investments in all the categories included in this analysis was £420,000. Investments in companies in the financial services sector were on average larger, at £775,000, than investments in companies in any other sector. These were closely followed by investments in electronic components companies, which averaged £771,000.

The average amount received by computer related companies as a whole was £336,000. Within this sector the average varied from £675,000 for computer peripheral companies to only £129,000 for 'other' computer companies. The average amounts invested per company in the energy and other manufacturing sectors were also well below average at under £300,000 per company.

Investment by region

The regions used for the geographical analysis of British investment are the standard regions of the Central Statistical Office.

Table 6

Investments by Region — 1986

Region	No. of Cos.	% of Cos.	Amount Invested (£m)	% of Amount
South East				
— North of Thames	67	11.2	81.6	21.3
— South of Thames	46	7.7	44.8	11.7
Greater London	164	27.3	119.4	31.1
South West	51	8.5	17.6	4.6
East Anglia	39	6.5	20.1	5.2
West Midlands	37	6.2	11.3	2.9
East Midlands	26	4.3	10.5	2.7
Yorks & Humberside	18	3.0	12.5	3.3
North West	26	4.3	16.6	4.3
North	18	3.0	11.9	3.1
Scotland	52	8.7	26.1	6.8
Wales	53	8.8	11.2	2.9
Northern Ireland	3	0.5	0.4	0.1
TOTAL	600	100%	384.0	100%

Companies in the South East and Greater London continued to account for the greatest part of overall investment by BVCA members, in 1986 they accounted for 46% of all companies financed, down from 52% of the total in 1985, though they still accounted for over 60% of the total amount invested during the year. Average amount invested per company in the South East and Greater London was significantly higher, at £887,000, than the overall average of £640,000. Companies in the South East-North of Thames region received an average of over £1.2m per company.

Wales accounted for the highest proportion of companies financed outside the South East, with 53 companies backed in 1986. The average amount invested per company (£211,000), however, was lower than in any other region apart from Northern Ireland. Total investment in the northernmost regions of England increased from £14m in 1985 to £41m in 1986. Companies in this area received an average of £661,000, which was approximately the same as the national average. This is in contrast with 1985, when the average for this area was significantly lower than for the UK as a whole.

STAGE DEFINITIONS

Start-up

Financing provided to companies for use in product development and initial marketing. Companies may be in the process of being set up or may have been in business for a short time, but have not sold their product commercially.

Other early-stage financing

Financing provided to companies that have completed the product development stage and require further funds to initiate commercial manufacturing and sales. They will not yet be generating a profit.

Expansion financing

Capital provided for the growth and expansion of a company which is breaking even or trading profitably. Funds may be used to finance increased production capacity, market or product development and/

or to provide additional working capital. Capital provided for turn-around situations is also included in this category.

Buy-out/buy-in/acquisition

Funds provided to enable operating or external management and investors to acquire an existing product line or business or to finance the formation of a holding company set up to acquire an existing company or companies.

Secondary purchase

Purchase of existing shares in a company from another venture capital firm, or from another shareholder or shareholders.

Appendix III

Negative Covenants and Warranties — Some Examples

NEGATIVE COVENANTS

The aims of and reasoning behind negative covenants included as part of risk capital investments are dealt with in Chapter 13. Their nature and extent will differ in each case; the type of covenants to be found in a typical risk capital investment where the investor wishes to take an active part in the affairs of the investee company may, however, include undertakings that the company will not, without prior permission of the investor, carry out any of the following actions:

Capital structure and shareholder rights

(a) Increase the company's authorised or issued share capital.
(b) Alter its memorandum or articles of association.
(c) Change the class rights attaching to any of its shares.

Compass of operation

(a) Invest or expend any funds of the company outside its existing business.
(b) Acquire control of any other company.
(c) Dispose of or transfer to third parties any part of its existing business.
(d) Dispose of any rights or property of the company other than in the ordinary course of business.
(e) Wind up the company.

Financial base

(a) Borrow any money in excess of previously agreed limits or alter the terms of any existing borrowings.
(b) Make any loan to or guarantee the debts and obligations of any other venture.
(c) Make any capital expenditure, or lease any capital equipment, in excess of an agreed amount.
(d) Declare the payment of any dividend or other distribution of profits or reserves.

Directors and employees

(a) Appoint or settle or alter the terms of service of any director or employee of the company.
(b) Enter into a contract with, or make any payments to, a director (or company in which the director has a material interest) outside the terms of an agreed service contract.
(c) Remove any director who is an appointee of the investor.

WARRANTIES

As in the case of negative covenants, the warranties required by the risk capital investor will vary from case to case. Nevertheless, the investor will usually, as a minimum, require the existing owners of the company, except as disclosed, to give warranties covering the areas described below:

Title

(a) The company's share capital is owned as previously stated to the investors, and there are no other provisions or rights (eg, to options, etc) which would dilute the investor's position.
(b) That the company's title to all its assets, intangible as well as tangible, is unencumbered.

Accounts

(a) The last audited accounts give a true and fair view of the affairs and operation of the company in accordance with generally accepted accounting principles.
(b) The latest management accounts on which the investor or his investigators have based their evaluation have been prepared on a basis consistent with that in the audited accounts, and give a similarly true and fair view. (In addition, the investor may ask for specific warranties on individual items within the accounts, for example, that stocks are not stated in excess of net realisable value, that debtors are collectable, and that all liabilities have been provided for. In particular, the investor may ask the warrantors to confirm that the company has no unprovided liabilities to taxation.)
(c) The investigating accountant's report is true and accurate in all material respects, and is not misleading, either by commission or omission.

Forecasts

The forecasts or estimates of profits examined by the investor or his investigators have been prepared after due and careful enquiry.

Events between the date of the last accounts and completion

(a) There has been no material adverse change in the business or affairs of the company.
(b) No dividends have been paid or other distributions made.
(c) There have been no other unusual or significant events.

Other matters

(a) All *pension* schemes, or other arrangements giving rise to similar obligations, are fully funded.
(b) All normal business risks are covered by valid *insurance*, and that no current or past claim under such policies has been disputed.
(c) The company is not in breach of the terms of any *material contracts*, all of which have been disclosed, and do not entitle any party to terminate or claim more onerous terms under such a contract by virtue of the investment.

(d) No *litigation* is in progress or threatened.
(e) The company has not breached any *legislation* (national or local) which might hinder or prevent the pursuit of its business.
(f) The investor has received from the warrantors all information which might reasonably affect his decision to invest.

(NB — this can give rise to a long list, if the investor wishes to be more specific!)

Appendix IV

Pricing Risk Capital Investments — An Example

Different risk capitalists will price their investments in different ways. One of the most common approaches is, however, set out below.

THE VENTURE CAPITAL INVESTOR

The venture capital investor's price calculation is not usually arithmetically difficult, once he has determined his target rate of return, and the method by which he will eventually recoup his initial cash outlay.

Example

As an example, let us take the case of the venture capitalist who is considering an all-ordinary equity investment in an early-stage company where:

(a) the total cash requirement is £400,000;
(b) the company is projecting post-tax profits of £700,000 in five years' time, at which stage
(c) the company plans to go public, thus giving the venture capitalist the chance to sell his shares and realise his investment. The venture capitalist is aware that the shares of comparable quoted companies in similar businesses are selling at a multiple of say 15–18 times earnings; he will assume for the purposes of this calculation that his own 'exit multiple' will be 12 (for a discussion of how the risk capital investor deals with the

uncertainties inherent in these figures, see the section 'The Question of Risk' below);
(d) the venture capitalist's target rate of return is 45% (before tax).

CALCULATION

The value of the company at the time of the venture capitalist's realisation (or 'exit value') will be £700,000 × 12 = £8,400,000.
The venture capitalist will require a sum equivalent to the £400,000 initially invested at a compound rate of interest of 45% for five years. Algebraically, this can be written as

£400,000 × $(1 + 0.45)^5$ = £2,564,000

Thus he requires an equity stake sufficient to ensure that he receives this value, ie,

$$\frac{2,564,000}{8,400,000} = 31\%$$

The venture capitalist may well therefore offer to subscribe his £400,000 for, say, 35% of the company in his initial offer letter.

ALTERNATIVE CALCULATION

An identical result can be obtained by using the same process 'in reverse', by the application of discounted cash flow techniques. By this method, the venture capitalist will discount the total future value of the company (£8.4m receivable in five years' time) to its present value, using a discount rate equal to his target rate of return, ie, 45%. This again can be written algebraically as

$$8,400,000 \times \frac{1}{(1 + 0.45)^5} = 1,310,507$$

Thus his required equity stake would be equal to his initial investment divided by the present value of the company, ie

$$\frac{400,000}{1,310,507} = 31\%$$

THE DEVELOPMENT CAPITAL INVESTOR

The development capitalist's pricing calculation is typically not so simple. It is often complicated by the fact that:

(a) He may be investing in a mix of securities, each giving him a different type of return.
(b) In such cases, his cash returns will be earned at different times.
(c) Certain specific rights attaching to his shares (eg, conversion rights) may make it more difficult to assess his likely return from them.

Nevertheless, the development capitalist will be able to use exactly the same approach as described above in calculating his offer price, ie, structuring the format and timing of his anticipated cash receipts in such a way that, when discounted at his target rate of return, his net present value will be positive.

THE QUESTION OF RISK

The risk capitalist investor will, however, need to take account of the fact that the figures used throughout this process will be estimates, and subject to all the uncertainties of business life. Whether he is considering a venture or development capital investment, however, the investor will use one or more of the following ways to bring these risk factors into his calculations:

(a) Altering (ie, reducing) the company's profit projections.
(b) Reducing his exit multiple.
(c) Increasing his required rate of return.

Appendix V

The Business Expansion Scheme

The provisions of the Business Expansion Scheme are set out in section 26 of the Finance Act 1983 and subsequent amendments. The summary below does not deal with all their intricacies or complexities, of which there are many, and anyone thinking seriously of taking advantage of the Scheme, either as investor or recipient of finance, should seek professional advice at an early stage.

The relief

Income tax relief is available in the tax year in which the investment is made, ie, in which the shares were issued (NB — where the individual invests by way of a BES fund, tax relief is only granted in the year when the fund invests in portfolio companies — not at the date he invests in the fund). Although due to expire in 1987, the Scheme was extended indefinitely by the Finance Act 1986. The relief is analogous to mortgage interest relief which, whilst beneficial to all income tax payers, is especially advantageous to higher-rate tax payers since it is given at the claimant's highest rate(s) of tax. This can be seen in the example given below on page 248.

Basic rules

Relief can only be claimed by a *qualifying individual* who subscribed for new eligible shares of a *qualifying* unquoted *company* which have been issued for the purpose of raising money for a *qualifying trade* which is being or will be carried on within two years by the company or a qualifying subsidiary. The subscription can be made on his behalf by nominees. Eligible shares are ordinary shares which carry no preferential rights.

For investments made after 5 April 1987, one half of any investment made before 6 October in a tax year, up to a maximum of £5,000 of relief, can be relieved in the previous tax year.

Qualifying individuals

An individual must be resident and ordinarily resident in the UK within the meaning of the tax legislation at the time when the company's shares are issued and must not be connected with the company (or become connected with it within the next five years) if he is to retain the relief.

The main rules relating to connection with a company are that:

(a) the individual or an associate of his must not be an employee, partner or paid director of the company; or
(b) he and his associates must not control the company or possess more than 30% of the ordinary share capital, or loan capital and issued share capital or voting power in the company.

For this purpose an associate includes a husband or wife, lineal ancestor or descendant (but not a brother or sister), a partner and certain persons with whom the individual has connections through a trust.

A director is not disqualified from relief if he is reimbursed travelling and other expenses allowable for tax purposes but he must not be entitled to any remuneration.

In addition an individual cannot claim relief if at the time when the shares were issued or, if later, when the company commences to trade, he is one of a group of persons that controls both the qualifying company and another company where both carry on the same or similar trades.

Qualifying companies

The company must have been incorporated in the UK and be resident only in the UK. It must not be listed on the Stock Exchange and its shares must not be dealt in on the Unlisted Securities Market. It can, however, be quoted on the 'Third Market' or one of the British OTC markets. It must not be a subsidiary of or be controlled by any other company and it must own at least 90% of any subsidiaries it has. All its share capital must be fully paid up. The subsidiaries may be resident or incorporated overseas provided that the trading activities of the group as a whole are carried on wholly or mainly in the UK.

Qualifying trades

Most trades qualify for relief. Those excluded are defined in the legislation, although the Inland Revenue have a wide measure of discretion in how the definitions in the Act are applied. Again, professional advice should be sought here in cases of doubt, and it may be advisable to obtain clearance in advance from the Inland Revenue on this point.

The main non-qualifying trades are:

(a) dealing in commodities, shares, securities, land or futures;
(b) dealing in goods otherwise than in the course of an ordinary trade of wholesale or retail distribution;
(c) banking, insurance, money lending, debt factoring, hire purchase financing or other financial activities;
(d) leasing, hiring or receiving royalties or licence fees (except for certain film production, research and development and ship chartering companies);
(e) providing legal or accountancy services;
(f) oil extraction activities.

A company will be regarded as having a qualifying trade if it raises money for research and development with a view subsequently to carrying on a qualifying trade.

The trade must be conducted on a commercial basis and with a view to the realisation of profit.

Companies with land and buildings representing a high proportion (in excess of 50%) of their assets as a whole are, subject to certain exceptions, excluded. This last provision was enacted in the Finance Act 1986 to stop the proliferation of 'asset-backed' BES financings. It followed amendments of a similar nature in earlier years excluding farming and property companies.

Claims

The individual must claim relief within two years of the end of the tax year in which the shares are issued or within two years after the end of the first four months of trading, if later.

Limits on the relief

Relief cannot be claimed on more than £40,000 invested in any one tax year including any amounts carried back from the succeeding tax year. Relief is not given for investment of less than £500 in any one company in any tax year where the claimant invests directly. This lower limit does not apply where the investment is made on his behalf by managers of an approved fund.

Withdrawal of relief

If the conditions attaching to the relief *relating to the company* cease to be satisfied within *three* years of the investment being made, or the commencement of the company's qualifying trade, if later, the relief will be withdrawn.

Relief will also be wholly or partly withdrawn if the *claimant* receives value from the company or disposes of the shares within *five* years of the issues of the shares. Value is received from the company if, for example, it redeems the shares or makes the individual a loan which is not repaid before the BES share issue or provides a benefit or facility. The provisions defining value received are complex, wide-ranging, and important.

Capital gains tax

A profit (or loss) arising on the sale of BES shares issued after 18 March 1986 is not a chargeable gain (or allowable loss) for the purposes of capital gains tax.

Tax avoidance

Relief is not available unless shares are subscribed for and issued for bona fide commercial purposes and not as part of a scheme of arrangement, the main purpose, or one of the main purposes of which, is the avoidance of tax.

This example of so-called 'anti-avoidance legislation' is capable of extremely wide application by the Inland Revenue. Indeed, it would be possible to argue that *one* of the main purposes of almost any BES share issue was the avoidance of tax by the investors! The attitude of the Inland Revenue to the issue is therefore of the utmost importance.

Clearance procedure

It is possible to canvass the views of the Inland Revenue before proceeding but there are no formal clearance procedures.

Returns to investors — example

The following example illustrates the effect of the available tax relief under the BES on the cost of shares to a qualifying investor who subscribes for 1,000 ordinary shares at 100p per share for a total subscription cost of £1,000. It is assumed that the full amount is eligible for relief at the rate of tax stated in the table.

Marginal tax rate of individual %	Amount of relief £	Net cost of investment £
60	600	400
50	500	500
40	400	600
30	300	700

If an individual holds his or her shares for the required five years after issue, and then even if the shares have not increased in value from their purchase price, a substantial return can still be achieved by the investor upon disposal as can be seen from the following table:

	60% £	50% £	40% £	30% £
Average rate of income tax relief				
Sale proceeds	1,000	1,000	1,000	1,000
Less effective cost of investment after tax relief under the BES	(400)	(500)	(600)	(700)
Effective surplus (no capital gains tax payable)	600	500	400	300
Average rate of income tax relief	60%	50%	40%	30%
Increase (compared to effective cost)	150%	100%	67%	43%

Annual compound growth rate over five years after tax	20.1%	14.9%	10.8%	7.4%

If the shares are sold after five years at double the cost price (ie, 200p, representing an annual compound growth rate of 14.9% before tax relief), the effective net of tax investor return will increase dramatically to:

Average rate of income tax relief	60%	50%	40%	30%
Increase (compared to effective cost)	400%	300%	233%	186%
Annual compound growth rate over five years after tax	37.9%	31.9%	27.2%	23.4%

Should such individuals dispose of any of their shares within five years, the relief may be withdrawn in whole or in part.

Index

Accountants
investigation by, 158, 169-171
role in raising risk capital, 116-118, 119-120
Aquisition of company
exit route for investor, 197-198, 204
number and value in 1986, 230, 231
stage definition, 235
Advisers. *See* PROFESSIONAL ADVISERS
Aftercare
hands-off monitoring style, 184-186
hands-on monitoring style,
  bad management, removal of, 191-192
  divestment, 191
  do's and dont's for entrepreneur, 192-193
  executive assistance, 188
  further financing, 189, 190-191
  growth, coping with, 189-190
  interference distinct from, 197
  investor's fiduciary duty to own subscribers, 191
  long-term investment decisions, 191
  management structure, 188-189
  meaning, 186
  policy input, 187-188
  problems of approach, 190-193
importance, 183
information systems of portfolio company, 185-186, 187
non-executive directors, 175, 185
reactive management style, 184
types, 183-184
Articles of association
changes required, 178

Banks
debt backed by personal guarantee, 37
development capital funds, 28, 29
lending policies, 13-14
Borrowing powers
restriction on, 178
Boston Consulting Group
growth/share matrix, 21-24
British Technology Group
joint venture project finance, 108-110
public sector fund, 33-34
British Venture Capital Association (BVCA)
approaching the funds, 122
code of conduct, 41-42
impact survey, 209-210
investment in 1986, 27, 228-236
membership, 17
report on investment activity, 209
role of, 41
Business Expansion Scheme (BES)
advantages of, 72-73, 79
amounts invested, 67-68
BES funds, 66-67
  amounts invested, 67-68
  case study, 221-223
Business Start-up Scheme, formerly, 4
capital gains generated, 78
competition from other risk capital funds, 74-75
conservatism of, 69-71
current and future trends, 75-76
direct investment by public, 66
exit routes, 204
fund manager remuneration, 76-77
hands-off style, 184-185
industry sector, 68

Business Expansion Scheme (BES)—*contd*
  legislation on, 65, 76
  marketability and liquidity, 78-79
  methods of raising finance, 66-67
  nature of scheme, 65-66
  poor performance and failures, 77-78
  price of, 73
  problems of, 73-74
  risks assumed by, 69-71
  share options, 77
  size and importance, 67
  size of investments, 71, 75-76
  stages of investment invested in, 69-71
  summary of scheme, 244-249
  tax advantages, 65-66, 72, 78, 244-249
  timing of investments, 72
  Wilson Report proposals, 3

Business plan
  accountant's role in preparation, 117, 126
  appendices, 136-137, 148-149
  confidential information, 132
  contents list, 140
  evaluation of plan, 151-153
  evaluation of proposals, 124
  financial analysis, 147
  financial projections, 127-129, 130, 132
  fundamental document, as, 121, 124
  history of business, 140-141
  inflation, 132
  length, 126-127, 136-137
  management, 132-133, 146
  manufacturing and operations, 145-146
  markets and marketing, 142-145
  measure of performance, 128-129, 137-138
  objectives and milestones, 125, 137-138, 148
  outline plan for equity finance, 139-149
  presentation, 136, 138-139
  products/services description, 141-142
  readability of, 136, 138-139
  risk assessment, 134-136, 148
  sensitivity analysis, 129, 135-136
  special nature of proposal, 134

Business plan—*contd*
  specific information required, 130-131
  summary, 137, 140
  who should write plan, 126
Business Start-up Scheme
  establishment, 4

Capital gains
  Business Expansion Scheme, 247
  income tax on, 165
Case study
  venture financing, 217-227
Cash profile of business
  finance to be matched to, 24
'Cash-cow' companies
  choice of finance, 21-23
City institutions
  BES funds, 69
  commitment to risk capital industry, 212
  composite funds, 32-33
  development capital funds, 18
  market quotation. *See* MARKET QUOTATION
  OTC Market, 108
  second round finance, 189
  sources of venture capital, 28
Competition
  BES and other funds, between, 74-75
  business plan outline, 143-144
  competitive edge of entrepreneur's business, 134
  competitive investment offers, 160
  non-competition agreements, 177
Confidentiality
  information supplied to funds, 42, 132
  management buy-outs, 54
Conflicts of interest
  corporate venturing, 95-96
  development capital funds, 30
  equity investor also holds loan stock, 161
  potential investors and confidentiality, 132
  professional advisers, 119
Consumer-related industries
  Business Expansion Scheme, 68
  investment patterns, 35, 232-234
Corporate finance
  types of, 10-15

Index 253

Corporate venturing
advantages for smaller company, 88–90
choice faced by entrepreneur, 80
conflicts of interest, 95–96
direct investment, 85–87
diversification of business by, 82
do's and dont's for entrepreneur, 96–97
exit routes, 89, 96
growing interest in UK, 81, 98
interference by host corporation, 92–95
matching potential parties, 90
meaning, 80–81
minority investment by large corporation in smaller company, as, 81
motives for, 82–84
NEDO survey, 81, 98
organisational advantages, 84
problems and pitfalls, 90–96
purpose, 81
resistance within large corporations, 90–92
sponsored spin-offs, 85, 88
staffing problems, 92
supplier/customer bases protected, 93–94
technology companies, 82–83, 86–87, 88
types, 81, 84–88
United States, in, 80, 81, 88
venture capital funds, via, 85, 88–89

Debt finance
capital structure required, 160–163
limits of, 12–14, 15
nature of, 12
Department of Trade and Industry
Loan Guarantee Scheme, 13–14, 37
Development capital
affiliated services, 30
captive funds, 28–30
choice of capital, 21–24
commitment to risk capital, 29
conflicts of interest, 30
evaluation approach of fund, 151–152
growth/share matrix, 21–24
hands on/hands off styles, 19, 20, 184–193
independent funds, 28–30
industries invested in, 30

Development capital—*contd*
investment patterns in 1986, 228–236
later stage investments preferred, 35
nature, 18–19
price of investment, 163–166, 241–243
realisation of investment. *See* EXIT ROUTES
return sought, 113, 243
second round financing, 29–30
semi-captive funds, 29
staffing of funds, 30, 39–41
stages of development of business, 21–24, 35–36, 69–71, 230–232, 235–236
types of funds, 28–30
venture capital distinguished, 17–20
Direct investment
Business Expansion Scheme, 66
corporate venturing, 85–87
Directors
composition of board, 178
investor's seat on board, 174, 186
non-executive directors, 175, 185
Disclosure letter
nature and purpose, 177–178
Diversification of business
corporate venturing, 82
Dividends
preference shares, 161
quoted companies, 201
Documentation
articles of association, 178
completion documentation, 171–172
continuing obligations, 174–175
disclosure letter, 177–178
indemnities, 176–177
negative covenants, 173–174, 237–238
preparation of, 171
service contracts, 179
subscription agreement, 172–173
warranties, 175–176, 238–240
'Dog' companies
choice of finance, 21–24
Due diligence standard
investigations, 169
lead investor's work, 39
prospectus requirements, 104
solicitor's duty, 120

Early stage investment
accountant's report, 169
availability of capital, 210–211

Early stage investment—*contd*
  Business Expansion Scheme, 70, 71
  choice of capital, 21–24
  concentration of funds, 214, 215
  investment patterns, 35–36, 230–232
  definition, 235
Employees
  management buy-outs, 50
  share options, 4, 189
Enterprise boards
  regional investment, 34
Entrepreneurs
  approaching the funds, 122–123
  business plan. *See* BUSINESS PLAN
  cash versus control dilemma, 9–10, 113–114
  choosing the financial package 15–16, 21–24
    case study, 222–223
  commitment required, 115
  demands on investor, 193
  desire to work for themselves, 9
  developments in 1980s, 3–4
  evaluation of risk capitalist, 153
    case study, 222–224
  expectations, 5
  involvement or interference by investor. *See also* INVOLVEMENT OF INVESTOR
    cash versus control dilemma, 9–10, 113–114
    do's and dont's, 192–193
  objectives, 6, 9–10, 148
  negotiations, 159–160, 179–180
  post-investment period. *See* AFTERCARE
  professional advisers, 115–121
  removal of bad management, 191–192
  sacrifices involved in raising finance, 113–114
  self-appraisal as manager, 192
  service contracts, 179, 204
  small businessman distinguished, 9–10
  stages of development of business, 21–24, 35–36, 69–71, 230–232, 235–236
  status of, 215–216
  surrender of flexibility, 113–114
  task involved in raising risk capital, 114–115

Equity finance
  business plan outline, 138–149
  capital structure required, 160–163
  choice of, 21–24, 74–75, 80
  development capital, 17–19. *See also* DEVELOPMENT CAPITAL
  growth and availability, 4
  nature of, 10–11
  syndications, 38–39, 42
  terminology, 17
  types of instrument, 14–15
  types of risk capital, 17–18, 28–34
  venture capital, 17–20. *See also* VENTURE CAPITAL
European Venture Capital Association
  database of contacts, 188
Evaluation of proposals
  ability of management to exploit potential, 114–115
  break-even analysis, 136
  business plan's importance, 124
  case study, 219–222
  development capitalist's approach, 151–152
  financial projections, 127–129, 130, 132
  fund evaluation by entrepreneur, 153
  initial interest by investors, 150–151
  investigations and reports, 156, 167–171
  management evaluation, 132–142, 152–153
  measure of performance, 128–129, 137–138
  offers. *See* OFFERS, INVESTMENT
  potential of business, 114, 125
  procedures to validate business plan, 151–152
  risk assessment, 125, 134–136
  sensitivity analysis, 129, 135–136
  special nature of proposal, 134
  techniques used, 125
  venture capitalist's approach, 151–152
Executives
  BES fund managers, 76–77
  corporate venturer's staffing problems, 92
  entrepreneur's management. *See* MANAGEMENT
  remuneration of fund managers, 36–37, 76–77

Executives—*contd*
staffing of risk capital funds, 30, 31, 39–41
training, qualifications and experience, 40–41
Exit routes
acquisition of company by third party, 197–198, 204
corporate venturing, 89, 96
importance to investor, 194
market quotation, 195–197, 200–203
re-purchase of own shares by company, 198–199, 205
third party sales, 197–198, 204
timing and manner of realisation, 194
types, 194–205
Expansion financing
BVCA survey in 1986, 230
definition, 235–236

Family companies
management buy-outs, 48
replacement capital, 99–100
Finance
choice of, 15–16, 21–24, 74–75, 80
BES funds, 74–75
case study, 217–227
corporate venturing, 80
costs of, 15–16
equity finance. *See* EQUITY FINANCE
loan-equity package, 15
size of, 36–37, 71, 228–229
stage of, 21–24, 35–36, 69–71, 230–232, 235–236
types of, 10–15
Financial analysis
business plan outline, 147, 149
Financial services sector
investment patterns, 35, 232, 233, 234
Flotation of companies. *See* MARKET QUOTATION
Future prospects
BVCA report and impact survey, 209–210
commitment of risk capitalists, 212
concentration of fund raising, 214
downturn in stock market, 213
early stage technology projects, 210–211
entrepreneur's status, 215–216
equity gap for smaller companies, 210

Future prospects—*contd*
internationalisation, 215
major problems to be resolved, 210–211
political climate, 212, 213
regional funds, 215
second round finance, 211
specialist funds, 215
supply and demand, 211–212
trends envisaged, 214–216

Gearing
management buy-outs, 49–50, 60, 63
Government measures
Business Expansion Scheme. *See* BUSINESS EXPANSION SCHEME
development of new business, 4
government and public sector funds, 32–34
Loan Guarantee Scheme, 13–14, 37
regional investment agencies, 34
Growth of company
finance to matched to rate of, 24
problems arising from, 189–190

Indemnities
nature and purpose, 176–177
offer letter's reference to, 156
Industrial and Commercial Finance Corporation (3i)
early role, 4
risk capital fund as, 32–33
Industry sectors
Business Expansion Scheme, 68
computers and electronics, 35, 233, 234
consumer-related industries, 35, 68, 232–234
financial services, 35, 232, 233, 234
focus of capital and development funds, 30, 31
industries invested in, 34–35, 232–234
investment patterns, 34–35, 232–234
leisure and franchising, 31, 233
management buy-outs distribution, 46–47
'people-based' industries, 35, 232–234
technology field, 31, 34–35, 232–234. *See also* TECHNOLOGY INDUSTRIES

Inflation
financial projections, 131
Information systems
monitoring by investor, 185, 187
Insider dealing
prohibition on, 203
Internationalisation
BVCA investment by country in 1986, 229
European Venture Capital Association, 188
risk capital industry, of, 31, 215
Investigations
accountant's report, 156, 169-171
types required by investor, 167-169
Investors
aftercare. See AFTERCARE
development capitalists, 18-19. See also DEVELOPMENT CAPITAL
interference or involvement. See INVOLVEMENT OF INVESTOR
international contacts, 188
lead investor, 39
long-term investment decisions, 191
management information required, 175
offers to invest. See OFFERS, INVESTMENT
prestige of, 159
rejection rate, 124
returns sought by, 15-16, 113
Business Expansion Scheme, 248-249
rights sought from company, 174-175
risk capitalists, 17
venture capital explosion of 1980s, 3-4
venture capitalists, 19-20. See also VENTURE CAPITAL
Involvement of investor. See also AFTERCARE
cash versus control dilemma, 9-10, 113-114
corporate venturer's interference, 92-95
development capitalist's role, 19, 184-193
hands-on/hands-off styles, 19, 20, 184-193
indirect pressures on entrepreneurs, 16
private placings, 102
source of problems, 5

Involvement of investor—*contd*
surrender of flexibility by entrepreneur, 113-114
type of finance determines, 10-15
venture capitalist's role, 20, 184-193

Joint ventures
form of financing, as, 108-110

Later stage investments
choice of capital, 21-24
investment patterns, 35, 230-232
Legal matters
completion documentation, 171-179
management buy-outs, 58
solicitor's role, 118-119, 120-121
Listing of companies. See MARKET QUOTATION
Loan Guarantee Scheme
debt finance, as, 13-14, 37
Loan stock
capital structure required, 160, 161

Management
ability to exploit venture potential, 114-115
appraisal of, 114-115
business plan, 132-133, 146
corporate venturer's resources and recruits, 89, 92
CVs of key managers, 146
development capitalist's role, 19, 20, 184-193
effort and staying power, 152
evaluation of, 152-153
executive assistance by investor, 188-189
expectations, 5, 6
finance to be matched to, 24
fund managers, 36-37
income tax on capital gains, 165
key man insurance, 177
leadership, 153
objectives in negotiations with investor, 159-160
proposals by experienced managers, 4
recruitment and remuneration, 189
removal of non-performing managers, 191-192
risk taking ability, 152-153
service contracts, 179, 204
structure of, and investor's advice, 188-189

Index 257

Management—*contd*
venture capitalist's role, 20, 184–193
Management buy-outs
advantages of management as buyer, 54–55
advisers needed, 57, 61
attractions for risk capitalists, 55–56
contribution and control by managers, 60, 63
definition, 49–50
development capitalist as main investor, 46–48
employee buy-outs, 50
example of, 62–64
failure rate, 55
family companies transferred, 48
financing the buy-out, 59–60, 62–64
golden rules, 61
industry distribution, 46–47
investment patterns, 35, 45–46, 230, 231
legal and tax implications, 58
leveraged buy-outs, 49–50
management buy-ins, 50
management team required, 56
mega-deals, 50
motives for parent to sell to management, 51–55, 61
nature of finance sought, 57
negative covenants, 174
number and value of, 35, 45–46, 230, 231
performance improved after, 55–56
personalities involved, 58–59, 61
price as main problem, 51, 60, 61, 62–63
process of, 58–59, 62–64
receivership buy-outs, 48
share rights, 60, 63
solicitor's role, 120
sources of, 48
sponsored spin-offs, 50
Stock Exchange quotation achieved, 44
subsidiary companies sold, 49, 51–55
success of, 44–45, 55–57
timing problems, 58–59
Manufacturing
business plan outline, 145–146
investment patterns, 35, 232–234
Market quotation of companies
advantages, 107–108, 200–201

Market quotation of companies—*contd*
Business Expansion Scheme companies, 66, 78
choice of markets, 195, 196
disadvantages, 201–203
downturn in stock market, 213
exit route for investor, as, 195–197, 200–203
management buy-outs, after, 44
methods of flotation, 197
new money raised, 196–198
Over-The-Counter Market, 104–107, 108
Stock Exchange, 195, 196, 202
suitability of business for flotation, 195
surrender of control, 197
Third Market, 105–107, 108
Unlisted Securities Markets, 4, 105, 195, 196
Markets and marketing
business plan outline, 142–145
policy input by investor, 187

National Economic Development Office
corporate venturing survey, 81, 98
National Research and Development Corporation
Wilson Report proposals, 3
Negative covenants
examples, 237–238
nature and purpose, 173–174
Negotiations
capital structure, 160–163
case study, 219–224
completion documentation, 171–179
do's and dont's, 179–180
investigations and reports, 167–171
objectives of entrepreneur, 159–160
price, 163–166, 241–243

Offers, investment
capital structure, 160–163
case study, 220–223
competitive offers, 160
deadline for acceptance, 158
evaluation by entrepreneur, 153
case study, 222–223
fee estimates, 158
heads of agreement, 154
initial offer, 153–154

Index

Offers, investment—*contd*
  investigations, 158, 167-171
  key issues, 155
  negotiations. *See* NEGOTIATIONS
  objectives of entrepreneur, 159-160
  offer letter, 154-158
    example, 156-157
  omissions, 158
  optimising, 159-165
  price, 163-166
  subject to contract, 154, 155
  warranties and indemnities, 157-158, 238-240
Offers for subscription
  shares, of, 103, 197
Options on shares
  BES funds, 77
  employee share options, 4, 189
Over-The-Counter Market
  quotations on, 195
  source of finance, as, 104-107, 108
Owners. *See* ENTREPRENEURS

Preference shares
  capital structure, 160-163
  fixed dividend, with, 14
  preferred participating shares, 14-15, 162
Price of investment
  case study, 225
  example of pricing calculation, 241-243
  management buy-outs, 51, 60, 61, 62-63
  negotiations as to, 163-166
  ratchet arrangements, 162-163, 164-165
  second round finance, 190-191
Private placings
  shares, of, 102-103, 197
Products
  decreasing life cycles, 82, 89
  description in business plan, 141-142
Professional advisers
  accountants, 116-118, 119-120
  approaches in using, 116
  approaching the funds, 122-123
  case study, 225
  change of, 177, 185
  conflicts of interest, 119
  costs and fees of, 119, 121
  lead adviser, 116
  negotiations, 179, 180

Professional advisers—*contd*
  range of, 115-116
  solicitors, 118-119, 120
Project finance
  joint ventures, 108-110
Prospectus requirements
  offers of shares to public, 102, 103-104
Public, going. *See* MARKET QUOTATION
Public sector
  risk capital funds, 33-34

Quasi-equity lending
  nature of, 14
'Question mark' companies
  choice of finance, 21-23
Quotation of companies. *See* MARKET QUOTATION

Ratchet arrangements
  investor's equity stake, 162-163, 164-165
Realisation of investment. *See* EXIT ROUTES
Receiverships
  management buy-outs, 48
  OTC market companies, 105, 107
Regional investment
  future prospects, 215
  investment patterns, 37-38, 234-235
  public sector funds, 34
Replacement capital
  buying out existing shareholders, 99-100
  'dog' companies, 23-24
Reports
  accountant's report, 169-171
  types required by investor, 167-169
Rescue capital
  regional bodies, 34
Research and development
  cash consuming companies, 23
  policy input by investor, 187
Risk capital
  3i(ICFC), 4, 32-33
  axioms and standards of funds, 41, 42
  British Venture Capital Association, 17, 41-42, 228-236
  capital structure required, 160-163
  case study, 217-227

Index   259

Risk capital—*contd*
choice of, 21–24, 74–75, 80
commitment of funds, 29
composite funds, 32–33
development capital funds, 28–30.
   See also DEVELOPMENT CAPITAL
emergence of funds, 27
executives of funds, 30, 31, 39–41
   remuneration of fund managers, 36–37
flexibility of debt and preferred equity, 161–162
government and public sector funds, 33–34
informal subscription for shares, 101–102
investment patterns in 1986, 228–236
issue of shares to public, 101–108
joint ventures, 108–110
lasting benefits, 216
market quotation, 104–108, 195–197, 200–203
offers for subscription, 103, 197
Over-The-Counter Market, 104–107, 108
price of investment, 163–166
pricing calculation example, 241–243
private placing of shares, 102–103, 197
professional costs, 121
ratchet arrangements, 162–163, 164–165
realisation of investment. *See* EXIT ROUTES
regional investment, 34, 37–38, 234–235
replacement capital, 99–100
return sought by investor, 113
size of, 36–37, 71, 228–229
small companies, 36–37
sources of finance, 27
sources of information, 43
stage of, 21–24, 35–36, 69–71, 230–232, 235–236
subjective assessment by funds, 43
syndications, 38–39, 42
Third Market, 105–107, 108
types of, 17–20, 28–34
venture capital funds, 31–32. *See also* VENTURE CAPITAL
Risks of investment
assessment of in business plan, 125, 134–136

Risks of investment—*contd*
Business Expansion Scheme, 69–71
business plan outline, 148
management of risk by investor, 187
pricing calculation example, 243
shared by syndication, 38–39

Sales
business plan outline, 144–145
Second round finance
access to as objective, 159–160
Business Expansion Scheme, 74
development capital funds, 29–30
disputes with investor as to, 190–191
future availability, 211
investor's involvement, 189, 190–191
private placings, 103
Secondary purchase
number and value in 1986, 230, 231
stage definition, 236
Service contracts
purpose and contents, 179
sale of company to third party, 204
Services
description in business plan, 141–142
Shares
arrangements for transfer or pre-emption, 177, 178
capital structure, 160–163
convertible preference shares, 162
informal subscription for, 101–102
issue to members of the public, 101–108
market quotation, 104–108, 195–197, 200–203
offers for subscription, 103, 197
options for executives, 4, 189
ordinary shares, 15
Over-The-Counter market, 104–107, 108
preference shares, 14, 160–163
preferred participating shares, 14–15, 162
private placing, 102–103, 197
prospectus requirements, 102, 103–104
quotation. *See* MARKET QUOTATION
re-purchase by company of own shares, 121
exit route, as, 198–199, 205
redeemable preference shares, 162
sale by investor, as exit route, 197–198, 204

Shares—*contd*
  share options, 4, 77, 189
  shareholder's agreement, 172-173
  Third Market, 105-107, 108
Small companies
  entrepreneurs and small businessmen, distinguished, 9-10
  equity gap, 210
  funds' attitudes towards, 36-37
  size of finance available, 36-37
  Wilson Report on financing of, 3
Solicitors
  advice on potential areas of conflict, 168
  completion documentation, 171-179
  fees, 121, 156
  role in raising risk capital, 118-119, 120-121
Specialist funds
  future prospects, 215
Spin-offs, sponsored
  corporate venturing, 85, 88
  management buy-outs, 50
Stage of business
  BES and risk capital industry, compared, 69-71
  choice of finance to be matched to, 21-24
  definitions, 235-236
  investment patterns, 35-36, 230-232
'Star' companies
  choice of finance, 21-23
Start-up investments
  availability of capital, 210-211
  Business Expansion Scheme, 70, 71
  choice of capital, 21-24
  definition, 235
  failure rate, 55
  informal subscription for shares, 101
  investment patterns in 1986, 35-36, 230-232
  Over-The-Counter Market, 104-105
  Third Market, 105-107
Stock Exchange
  Business Expansion Scheme companies, 66, 78
  choice of markets, 195, 196
  market quotation. *See* MARKET QUOTATION
  OTC market as alternative, 104-107, 108
  rules and regulations, 202

Subscription agreement
  purpose and contents, 172-173
Success rates
  figures, 5, 124
Syndications
  venture capital funds, by, 38-39, 42

3i
  previous role as ICFC, 4
  scope of operations, 32-33, 99
Taxation
  Business Expansion Scheme, 65-66, 72, 78, 244-249
  employee share options, 4
  income tax on capital gains of managers, 165
  indemnities as to, 177
  inheritance tax, 99, 202
  loan stock interest, 161
  management buy-outs, 58
  preference share dividends, 161
  professional advisers, 117-118, 119
  re-purchase of own shares by company, 199
Technical Development Capital
  Wilson Report proposals, 3
Technology industries
  3i ventures, 33
  British Technology Group, 33-34
  Business Expansion Scheme, 68
  corporate venturing, 82-83, 86-87, 88
  funds invested in, 34-35
  investment patterns in 1986, 232-234
  joint venture project finance, 108-110
  venture capital investment, 31
Third Market
  quotation on, 195, 196
  source of finance, as, 105-107, 108

United States of America
  BVCA survey, 229
  corporate venturing, 80, 81, 88
  cyclical trend in risk capital investment, 212
  upsurge in venture capital activity, 3
  venture capital funds, 31
Unlisted Securities Market
  formation, 4
  history of entrants, 105
  quotation on, 195, 196

Venture capital
British Venture Capital Association, 17, 41-42
survey, 228-236
captive and independent funds, 31
choice of capital, 21-24
corporate venturing via fund, 85, 87-88
development capital distinguished, 17-20
evaluation approach of fund, 151-152
explosion of in 1980s, 3-4, 27
focus of investments, 31
growth/share matrix, 21-24
hands-on/hands-off styles, 20, 31-32, 184-193
industries invested in, 31. *See also* INDUSTRY SECTORS
investment patterns in 1986, 228-236
nature, 19-20
overseas links, 31, 189, 215
price of investment, 163

Venture capital—*contd*
pricing calculation example, 241-243
realisation of investment. *See* EXIT ROUTES
return sought, 113
roots of, 4-5
staffing of funds, 31, 39-41
stages in development of business, 21-24, 35-36, 69-71, 230-232, 235-236
syndications, 38-39, 42

Venture Economics Limited
survey of investment in 1986, 27, 228-236

Warranties
management buy-outs, 54
nature and purpose, 175-176
offer letter's reference to, 156

Wilson Report
financing of small firms, 3, 209
public sector funds, 33